£14.99
WS

The C
Writi   k

D0865813

The Creative Writing Handbook

Techniques for New Writers

Second Edition

Edited by
JOHN SINGLETON and
MARY LUCKHURST

First published 1996
Second edition 2000
MACMILLAN PRESS LTD
Houndmills, Basingstoke, Hampshire RG21 6XS
and London
Companies and representatives throughout the world

ISBN 0-333-79226-2 paperback

A catalogue record for this book is available from the British Library.

10 9 8 7 6 5 4 3 2 1
09 08 07 06 05 04 03 02 01 00

Printed in Great Britain by CPD Wales, Ebbw Vale

Contents

How to Use This Book

If you are following a creative writing course, or belong to a creative writing group or are writing on your own you will find this book essential reading. It's about learning the craft of writing. It is not a textbook. Neither is it a 'How To' book. It doesn't *tell* you what to do. We don't believe in prefabricated writing assembled from step-by-step instructions.

What we do believe is that the imagination drives writing and that it is most effective when harnessed to craft. We feel writers come to good writing in different ways but the best way to improve is by constant practice; by trying out and experimenting with new forms and strategies; by rewriting. So what this book offers is not writing-by-numbers but a whole variety of suggestions and ideas for every kind of writing you can imagine. It's a rich resource book packed with possibilities.

Most taught creative writing goes on in practical group sessions. This book shows you how to get the best out of such workshops and how to build on that experience by developing your writing in your own time.

We believe good readers make good writers so we have recommended hundreds of books and authors for you to select, browse through and learn from. Accomplished writers read as well as write because they've learnt their craft by imitating the good practice of others. Writing is something you can catch through reading.

The Handbook is sequenced and the chapters take you through each stage of the writing process from first acquiring basic skills with words, finding ideas and developing them through different forms and genres to the final crafting stages of revision and editing. But don't feel you have to work your way through it systematically. Pick and mix. Select from it what appeals. Adapt the material to suit your needs.

We feel strongly that writers should not work in intellectual isolation. So, Chapter 1 considers some general issues of practice and theory and puts writing in a broad cultural, historical and ideological context. Each of the subsequent chapters starts with a short discussion on aspects of language and genre and is followed by a workshop section where up to ten workshops are described in detail. You can use them to structure your own course with a small group of friends or follow them as part of a taught school, university or community writing programme. The third and final section of each chapter offers you a whole range of writing suggestions to try out in your own time. Some of them could be workshopped as well. The point is you use the book the way you want.

1 Making a Mark

MARY LUCKHURST AND JOHN SINGLETON

The English word for writing derives from the Old German verb, *writan*, to scratch. In a sense all writing starts from scratch, and though this origin emphasises writing as a material activity, the process described also involves thinking and imagining. Joan Didion, the American novelist and journalist, defines writing as 'pictures in my mind', and says her purpose is, 'to find out what I am thinking... What is going on in these pictures in my mind'. Here then is one of our major objectives as writers – to find out who we are and why we think and feel as we do.

The very first mark we make is our name, scrawling it slowly on paper, drawing the pencil down, then up, then round and across, till it's there. Our signature, the sign of self. As a child making our first letters we have written ourselves into existence, marked ourselves out, announced our arrival in the world. It's a way of saying I am here and making the world sit up. Like Kilroy leaving his trace on walls or like Kevin or Shirley or JR who loves PC and wants the world to know.

First writings establish our identity; later ones may validate it as in signatures on cheques. After naming ourselves, me John, we name our family, Mum and Dad, sister or brother, best friend, gran, the baby, our house, our pet, the sky, cars, apples, rivers, trees, roads, kites, flies, astronauts and pterodactyls and before long we have named the world. In one sense, for us anyway, we have brought it into being. Writing then is the act of naming and creates, through mind pictures, the world about us. Put another way it joins us to the world – of family, history, culture and nation.

1

It is also an act of piracy. Child crayons small, brown squiggle on stilts and names it, '*My* dog'. Now it is possessed. And the world hears, recognises the familiar public ritual of ownership. Dog is dragged off to show Mummy who confirms symbolic act of possession. For the child writer it's not just an assertion of place and presence in the world, this labelling is an act of control over the world. It's an ordering, a making sense of. William Goyen was very clear about the writer and the world. 'Writing is a way of life to me,' he wrote, '. . . a way to observe the world and to move through life, among human beings, and to record it all and shape it, to give it sense, and to express something of myself in it.'

Scratching the surface is obviously the first stage in getting deeper and as a metaphor has something to say about writing as an exploratory process, a search into self, or more accurately, into self and the world together. In the Preface to her autobiographical novel *That's How It Was*, Maureen Duffy explains her reasons for writing the book. 'I was trying to make psychological sense of myself,' she writes, 'and to do this I was rerunning those events and emotions that had formed me.'

This quest for self-knowledge is as difficult for the writer as it is for anyone. Writing can be as self-deceiving as it can be self-revealing. Writers can invent ideal selves, alter egos, the fantasised heroes and heroines of their fiction and thus evade the problem of finding out who they really are. Other writers are more confrontational. The follies and failures of self are met head on. The empowering therapy of facing up to life in this way is regarded as the prime function of the writing. As one of our students wrote, 'Writing lets out the evil dragons in me.' But as another shrewdly observed, 'That's OK for starters. Then where do you go?' Though writing for therapy may be limited at least it is an honest way of looking. And it touches on an important truth about writing. You should write not about what other people want, nor about what you think other people want, but about what *you* want. Of course you have to write first to find out what that want is.

We are back with Joan Didion's notion of finding out what's going on in the pictures in the head. These images make up the writer's vision. It is our view on the world, as if out of a window, our distinctive way of seeing. Some regard writing as a prime way of expressing this vision. Others talk of finding a voice. Both notions highlight a central aspect of the writing process – it is about perception. Looking into things. Not at things, into. Getting below the surface. And it's about voicing or communicating what you see through the medium of words.

In his essay, 'On Writing', the American short story writer and poet, Raymond Carver, saw vision as the essential element in writerly success. It is 'a unique and exact way of looking at things and finding the right context for expressing that way of looking...' he asserts. 'It is the writer's particular and unmistakable signature on everything he writes. It is his world and no other.'

Alice Walker, author of *The Colour Purple*, was blinded in one eye by an air-gun pellet when she was eight. Now one eye has a glob of whitish scar tissue at its centre. She tells a beautiful story about her daughter Rebecca. Every day when she was three the little girl watched a TV programme that began 'with the picture of the earth as it appears from the moon. It is bluish, a little battered-looking, but full of light, with whitish clouds swirling round it.' One night, as she is put to bed, Rebecca holds her mother's face in her hands and says 'Mommy there is a *world* in your eye...Mommy, where did you get that world in your eye?' It was from that moment that Alice Walker says she was able to face up to her scarring and disability. That night she says she dreamt of dancing with a bright-faced dancer. 'The other dancer has also come through all right, as I have done. She is beautiful, whole and free. And she is also me.'

In this account, 'Beauty: When the Other Dancer is the Self', Alice Walker traces how we ourselves can obscure our vision of the world and never realise it. Most commonly by not accepting the voice within, the other dancer. Mary Gordon, the American novelist, describes how her writing development was also about overcoming self-imposed obstacles. 'Spectres' haunted her as a young writer. They told her to write like Henry James, be like a man, be serious, be distant. Wanting to be a 'good girl' and please the patriarchal voices of the literary establishment she tried writing Jamesian fashion and failed. She really wanted to imitate women writers

– 'Charlotte Brontë, Woolf, Mansfield, Bowen, Lessing, Olsen.' Gradually under their influence she 'discovered that what I loved in writing was not distance but radical closeness; not the violence of the bizarre but the complexity of the quotidian.'

All writers start with impediments of some kind or another, which may be as difficult to break as the 'mind-forged manacles' of William Blake. Nadine Gordimer, the South African novelist and Nobel Literature prize-winner, who all her life fought against apartheid, characterised her early efforts at writing as 'a clumsy battle to chip my way out of shell after shell of ready-made concepts and make my own sense of life'. If anyone got below the surface it was Nadine Gordimer. It was writing that woke her up to the 'shameful enormity' of racial oppression in her country and sent her 'falling, falling through the surface of "the South African way of life"'.

She, like Mary Gordon and Alice Walker, stresses the importance of models for young writers. She read Maupassant, Chekhov, Katherine Anne Porter and Eudora Welty. These writers gave her a completely new sense of history and political truth. For Alice Walker it was the early twentieth-century black writer, Zora Neale Hurston, novelist, essayist, anthropologist, and autobiographer, who lit the path and showed her a way to explore the black experience, and who rose above racial oppression to celebrate life itself. Reading other writers, 'enlarges one's view of existence... enlarges the private and the public world'. Such an experience is essential she argues because, 'in our particular society, it is the narrowed and narrowing view of life that often wins'. Much of Alice Walker's writing is a celebration. For writers like the South American Jorge Luis Borges, writing serves to 'ease the passing of time'. But Alice Walker takes a more optimistic and engaged position. For her writing is about 'saving the life that is your own'. It was Albert Camus who talked of the writer reaching for the 'invincible summer' that is in us all and in life.

For Ian McEwan both writing and reading are energising experiences. After reading Kafka, he says in an interview, he felt 'a great surge of liberation'. He no longer felt guilty 'at not being able to do the classic thing that English writing does: closely textured social commentary'. In her essay, 'Nine Beginnings', Margaret Atwood turns this learning experience into a precept. 'You learn by reading and writing, writing and reading,' she argues. 'As a craft it is learnt through the apprentice system, but you choose your own teachers. Sometimes they are alive, sometimes dead.'

It's not just ignorance or innocence that deadens writing and enfeebles our invincible summer. George Orwell in his essay, 'Why I Write', considered all writers to be egotistic, driven by, 'The desire to seem clever, to be talked about, to be remembered after death, to get your own back on grown-ups who snubbed you in childhood . . .' Certainly most new writers find it difficult to resist the temptation to impress; to write grandly. One of our students defined his lapses into 'purple' writing as 'trying-to-be-a-writer writing or, me-as-the-great-writer writing'. In 'Why I Write' Orwell also argued, like other commentators on the writing process, that the ego should be eliminated from writing. 'One can write nothing readable,' he claims, 'unless one constantly struggles to efface one's own personality. Good prose is like a window pane.' He goes on to say that in his own work where he lacked real purpose his writing became lifeless, full of 'purple passages, sentences without meaning, decorative adjectives and humbug generally'. Boris Pasternak, the Russian poet, in his autobiography pours scorn on the 'fine' writing of those who write literature, which in his view is 'a world of rhetoric, triteness and rounded phrases'. 'Whenever, in this kingdom in which artificiality is so established it goes unnoticed,' he writes, 'anyone opens his mouth not out of a taste for verbal eloquence but because *he knows a thing and wants to say it*, the result is an upheaval, as if the doors had been flung open and let in the noises of the street; not as if the speaker were reporting on the events in the town but as if the town itself were giving notice of its presence through his lips.' Take note, write the real.

The metaphor of surfaces and marks illuminates other aspects of the writing process; scraping away the surface clutter of writing for instance. After all we are surfacing so often, riding language thoughtlessly in the commonplaces of cliché. Real writing cuts through familiarity and the dull patina of habit to startle readers with a new and unexpected view of things. The English poet Philip Larkin puts it like this, 'it seems as if you've seen this sight, felt this feeling, had this vision, and have got to find a combination of words that will preserve it by setting it off in other people.' He seems to be saying writing is not just a matter of handing on a message, it is a question of ignition, and setting your reader alight. None of this is possible without finding the right 'combination of words'. You need to craft and shape your writing before it can be revelatory and inflammatory. The following chapters tell you much about the crafting. It should make you warm to the task.

Raising your Voice

Writing is not solely about self-expression and the exploration of the writer's private world. Writers also write on behalf of others. They are representative in the sense that they express what others find difficult to say. As Anaïs Nin put it, 'The role of the writer is not to say what we can all say, but what we are unable to say.' But writers speak on behalf of others in a political sense, as witnesses and advocates. Margaret Atwood sees this social and political role very clearly. Addressing new writers she says, 'As for the particular human society to which you yourself belong – sometimes you will feel you're speaking for it, sometimes – when it's taken an unjust form – against it, or for that other community, the community of the oppressed, the exploited, the voiceless.'

Confirming identity was Grace Nichols' purpose when she rewrote and published a collection of folk tales from her native Guyana. She wanted to give a tongue to the distinctive voice of her culture and preserve its identity and resist the forces of global conformity. Much of her own writing has been a struggle to assert her own identity in the face of the colonial experience that demeaned her native language and supplanted it with standardising English and the literary canon of Shakespeare and Dickens. Nigerian writers such as Chinua Achebe and Wole Soyinka have faced the same problem of identity in a postcolonial world and have sought to establish a literature that is expressive of the new Nigeria and not just a pale reflection of old imperialist values.

The other side of asserting the truth is exposing folly, hypocrisy and lies in each one of us but especially in those in high places where these vices supposedly flourish. In one sense all writing is an exposé whether of self or others but in some contexts writers have little choice but to take a stand against government. In our own permissive society literature has limited subversive value. As Italo Calvino says in his essay, 'The Right and Wrong Political Uses of Literature', writing in the liberal democracies, 'is being used merely to create the occasional pleasing contrast to the general ballooning of verbiage'. Russian writers like Alexander Solzhenitsyn were imprisoned in labour camps for challenging the communist dictator Stalin. Vaclav Havel, playwright and now president of the Czech republic, was imprisoned for seven years in the 1980s for defying the authority of the state and in his words, 'championing the power of the powerless'.

'Words are only words,' writes Calvino. 'They produce no friction in the world.' Except when they blow on the most powerful. You can look to authoritarian rule across the world and you will find writers raising their voices against oppression and rulers censoring and imprisoning them. Even in our own democracy the state has sought to silence the voices of writers. The celebrated 1950 obscenity trial of *Lady Chatterley's Lover*, the novel by D. H. Lawrence, saw John Mortimer the advocate and later novelist defending the right to freedom of expression against the paternalist suppression of the state. After the successful defence of the publishers against the charges of obscenity and offending public decency Mortimer pointed out that in his view the main purpose of literature was to offend and disturb. To disturb the comfortable classes out of their torpor and indifference, to unsettle the privileged and shake them into sympathy if not action.

Being a Writer

Most new writers are loath to confess to the supposedly tawdry secret of putting pen to paper, or to tapping the computer keys. Being a writer in Western culture has come to mean being cool, macho and well supplied with cash – at least that's the dominant cultural icon. Hand in hand with this image goes the notion that a great novel, poem or play must somehow flow miraculously from brain to page without sweat, tears or the consumption of too much time. In other words, the mythology is that you are only a 'writer' once you're published and earning money. There is, of course, the other extreme alternative that we instantly recognise: that of the unfêted genius bashing away in the dead of night, unpublished, poor and wracked with existential self-doubt.

Let's dispel these myths once and for all. You don't have to slick your hair or hang around chic cafés reading Hegel. Nor do you have to take to wearing a hair shirt. Being a writer means that you write and take yourself and your writing seriously. The credentials are persistence and passion. You will have periods of frustration and anger, but equally you will have times of delight and joy; what matters is that (a) you enjoy it and (b) that you stick at it no matter how difficult the circumstances and no matter what anyone else says or thinks of you – though hopefully you'll find people who can share and understand your endeavours. So, from now on think of yourself as a writer: you do have something to say, something entirely of your own. Don't apologise for this and don't feel guilty about it, but do get on and learn about the business of *how* you can best say what you want to say.

Writing is a craft and takes years of apprenticeship; with practice you get better. Yes, of course, there are exceptional writers who have a gift – no one can teach you style – but they too refer to the mental and physical effort involved in writing. T. S. Eliot considered it an 'intolerable wrestle with words', and all writers speak of learning a craft and of acquiring the discipline to sit down and write whenever possible.

'Constant toil is the law of art', said Honoré de Balzac, the nineteenth-century French novelist, and this is certainly borne out by a writer such as Franz Kafka, who worked for an insurance firm by day and wrote by night. Or Herman Melville, who was nearly 70 before he could give up working and for years was only able to write in the evenings and at weekends. Whilst Jane Austen had the privilege of leisure to enable her writing, she was still confined to working in the living room and had to hide her manuscripts under blotting paper so that the servants and visitors should not see her engaged in an activity then regarded as unsuitable for women. Novelist Beryl Bainbridge began writing in secret at the age of ten and glued her work inside a book, which she tried to burn in a panic of it being discovered and set the back door on fire. In a letter Joseph Conrad wrote of his despair at sitting at his desk for eight hours and managing to pen just three lines. Virginia Woolf, on the other hand, speaks of her 'rapture' when writing. If you're thinking it's all too late think of Mary Wesley whose first novel was published in her seventies; she is now a best-selling writer and has never looked back.

Clearly, finding the time to write can be a major obstacle in most people's lives. In her book *A Room of One's Own* Virginia Woolf argues for the necessity of economic independence for women writers to allow them the time and space to be creative. This is still something that most writers, whether female or male, crave. There will always be distractions, always pressures, always reasons to delay your writing for another hour, another year. Don't fall prey to avoidance tactics. Pick up that pen and write!

Work need not be a counterforce in your writing: on the contrary, it can inform and enrich. What are the situations you find yourself in? Who are the people you meet? Do you hate/ love what you do? Why? Most published writers do not earn enough to enable them to give up work, so whatever your feelings about your job or your situation you could use them in your writing. Fred Voss, a Californian poet, is an itinerant factory machinist who writes about his experiences on the factory floor. Many writers are also teachers, the Caribbean poet and Nobel prize-winner Derek Walcott being just one example.

There are writers who cannot write even though they do have the time. Irina Ratushinskaya was held in a Russian gulag for years; she composed poetry in her head and memorised it, writing down what she could on tiny fragments of cloth or paper which she concealed wherever possible. Dennis Potter, the screenwriter, was only able to write in the periods when his skin disease, psoriasis, was not reducing him to agony and inertia.

You may think that these are rather remarkable examples, but completing any piece of writing to a point where you are honestly happy with it is a considerable achievement. There are plenty of female writers who still manage to work, bring up children and somehow write their novels around everything else. The important thing is to keep at it regularly, set your own time-scale and make it realistic. If you can only spare ten minutes a day so be it, but be absolutely unmoving about those ten minutes and don't allow anything else to crowd them out. If you want to be published don't think it's beyond you. Go for it, but recognise that it doesn't happen quickly or easily for the majority. You'll have many more rejection letters than acceptances and you mustn't let them deter you. Richard Adams's novel *Watership Down* was rejected about thirty times before finally being taken on by a publisher.

Insecurity and dread as a new writer are not things that should hold you back either! Every blank page is a challenge whether you are a seasoned writer or not. You are not going to write well every time you sit down and very few writers allow themselves the freedom to write without nagging worry and self-criticism. Just write! Don't paralyse yourself with the thought that you've nothing to say. Write because you want to. In his novel *Tropic of Cancer* Henry Miller sees writing as a song sung, something you do naturally. His writer/narrator says 'To sing you must first open your mouth. You must have a pair of lungs, and a little knowledge of music. . . . The essential thing is to *want* to sing.'

So write and take risks. Stop worrying whether it has potential – that's a decision you make when you read and reject. Besides, if it doesn't suit your present purposes it may be useful for another piece later on.

The concept of writing and redrafting is horrifying to some. 'But it's finished!' you cry when you reach the end of the first draft. It isn't. In fact, the core of your work hasn't even begun. There are established writers who throw away two thirds of their work on a novel and rewrite the rest. A playwright can be engaged in significant changes well into the rehearsal period. Fay Weldon usually redrafts her stories eight or nine times. Beryl Bainbridge reads her work out aloud to herself at night over and over again and makes corrections there and then. Rudyard Kipling revised his prose work by repeatedly striking out words he considered unnecessary, and as a result his prose is lucid, economic and deceptively simple. Comparatively few final drafts resemble first drafts.

You may be someone who writes on loose sheets of paper or has a notebook. You may have a journal. Some writers find that whole chunks of dialogue come to mind and find it easier to speak into a dictaphone to record them. Your processes will inevitably differ from anyone else's; try things out and see how it aids your writing. All of it helps you to discover ways of working as a writer. What time of day do you write best? Do you have a favourite place for working? Is there anything you like to have near you when you write? Make notes on the books or newspaper articles that interest you. List the films or exhibitions you've seen recently. Why did they appeal to you? What did you learn about craft from them? As a writer you draw on life; just thinking and observing will take a lot of your time.

All this is the *process* of writing, which has increasingly been recognised and articulated this century. Traditionally, it has always been far more fashionable to claim that a novel was written in matter of weeks, a film in a fortnight, or a poem in a single sitting. This is perhaps understandable: the idea of a person sitting at a desk for months or years, quite alone, doesn't exactly project a dynamic image. This isn't what we expect to hear. It is perhaps a mark of how difficult some writers find it to articulate the way they work: documenting the process of playmaking or the evolution of a poem *is* difficult. Sometimes that process is fast, mostly it's protracted.

In the introduction to her book *The Agony and the Ego* Clare Boylan battles with Romantic descriptions of process, using terms like 'mystery' and 'magic' to describe it. Where do ideas come from? From the Muse the Romantics would say. How do we hit upon a certain sequence of words? Divine inspiration they would reply. Much twentieth-century psychology, however, argues that the writer's unconscious is the wellspring of creativity. Whatever the source of the ideas, process – the actual crafting of those ideas – is very much about technique and structure. Read any interview with a writer and you'll soon realise that writing never tumbles onto the page in complete form.

Do you call yourself a writer? Or are you bitten into denial by the sadly prevalent view that writers are both self-indulgent and useless to society? Ignore all platitudes about writers. Tony Harrison famously describes himself as a poet in his passport. What would you declare?

Locating Yourself as a Writer

There is a dramatist in America called Louis Catron who asks new writers to draw up their personal creed, starting each sentence with *I believe*. For however long it takes, each writer has to search inside themselves for their deepest convictions about life. This creed, Catron argues, can reveal a set of passions, a sort of manifesto, which may then guide the writer to what they want to or have to say.

Knowing what you want to say relates to how you perceive the world. In order to adopt informed opinions and judgements you need to have as much information as possible; you need to be alert to everything going on about you. How do you relate to your environment? What and whom do you believe and why? What exactly do you want to impart to your reader/listener/spectator?

Every writer has a point of view and politics cannot be avoided in writing. If our sense of self is constructed through language as current theory asserts, then it is impossible to exist outside our cultural history and environment. And no language is neutral, because there is always a speaker or a writer behind it, always someone making decisions and trying to manipulate your response. In the Western world that manipulating voice has historically been white, male and educated, or to put it another way, we have been dominated by the discourse of capitalist patriarchy. Discourses attached to race, gender and class are the most obvious and many of us have been made aware of the oppression of certain sectors of society either through personal experience, the media, or through implementation of equal opportunities schemes and the advent of political correctness.

The postmodern debate, among others, has not only critically validated the voices and experiences of writers who have traditionally been marginalised but has also celebrated this multiplicity of viewpoints. In doing so it has challenged the so-called canons of literature and sought to redefine them.

One way of looking at the canon is as the body of literature which has been/is taught within a culture. This body of literature is seen as enshrining that culture's values. In English literature indigenous critics, reviewers, and academics have persistently hailed writers like Shakespeare and Jane Austen as 'great', on the basis of their apparent universality and moral seriousness; on their 'Englishness'. As a result, they are often compulsorily read in schools and universities as though they are untouchable, and many of us feel intimidated in their presence.

The canon, however, does not yield to the rigid definitions promoted by so many of the political and ideological movements of this century. Its existence has to do with an accumulation of state-institutional decisions made in the name of, for example, taste and morality (censorship) or appropriate reading for children in schools. Why, for instance, are certain poets on the reading lists at school and not others? Why is Ted Hughes there and not Derek Walcott? Why do we have to read Dickens but are not allowed Virginia Woolf? Why is there no room for Nadine Gordimer? Selections and exclusions like these can lead to a narrow and biased view of 'literature' and could clearly be used ideologically – to promote nationalism for instance or white suprematism.

Some have argued that the canon has been created through standards of 'literariness'. This debate addresses the question, what is good art? and tries to discriminate between so-called high and low art. Who sets the standards? Who draws up lists of Nobel prize-winners? Who decides which writers to hype? And why is there a persistent snobbery about books labelled 'genre fiction' – sci-fi, romance, horror and so on?

Whatever the canon is, it is certainly protean. Postmodernism has allowed for a plurality of voices and a variety of 'Englishnesses'. What we should welcome is that more minority voices are being heard than ever before and more 'lost' histories are being uncovered. Books such as Tillie Olsen's *Silences* have chronicled the history of women's oppression and had widespread impact on readers and writers. And writers like Chinua Achebe and Alice Walker must smile at the fact that they have become part of the very exclusivity they fought against, the literary canon. Perhaps the questions you might ask yourself are by what authority you speak, and who your readers are?

With the advent of postmodernism authority has become a problematic term. In this secular, traumatised century that has known two world wars and seen the devastating consequences of technology in the nuclear bomb, the notions of History and Truth have been seen to vary according to whose side you support. The Romantic era perceived 'great' writers to be custodians of the Truth, as though they had access to a wisdom that was beyond the merely mortal. The writer, if you like, had the key to unlock the mystery of the universe.

This is not the view held now. Think of Auschwitz. No one account of an individual survivor of a concentration camp is held up as exemplary; instead we look at the mass of stories and testimonials and appreciate the significance of them all. We are aware too of those who did not survive to tell their tale. History is full of oppressive silences. How do we verify history? Whose history is it? Certain revisionist historians are already arguing that the Holocaust never happened; that it was simply a Jewish conspiracy. Single, unified versions of the past and present have brought about and justified dictatorships and colonisations, the oppression of women and the marginalisation of children – to name a few horrors. There are no absolutes. History with a capital H has been usurped by individual *histories* each valid in their own right; Truth with a capital T is a chimera and only a multiplicity of *truths* exist. There is no ultimate meaning to be divined in man nor the universe; there are no solutions to anything. Self and identity as fixed concepts have been challenged; we can theorise to our heart's content but the self is fluid, perplexing and ever-changing.

So how does a writer get to grips with any of this? You might look at Stephen Connor's book *Post-modern Culture* for a

useful way in. Or you might read Roland Barthes' essay 'Death
of the Author', which declares the age of the omniscient author
as over. Gone are the days of the reassuring if fake objectivity
of narrative style. Gone too are the days when authors can
make pronouncements like sages or prophets. Text, Barthes
argues, is sufficient in itself: the notion of author imposes a
limit or closed meaning on the text and originality is impossible since text is 'a multi-dimensional space in which a variety
of writings... blend and clash'. Here Barthes is simply drawing our attention once again to the notion that none of us exist
as islands in the world. Language is the result of many influences in our lives. It does not emerge out of nowhere but is
learned and should be treated with caution. It is language,
Barthes argues, that gives us access to ourselves and the
world. It may be frustratingly limited but it is all we have.

Elsewhere in his work Barthes makes a useful distinction
between what he calls 'readable' and 'writable' text: the former
is a description of the text which is apparently transparent and
'objective', asking the reader to be passive; the latter applies to
modern text which demands the reader's participation in the
production of meanings which are seemingly inexhaustible.
The overt manipulation of the reader is very much a trait of the
postmodern novel. Italo Calvino's *If on a Winter's Night a
Traveller* is a fine example of this where he gleefully refuses
to indulge the reader's expectations of novelistic convention.

Similarly, other postmodern writers refuse to be drawn on
the standardisation of narrative. John Fowles offers alternative
endings in *The French Lieutenant's Woman*. Often you'll find a
circular structure as opposed to a linear one. Perhaps certain
questions haven't been answered or others have been raised.
There isn't a definitive resolution to the story where everything is tied up neatly. And these days you'll find it is as
common in novels as it is in screen and stage plays to have
multiple, episodic narratives. We have no difficulty interpreting the fast-paced, fragmentary narrative structures of soap
operas; most of us are sophisticated postmodern readers and
viewers without even realising it!

Narrators, on the other hand, are an unreliable, disturbing
lot in postmodern fiction. They can contradict themselves, tell
blatant untruths or present such a confusing collection of

information that we're left wrestling with a story that simply won't fit together. Robert Coover's short story 'The Babysitter' seems to change viewpoint a number of times and it is impossible to work out how many narrators are involved in telling the story. Neither can you work out what, if anything, has happened, though sinister things are in the air.

Writers of postmodern fiction are, as you see, very self-conscious in their crafting. They make their presence felt, but in a way that blurs and confounds. Whatever you think of postmodernism it's all around you. Our point is simply this: if you want to be a writer you need to know about past and, in particular, about present developments in your artistic culture. Writing like Charles Dickens in the late twentieth century is unlikely to attract many readers, and you have to find appropriate forms and language for what you want to say.

This is a challenging era for a writer. On the one hand, there is a strong camp arguing that the process of writing is one of self-discovery and a means of understanding yourself in relation to the world. On the other hand, postmodernists are telling us that the search for a fixed self is pointless; that we will discover only selves and that none of them will be 'real'! So theoretically we're in a double-bind: but don't let it stop you writing! Read postmodern works. Explore postmodern writing through experimenting and with this experience decide where you stand as a writer.

Booklist

Atwood, M., 'Nine Beginnings' in *The Writer on Her Work*, ed. J. Sternberg (Virago, London, 1992).

Bainbridge, B., 'Interview' in the *Guardian*, 8 April 1995.

Barthes, R., 'The Death of the Author' in *Modern Criticism and Theory*, ed. D. Lodge (Longman, New York, 1988).

Boylan, C., *The Agony and the Ego: the Art and Strategy of Fiction Writing Explored* (Penguin, Harmondsworth, 1993).

Calvino, I., *If on a Winter's Night a Traveller* (Picador, London, 1982).

Calvino, I., 'Right and Wrong Uses of Literature' in *Literature and the World*, ed. D. Waller (OUP, London, 1990).

Catron, L. E., *The Elements of Playwriting* (Macmillan, New York, 1993).

Connor, S., *Post-modern Culture* (Blackwell, Oxford, 1989).

Coover, R., *Pricksongs and Descants* (Minerva, London, 1991).

Didion, J., 'Why I Write' in *The Writer on Her Work*, ed. J. Sternberg (Virago, London, 1992).

Duffy, M., *That's How It Was* (Virago, London, 1990).

Gordimer, N., *The Essential Gesture* (Cape, London, 1988).

Gordon, M., 'The Parable of the Cave: In Praise of Water Colours' in *The Writer On Her Work*, ed. J. Sternberg (Virago, London, 1992).

Goyen, W., Quoted in *The Writer's Chapbook*, ed. G. Plimpton (Penguin, Harmondsworth, 1992).

McEwan, I., Interview in the *Independent Magazine*, April 1990.

Miller, H., *Tropic of Cancer* (HarperCollins, London, 1993).

Nichols, G., *Come On Into My Tropical Garden* (Black, London, 1988).

Olsen, T., *Silences* (Virago, London, 1980).

Orwell, G., 'Why I Write' in *Collected Essays, Journalism and Letters*. Vol. 1 (Penguin, Harmondsworth, 1970).

Pasternak, B., *Poems 1955–59 and an Essay In Autobiography* (Collins, London, 1990).

Walker, A., *In Search of Our Mother's Gardens* (The Woman's Press, London, 1984).

Woolf, V., *A Room of One's Own* (Grafton, London, 1977).

2 The Workshop Way
LIZ ALMOND

For many writers the time spent in workshops is time they spend experimenting and trying out new ways of approaching their writing. That word experiment brings to mind the laboratory, a place where transformation takes place under controlled conditions. We all have at our disposal the basic elements – language – but perhaps unlike experiments conducted in a laboratory, with writing, the results are less predictable and measurable. It's important for you to realise that the work you are expected to produce in workshops is first draft raw material for reworking and extending in your own time; a workshop is more about process than product.

What other ways are there of defining a workshop? I put this question to people who regularly participate in them and their response was unanimous:

'It's practical, isn't it?'
'It's a hands-on approach.'
'It's collaborative, a shared experience.'
'It's reading, writing, discussion, all rolled into one.'

The atmosphere in a workshop should encourage both experiment and application to a particular task. It should provide a safe environment whereby you can get to know and respect other people through their work and begin to develop an ability to offer constructive criticism. Sometimes a workshop leader might suggest passing round written work so that comments can be written down and more time is allowed for a considered response. You might find it helpful to make friends with someone in the group whom you feel comfortable with, whose own work you like and admire and whose critical perception you can trust. Sharing work with another writer outside the larger workshop context can build confidence and help overcome fear and reticence.

Workshops are usually devised in order to focus on a particular aspect of your writing and the technique may be applicable to poetry, prose or anything else you may be working on at the time. Exemplary texts are often used as a starting point for discussion and are chosen to provide a model for what you may subsequently be asked to write. A large percentage of the workshop may well be spent writing and the advantage of being made to write rather than waiting until you feel like it, is that by allowing the pen to move quickly across the page you may access material you didn't know was there. Decisions about style and form can then be made later, either at a later stage in the workshop, or outside the workshop if you choose to continue with the work. Inevitably one of the main benefits of regular workshop practice is that you become less dependent on the idea of inspiration and increasingly confident that the more you write the more you have to say and the more you write the more fluent your style will become. Of course sometimes people's exposure to new ideas and working methods in workshops results in a period of confusion before their own voice re-emerges stronger and more distinct.

Because writing is such a solitary activity, you may find that the workshop's value to you is less the writing element and more the contact with people who share your enthusiasms, preoccupations, problems and passions. Your immersion in the world of the imagination that adds a whole dimension to your life is validated and nourished by this contact. If you're suffering from self-doubt about why you write, someone else may be feeling the opposite and their optimism and energy can refuel yours! Exchanging ideas about what you've read and why you like or dislike it, information about competitions, courses, new outlets, swapping anecdotes about circumstances that can inhibit creative work, are all necessary to writers as an antidote to working alone, and help to make them feel connected to a wider community of writers. Talking to other writers about the writing process and learning how to evaluate what works and what does not, as well as being able to identify strengths and weaknesses, will foster a more focused critical attention to your own and other people's work. New writers in particular may suffer from demotivation and loss of confidence, but as writing becomes more and more a part of your whole identity, you'll recognise that you're driven to write and routine practice will become part of your lifestyle.

In workshops attached to festivals or conducted as part of residential courses there is obviously no opportunity to develop close working alliances with other writers. Workshop leaders in these contexts know that they will be faced with a diverse group ranging from novice to seasoned writer and that any exercise will have to cater for that broad spectrum. Occasionally participants respond by being unhelpfully competitive as a defence mechanism which can be intimidating for beginner writers – don't be deterred!

Evening classes in adult education or through the Workers' Educational Association or extra-mural departments of colleges will similarly be made up of a wide variety of writers drawn from all walks of life. With no academic assessment involved, these kind of sessions can be very enjoyable and are a great way to meet other writers in your area.

In academia, the structures of course and degree routes establish a certain ethos which includes formal assessment. The needs of students in their first year will differ from those in their final year who will have decided what kind of writing they want to be engaged in and who may find detailed discussion of their own work, and issues surrounding it, to be the most useful focus for workshops, rather than the generation of new work. By this stage in your career you may have developed an interest in critical theory which you are keen to relate to your own creative work: theories of authorship, of the nature of the postmodern text and so on.

As you and your writing mature, personal change and growing self-awareness may have forged an understanding of the deeper psychological motivation behind your work and how that might be translated and expressed. Robert Olen Butler, a sceptical workshop leader who nevertheless runs a master's degree in creative writing, is adamant that writers must be brought back to 'the locus, the location and how to get into and stay in their artistic unconscious... how to nakedly confront their deepest feelings and not let them write about anything else'.

Getting into your artistic unconscious is not easy in the workshop situation until you have become comfortable with the idea of exposing not only your writing to group scrutiny, but something of yourself as well. What do we mean by 'artistic unconscious'? One definition would be the psychological motivation and driving force behind your writing. It involves tapping into an intuitive mode of thinking, coming to understand the meaning of what your imagination produces and how to control and shape, and make it coherent to readers. It can be unsettling or disturbing or even frightening when memories come to the surface and it is sometimes the act of writing which recovers those memories. However, writers who draw on their artistic unconscious often produce writing that has psychological realism and potency. Perhaps this is why some people writing in workshops tend to self-censor and write material which might be technically impressive but devoid of feeling or depth. Writing that is both technically proficient and has emotional impact, does not come without effort and deep thinking. Many workshop ideas that seem strange to you when you are presented with them may actually be designed to help access these deep levels of consciousness: guided fantasies, exercises to do with childhood memory, to name but two. People are often surprised by the work that arises from such workshops and the accompanying emotional content.

Six Good Ground Rules

1 Observe silence when writing in a workshop – creative thought is impaired by superficial conversation.

2 Always try to write as much as possible in the given time – the movement of pen on page sometimes produces material you had no idea was there. You are not just working with the conscious mind.

3 Don't be too self-conscious about the work produced – it's raw, waiting to be worked on, you're not trying to prove anything.

4 Be supportive of each other, be constructively critical, not negative.

5 Do not use the workshop as an opportunity to show off technical virtuosity – it intimidates other people.

6 Do not refuse to read your work out week after week or it will become an increasingly frightening prospect.

It takes time to develop a critical vocabulary if you're not used to responding to other people's work. Sometimes it's useful to ask them questions about their intention and purpose so that they can begin to gauge how readers are responding. You might find it helpful to begin by commenting on stylistic successes; an image that works particularly well or an outstanding phrase that stays with you. Common criticisms are the over-liberal use of adjectives or adverbs, sentences which are too long and complicated, dialogue that fails to be idiomatic.

Keeping a journal or notebook is an invaluable support activity to workshop sessions. Most importantly, it builds regular writing activity into your life and helps you remember small details which might otherwise be forgotten. It's portable too, so you can jot down snippets of conversation heard on buses, in cafés, anywhere. You can keep it beside your bed for recording dreams or thoughts on waking, that time of the day when we are often closest to our unconscious processes.

Many professional writers keep such a journal, one of the best known is Virginia Woolf's *A Writer's Diary*.

Workshop Writing

1 'This Is the Indelible Place You Lived In' (quotation from 'The Return' by Jamie McKendrick)

This workshop is designed to access memory of a house, possibly from childhood. Two model texts form the basis of the workshop by demonstrating close attention to physical detail, the use of the senses and a symbolic use of threshold and keyhole for heightened dramatic atmosphere. Although both pieces of writing use keys in a literal way, both too are about the symbolic unlocking of memory and the unconscious. One piece is fictional prose and the other a poem, thus catering for a range of writing within the group: 'The Cellar Key' by Michèle Roberts from *Daughters Of The House*, 'The Return' by Jamie McKendrick from *The Kiosk At The Brink*.

A The first part of the exercise takes the form of a guided fantasy which your tutor will talk you through as you write in the first person without stopping to think about any stylistic features. The aim is to get as much raw material down on paper as possible.

You are returning in your mind to a house you know well from your past whose geography you always carry with you in your imagination. Why is that? Was it a happy or an unhappy place? You are outside this house walking towards the front door. You notice a detail about the outside, maybe from your peripheral vision, and you pause for a moment to concentrate on it more fully. You move right up close to the door and take a key to open it. As the door opens, you are conscious of a smell in the house that you associate with someone. Describe it. You enter the house and make your way to the kitchen where a familiar view through the window reminds you of a particular incident. Notice how you feel about this incident, can you locate the emotional atmosphere of it? You turn away from the window and see an object on the table. It is well known to you and you make some notes about it. You leave the kitchen and go upstairs. On the landing you have to choose which room to go into. When you have made a decision, enter that room and let another memory come to the surface. You take a last look around the room, go back downstairs and leave the house. How do you feel as you leave it – reluctant, sad, relieved, disturbed, nostalgic?

B Now read through this material and circle any parts in pencil that you don't like and underline those parts which you like because of their accuracy, emotional potency or the way the writing brings the place to life. Then rewrite using third person narration, that is 'he' and 'she', remembering that you can now change and invent as much as you like. Michèle Roberts when talking about her novel, *Daughters Of The House*, on radio, said that some of the domestic objects she used were based on actual things she owns while others were pure invention, but the reader cannot distinguish between them. One condition that is helpful with this particular exercise is not to vary what is sometimes called 'psychic distance' – stay with the close-up point of view, don't pull back or alter the focus but concentrate on recreating the three-dimensional, fully realised place. Think also of the relationship between fiction and autobiography, the way 'objective truth' if you like, becomes a more and more elusive concept. Nevertheless the emotional resonance of your piece of writing should aim to demonstrate Virginia Woolf's belief that our imaginations are structured by 'moments of being' that weld emotion and the physical world into a symbolic whole. Talking and thinking about the interrelationship between fiction and autobiography problematises the opposing pieces of advice often offered to writers, to write about what you know or to write about what you don't know. Of course all writers do both.

2   Everything Happens Somewhere

As Julia Casterton remarks in her book *Creative Writing*, many people have a tendency to write in a vacuum. They neglect to pay attention to context or ignore the creative possibilities of exploiting landscape, place, weather or season. These elements can all add dimension and texture to writing, particularly if made to serve a quality of feeling, or a dramatic incident. I often choose examples from contemporary small press publications to introduce students both to new writers and also to the outlets themselves, so that they can see the kind of work getting published now. I have used a short, short story, a form that lends itself particularly well for use in workshops, 'In The Mountains' by Kathy Janowitz. The story's themes of illness, fragility and isolation, are perfectly matched by use of its alpine setting which exploits colour, temperature, the contrast between indoors and out and texture, to build a relationship between the rarefied atmosphere of the place and the heightened moment experienced by the main character.

A   First, choose an emotion or a dramatic situation and then think carefully about an equivalent in terms of landscape or terrain. Brainstorm several possibilities including the use of colour and its associations. Make notes too about the particular features of your chosen landscape. When you've exhausted those possibilities, create a fictional character who has that emotion or is in that situation and write a short biography of that character. Make sure you describe their physical appearance also. Now, why might they be in this particular place? How did they get there? Who do they meet when they get there? What happens to them while they are there? You can begin now to structure a short story incorporating detail from your working notes as is appropriate. Concentrate in particular on the opening paragraph. The intention is to set the scene and establish the tone of the whole piece right at the start. Remember that a short story traditionally focuses on a character and a moment of revelation or a significant turning point in their lives.

3   Black and White

A workshop that uses the black and white photograph as a starting point for writing and also draws on the vocabulary of photography – frame, composition, negative, positive, closeup, portrait, landscape, cropping, enlarging, and so on.

A   Everyone is given an image to work from as an impetus, preferably ones that make strong aesthetic statements. A suggested exemplary text for looking at, prior to writing, is 'Photograph: Dairymaids' by Jo Shapcott from *Electroplating The Baby*, in which the writer has used an image as a basis for a poem. She describes what is actually there and restricts herself to black and white before going on to develop a sense of what is not seen, or to consider the latent meaning. It's useful when looking at your image to focus on the frozen moment rather than the before or after implied by a developing narrative.

B   With your black and white photograph in front of you, what is the first detail you notice? Think about what might be happening just outside the frame and to the right. Do not use any colour in your writing, but only black and white and what those colours may suggest to you in terms of metaphor or simile. Draw attention to the composition of the whole image and think about what it means. Is it composed or has the photographer crept up on the subject unbeknown to them? Try to exploit the technical vocabulary of photography if it appeals to you. If you are working on a poem, then consider the importance of end-line as a means of introducing your central thoughts about the image and what it really says to you when you get beyond the surface.

C   Now try something different. Pretend that you, or a character you invent, have found this photograph somewhere, lying in the street, between the pages of a book, in a newspaper... You look at it in a completely different way, use it more imaginatively, construct a fantasy around it. You might like to use the found object as a structure for a story because it's got potential for movement and change, it can be a catalyst for plot development. You can introduce a restrained use of colour if you wish.

4   Becoming Someone Else

A workshop that explores the device of fictional personae in poetry in order to set up a discussion on authenticity, authorship, autobiography and poetic voice. There seems to be a deep-seated resistance to transferring the methods of fiction to poetry and a widely held belief in the convention that the poet's concern is only with articulating personally felt emotion. This is a limiting and anachronistic view of the poet which derives from the Romantic tradition which modernism called into question and transformed. In my workshops I like to encourage writers to be more experimental in terms of the poetic voice they choose to adopt. There are plenty of examples of poems that adopt a mask or persona: Lorca's 'Barren Orange Tree', Carol Ann Duffy's 'Warming Her Pearls' to name a couple. The one I've used recently is Paul Durcan's 'Portrait Of Greta Moll' from his new collection *Give Me Your Hand*, because not only is the voice that of Greta, so we have a man adopting a woman's voice, but the poem was inspired by a Matisse painting and portraits can be a useful stimulus for this kind of work.

A   Choose someone from a film, or from a newspaper story, or someone from a portrait painting, or someone from history who interests you. You have to identify imaginatively with that figure. Consider the idea that this method of approaching poetry enables you to extend your work out from the personal. Begin by making notes about the character, what is particularly interesting about them, what drives them, what preoccupies them, does what they look like matter? If you're working from an image, try to look beyond it, to find more than is there. You have to push the imagination to work hard, to let association and suggestion have free rein.

B   You may need to do some research. For example, the life of the artist who painted the picture may provide information which you may want to incorporate in your work. If you're writing from the point of view of someone who lived abroad, you may need details of flora, fauna, topography, food, and so on. Again, this approach to writing combines what you know with what you don't know. The person may have been put into an imagined situation by you but their psychology will be informed by your own experience. You may find this method of 'emptying' your feelings into a fictional character oblique at first but it can be a powerful way to explore yourself. In this way, public and private worlds are collapsed into each other rather than kept separate and distinct.

5 'The Poetry of Household Objects'

The title of this workshop is a quotation taken from a short story by Gabriel García Márquez called 'Light Is Like Water'. It is a favourite theme of his, since in *100 Years of Solitude* he says 'things have a life of their own, it's simply a matter of waking up their souls'. Márquez has a particular talent for making the ordinary magical and fantastic and in this story extended metaphor is used as a structuring device. In fact thinking metaphorically is the demand that this workshop makes of you in your aim to defamiliarise and thereby invest objects with a meaning that exceeds their normal usage.

A   As a starting point imagine you are given a brown cardboard box tied up with string and sealed with wax. When you open the box there is a yellow pottery jug. Inside it is a Swiss army knife and a string of amber beads. Describe each object in as much detail as you can. One or all of these objects are going to be central to your writing. Now try and make notes about possible strange contexts, changes of use, alteration of scale; exploit the bizarre and surreal as much as possible.

B   Then try to describe a sequence of actions involving an object, so that human agency is brought to bear and there is movement of some kind. The people moving the object(s) may be shadowy, still at the margins of your imagination. Shift your attention from object to person. Who are they? Where are they? Think about location in more detail, since it must be developed in terms of its potential to enhance the visual impact of the writing.

C   Another approach to defamiliarisation, or the making strange, is to adopt a 'Martian' point of view and pretend you are an alien confronting an object that is familiar to you but not to it and who may be able to make no sense of it whatever. Read Craig Raine's 'A Martian Sends A Postcard Home'.

D   Alternatively, how might people react when a new invention is made available to a population for the first time? The impact of radio for instance, or electricity, or the magnet. Look at Kathleen Jamie's poem 'Crystal Set' as an example of this kind of approach.

6   A Poem Doesn't Have to Begin with an Idea

A workshop that begins with a discussion about where ideas come from and looks at how writing itself, and the material conditions necessary for it, can be turned into content. Jo Shapcott's poem 'Writing Positions' is useful as a model in that it claims writing has no mystique, 'there's no magic in it', creative work is seen to happen in the context of ordinary domestic life.

A   Look at a piece of writing and imagine working back to its first draft – what might have been the starting point? I chose 'Mrs Midas' by Carol Ann Duffy because it suggests brainstorming around the colour gold and discovering a narrative in the process. Or take a myth and use it as a way of articulating something personal. In conjunction with this poem look at the section on silver and gold in Derek Jarman's *Chroma*, which shows how rich a texture of ideas can arise from scraps of language, phrases, associations and common-place sayings. Now, think of a colour, a particular colour that has an affinity for you and try to write some notes for each of the following categories:

> myth,
> a well-known saying or proverb,
> something ordinary,
> something exotic,
> food or drink,
> a famous painting,
> a country,
> a quote from another writer,
> a dictionary definition,
> a scientific association,
> why it is personal to you,
> anything else that comes to mind.

B   Using these notes as your resource, begin to shape a piece of writing that is aiming ultimately to pivot on a contradiction or antimony. For example, 'Mrs Midas' explores the idea of desiring something and then discovering that it's unpalatable or intolerable. In order to help you structure the piece, think of it having a crisis point where the positive begins to descend towards the negative.

C   As another way of generating raw material, take a coloured image, preferably a reproduction of a painting. I have a collection of postcards that I distribute at random when working with a group. Take the top right-hand corner and describe it. Take the top left-hand corner and describe that. Take the two-inch square at the bottom centre and describe it. Also, concentrate on the dominant colour in your picture – what does it make you think of? Go beyond the details and now contemplate the whole. See if you can forge a relationship between each element.

D   Look at Mimi Khalvati's 'A Persian Miniature' which operates within the same parameters. It also makes statements about the poem being produced in a workshop where she was asked to do exactly what you've been asked! She very cleverly opens out from the particular to the universal by making a political reading of her image that relates to cultural identity and imperialism.

7   A Curious Room

Angela Carter, when talking about formative influences on her work, cited Hollywood film, fairy story and her own curious idea that before we are born a room is created for us which contains everything our imaginations need and objects which have symbolic meaning for us. This workshop draws on the idea of the curious room as an imaginative resource and aims for writing which fits the tradition of magic realism.

A   Think about a room like no other room you've ever been in, which has no obvious function, does not contain conventional furniture, but is furnished instead with things that express your particular interests or obsessions, things which might symbolise the unconscious and which conform to the logic of dreams. This is a room designed to nourish the imagination – you can play with scale in order to fit things into it which might otherwise be too big, you can bring back from the past things that have been lost or discarded, you can play with the future in terms of its possibilities.

B   Think for a moment too about your own writing – are there recurring themes, words, things, that could be translated into symbolic objects and put in the room to remind you of their importance? Now you are ready to write a description of your own curious room. The process of completing the furnishing of this room may take several sessions, items may occur to you out of the blue or in dreams, so keep returning to your room in your mind from time to time and draw on it as a creative resource for your work.

Use this piece of writing as a way of taking the emotional temperature of your work. How do you feel when you read it back? Does it have a tangible effect? If not, can you expect other readers to respond positively to it? Is there something missing and if so, can you identify what it might be?

8   Poet's News

This is a workshop which considers the role of writers in society. BBC TV (Poet's News) recorded poets reading work which they wrote in response to a news item, a response which in most cases was more critical, more unashamedly biased than an 'objective' newsreading. Consider how the role of writers changes in a culture which heavily censors the written word. Does writing have a subversive role to play in the contemporary world?

A   Using newspaper stories as an initial stimulus, try to imagine the story as told from another angle or point of view. It may be useful to make two lists which may come to represent two different narrative voices in the same piece of writing. Your alternative version of the story should aim to make a relationship between 'rhetoric' and 'reality'. Look at the poem 'Two News Stories In *The New York Times*' by Michèle Roberts which does exactly that with its alternation of voice of the establishment and its rhetoric of exclusion and the imagined account of a victim of that policy of exclusion. Stylistically there is a contrast so that we can see how form and content can be manipulated for maximum effect.

9   'I Forgot What Things Were Called and Saw Instead What They Are' (from 'Strawberries' by Margaret Atwood in *Murder In The Dark*)

This workshop is intended to help shape a memory that is linked with the physical world.

A   Choose a moment of extreme emotion and remember how it affected you physically. Be precise and clear about where you were, what season it was, what time of day and what object has become inseparable from that feeling.
B   Now, having read 'Strawberries' and noted the way it falls into two halves, the first distorted by anger and the second focused and displaced, or 'cooled' bring your emotion and the object together in a piece of concentrated writing the aim of which is to be complete in itself like a still-life, an

arrangement of elements, a composition that has discarded anything extraneous to its purpose.

In order to weight the object, and give it particular significance, make it noticeable to the reader, try clustering adjectives, while omitting them elsewhere. Raymond Carver is a writer who uses this method in his short fiction.

Writing On

Self and Creativity

Psychological realism and an understanding of what motivates character and drives plot can be achieved through scrutiny of one's own life and key structuring events. This strategy is close to Virginia Woolf's theory that every life is shaped by 'moments of being' and that the writer's imagination returns to these moments again and again as an emotional resource.

The following exercises are designed to help you access your own moments of being and to appreciate how contradiction and ambivalence can enrich your writing.

- Were you happiest indoors or outdoors as a child? Why was that? Can you recall incidents that explain why? Has this preference stayed with you, carrying the past into the present? Write a piece of prose in which you visit a place with the express intent of reliving some past event. Perhaps it is a corn field where you always walked with your grandfather. Or may be it's the barn where you were kissed for the first time.

- Describe the atmosphere in a house from two points of view, happy and sad. Think of an incident from your past whereby another member of the family creates a drama. You are the passive onlooker. Write the incident from your point of view. Then from the other person's point of view. This exercise encourages imaginative flexibility in terms of inhabiting another person's point of view. Try looking at 'House Of Changes' by Jeni Couzyn for inspiration.

- Think about where you live now. Is there anything you'd like to change about it? What and why? Write a letter to someone abroad telling them what you've done. How might this exercise relate to the previous one? Changing our physical environment is believed by psychologists to indicate a mental attitude that is not fixed or stuck in old habits. The use of the letter-writing mode is an intimate, confessional one, supposedly addressed to one reader only but sometimes used in fiction to expand the 'inner voice' of a character. If you need an example read the short story 'Dear George' by Helen Simpson in *The Minerva Book of Short Stories*, No. 5.

• Keep a notebook with you to record one day's thought processes. What are you thinking about while washing up? How do you react to a telephone call? Record what interests you, and which memories replay themselves in your imagination. Fragments of what you write may be incorporated into what you are currently writing or used as the basis for a stream of consciousness prose piece, where the writing attempts to emulate patterns of thought. Look at Katie Campbell's *Live, In The Flesh*, which illustrates a fragmented, dislocated approach to fiction, time and subjectivity.

Where and Why There?

• What kind of places inspire you? Choose one that means a lot to you and use it as a fictional setting. Why does it inspire you? Does it have certain resonances or memories? Perhaps you visited a house which frightened you as a child, or maybe you have a secret place where you go to escape from everyone. You might find Derek Walcott's 'Sea Chantey' in *The Rattle Bag* helpful or Janette Turner Hospital's collection of stories called *Dislocations*.

• Use indoors and outdoors to create dramatic movement in a piece of writing. Perhaps someone is watching a house from a distance, unknown to the people inside it. Perhaps someone leaves a church in a great hurry, watched by someone from the tower. Consider how your choice of building can lend drama to your piece and describe the exterior of the building or refer to one of its architectural features.

- Use weather as a way of endorsing the emotional tone of a piece of writing. For example, storms have traditionally been a way of depicting emotional tumult within a character. A lonely character staring out to sea might make us think of someone who has something on their mind. Try reading 'The Happy Autumn Fields' by Elizabeth Bowen.

- Choose a place which is associated with holidays/leisure/ sport and attempt to construct it in terms of opposites. There is its surface attraction but also a darker, more sinister aspect which could be exploited for dramatic effect.

Texts and Images

- Take a photograph or a postcard and restrict yourself to writing a caption for it. You must add a caption that gives the image a new meaning or expands the meaning that is already there. This is an exercise in clarity of expression, but not just that; it's also an exercise in making less equal more. Look through newspapers and magazines and consider what happens when word and image are juxtaposed. Can you play off one against the other?

- Look at writing which has been inspired by photography such as George Szirtes's poetry in *Blind Field*, or Tony Harrison's Gulf War poem 'A Cold Coming' inspired by the photograph of the charred body of an Iraqi soldier at the wheel of his jeep.

- Write a short piece to mark the millennium and think about an image to go with it. That image may be inspired by something you fear, perhaps more ecological disturbance or technological invasion in our lives, or it might represent a hope of some kind. Take a look at Andrzej Klimowski's graphic novels to give you some ideas.

- Take a colour postcard or picture from a magazine. Do the colours cause any positive or negative sensations in you? Do they dazzle or intoxicate? Take one of the colours and look it up in a thesaurus. Red, for example, will have a list of adjectives after it. Write a eulogy to a colour of your choice. Or write a rant against a colour you loathe.

- Consider a black and white image. What do you notice about your reaction to the picture? Does it offer a kind of neutrality or freeze the image in some way? Pull out some old black and white photographs of your family and write a monologue for one of the faces.

- Look at some examples of collaborations between writers and photographers like Fay Godwin and Ted Hughes. Perhaps you know someone who paints or draws, or someone who is a photographer. Ask them if you could write about one of their images. Don't let them tell you anything about it before you write. Afterwards ask the artist to read your work. Have you interpreted their work in a way that is unexpected? Have you perhaps lighted on something that they hadn't been aware of? Has your own response been quite different to theirs? If so, discuss why this might be the case.

- In order to change your habitual view of the world and alter perspective and distance, try to write from the point of view of a bird flying over a landscape, or an animal moving at ground level. In prose it is often the dynamic created by a shifting point of view that energises the writing.

Who Are You?

- Looking through a classical dictionary for ideas, assume the voice of a character from ancient myth and tell your story. Try to choose a character whose narrative accords with some aspect of you and your life now, or who can be made to serve that purpose. Mythic and heroic paradigms can lift the personal into a more universal context. For example, you may long to be stunningly beautiful and so become Helen of Troy. Or you may yearn to be far away from your present situation and so choose the explorer and adventurer Odysseus.

- Pretend you are someone who has previously been 'hidden' in history, someone whose ordinary existence was made invisible by official accounts. You might be a galley slave, a vagabond, or a travelling entertainer. Write their story.

Look at Carol Ann Duffy's poem 'Warming Her Pearls' in which a servant speaks of her mistress. Similarly, you might be interested in Timberlake Wertenbaker's play *Our Country's Good*, in which a collection of convicts sent to Australia rehearse a show.

- Imagine that you have just woken up and cannot remember who you are or where you live. Where are you now? Perhaps on a beach or lying on the floor of a house that you don't recognise. What's the first thing you do? Perhaps you check your pockets in search of some kind of identity or try to find someone who can help.

Making the Familiar Strange

Sometimes as writers we need to be forced to take risks and allow our certainties to be disrupted. The following three exercises experiment with the order of words and with the conventional associations of language.

- Attempt to write in a surreal style by disrupting the syntax of ten lines of writing, dropping any punctuation. Think of the words as all having equal weight and no logic that determines their order. Write without stopping and then read out the result aloud. The unexpected juxtaposition of words can often make you think about certain words in a very different way.

- This is an exercise for which you'll require a partner with a sense of fun. You each choose a topic for each other. That topic can be as abstruse as you like: it might be on cabbages, or dinosaurs, or the day in the life of an ant. Choose who will go first and give them their topic. They now have to talk non-stop on that subject for three minutes. Meanwhile the other person writes down any words or phrases that strike them as interesting. Now swap. Once you each have your sets of words or phrases, draw up a list of ten. You now each have twenty minutes to compose a prose piece using your list. Don't write nonsense. That's the easy way out! Try and write a piece that has a coherent strand however stretched it may be. Read your pieces aloud to each other at the end. The results of this are often very funny and can be quite enlightening.

- Take three or four objects that are wildly incompatible, perhaps a stuffed owl, an abacus and a potato-peeler, and put them together in a piece of writing.

Playing with the Postmodern

- Look at authors whose writing draws attention to its own processes and refers to creative decisions being made during those processes. In these works the reader is constantly denied the comfort of forgetting that they are reading, and attention is drawn to the artifice of writing as well as the writer's ability to manipulate storyline at any point. Contemporary fiction, particularly American fiction, illustrates this 'self-reflexivity'. Read the first chapter of *Slaughterhouse Five* by Kurt Vonnegut, in which the narrator/writer speaks of the impossibility of writing the novel and discards certain options.

- Experiment with the opening paragraph to a piece of prose or a short story that you have already written. Write two other versions, in which you change certain details. Read out your three versions. How does the process 'dislocate' you as a reader, that is render you unable to find a way of interpreting the piece?

- Write an opening paragraph of ten lines in the first person narrative. Now write a second paragraph continuing the story, still using 'I' but with a different voice, making it seem as though someone else is now telling the story.

- Take two pens which each have a different colour of ink. Write a three-line paragraph opening a story with one of the pens. Now pick up the other pen and write a second paragraph in some way denying or contradicting the first. If you have a computer use different fonts. Don't contradict wildly, the effectiveness of this exercise depends on subtlety. For example, you might begin with: I am sitting on this chair, looking out of the window. I am calm. I know she will come. And your second paragraph may be: *You are sitting on that chair, not looking out of the window. You are calm. You think she will come.* Now continue your story alternating the speakers. Write for an hour. Read out what you've written. What is the effect of the double narrative? Are you able to believe either one of the speakers? Do you feel more sympathy for one in particular?

• Many writers of novels and films refuse to adopt the conventional device of narrative closure, and do not resolve their works neatly, tying up all the loose ends. Some writers pose alternative endings, some do not lead the writer to the place that the novel or short story appeared to be taking them in. Write several different endings of a short story. Experiment with self-conscious references to artistic decisions in the text itself.

Passions and Politics

• Write on a cause or an issue about which you feel passionately. Give vent to your outrage without letting it obscure the direction of your piece. You may choose environmental issues, or a piece about the death penalty, date rape or sexuality.

• George Orwell's *Animal Farm* is a political satire on communism, in which the pigs finally gain ultimate power. Orwell described it as a 'fairy tale'. Write a political fable. *Sleeping Beauty*, for example, lends itself well to a particularly scathing feminist attack!

• Write from the point of view of someone whose life is endangered by their writing. Amnesty International have lists of hundreds of writers who are imprisoned for their beliefs. Think of Vaclav Havel or Solzhenitsyn. Imagine that you are one of these writers and write a journal entry of your hope or despair. Read the poems of Anna Akhmatova.

• Write a lampoon of a political figure whose policies you detest. Look at cartoons in newspapers and consider how certain figures are parodied. Perhaps you know of *Spitting Images* or *Yes, Minister* on television which satirise those in power. Collect from friends other examples of satire.

- Listen to or watch the news for several days, concentrating especially on interviews with politicians. How do they evade answering tricky questions? What tactics do they employ to persuade others that their views are right? You could watch for the use of soundbites, or repetition, or the citation of statistics. Write a party political broadcast of no more than five minutes for radio or television which is aimed at the public the night before a general election.

Booklist

Akhmatova, A., *Poems* (Norton, London and New York, 1983).

Atwood, M., *Murder In The Dark* (Virago, London, 1994).

Auster, P., *New York Trilogy* (Faber & Faber, London, 1995).

Bowen, E., *Collected Stories* (Penguin, Harmondsworth, 1991).

Campbell, K., *Live, In The Flesh* (Bower Press, London, 1992).

Casterton, J., *Creative Writing* (Macmillan, London, 1986).

Coover, R., *Pricksongs and Descants* (Minerva, London, 1991).

Couzyn, J. (ed.), *Bloodaxe Book of Contemporary Women Poets* (Bloodaxe, Newcastle-upon-Tyne, 1985).

Couzyn, J., *In the Skin House* (Bloodaxe, Newcastle-upon-Tyne, 1993).

Duffy, Carol Ann, *Selling Manhattan* (Anvil Press Poetry, London, 1987).

Duffy, Carol Ann, *Poetry Review* (Spring 1994), 84, no. 1.

Durcan, P., *Give Me Your Hand* (Macmillan, London, 1994).

Fowles, J., *The French Lieutenant's Woman* (Picador, London, 1992).

Godwin, F. and Hughes T., *Remains of Elmet* (Faber & Faber, London, 1979).

Gordon, G. (ed.), *Minerva Book of Short Stories 5* (Minerva, London, 1993).

Harrison, T., 'A Cold Coming' in *Poetry With An Edge* (Bloodaxe, Newcastle-upon-Tyne, 1993).

Heaney, S. and Hughes, T. (eds), *The Rattle Bag* (Faber & Faber, London, 1982).

Hospital, J. T., *Dislocations* (Virago, London, 1994).

Jamie, K., *Queen Of Sheba* (Bloodaxe, Newcastle-upon-Tyne, 1993).

Janowitz, K., *In the Mountains*. Panurge Magazine (1993).

Khalvati, M., *In White Ink* (Carcanet, Manchester, 1991).

Klimowski, A., *The Depository: A Dream Book* (Faber & Faber, London, 1994).

Lee, H. (ed.), *The Secret Self 2* (Dent, London, 1991).

Lorca, F. G., *Selected Poems* (New Directions, London, 1961).

McKendrick, J., *The Kiosk At The Brink* (OUP, Oxford, 1993).

Márquez, Gabriel García, *One Hundred Years of Solitude* (Cape, London, 1991).

Márquez, Gabriel García, *Strange Pilgrims* (Cape, London, 1993).

Orwell, G., *Animal Farm* (Penguin, Harmondsworth, 1951).

Raine, C., *A Martian Sends A Postcard Home* (OUP, Oxford, 1979).

Roberts, M., *Daughters Of The House* (Virago, London, 1993).

Roberts, M., *Psyche and the Hurricane* (Methuen, London, 1991).

Shapcott, J., *Electroplating the Baby* (Bloodaxe, Newcastle- upon-Tyne, 1988).

Szirtes, G., *Blind Field* (OUP, Oxford, 1994).

Vonnegut, K., *Slaughterhouse Five* (Cape, London, 1991).

Wertenbaker, T., *Our Country's Good* (Methuen, London, 1988).

Woolf, V., *Moments Of Being* (Grafton, London, 1978).

Woolf, V., *A Writer's Diary* (Grafton, London, 1978).

3 | Words Words Words

JOHN SINGLETON AND
GEOFF SUTTON

A thousand years ago we had about 30 000, now English has 500 000 and the figure is rising daily. They belong to the nation, are listed in dictionaries and each one of us has a usable store or word-hord, as the Anglo-Saxons called vocabulary, of about 15 000. This is 3 per cent of the total in *The Oxford English Dictionary* and only half the number used by Shakespeare.

His word-hord was made up of 'native' Anglo-Saxon words, often short and concrete, and Latin and Greek words, often polysyllabic and abstract. These two currents in our language, words for things and words for ideas, give English its extraordinary flexibility and variety.

After murdering King Duncan, Shakespeare's Macbeth looks guiltily at his bloodied hands and agonises:

> Will all great Neptune's ocean wash this blood
> Clean from my hand? No; this my hand will rather
> The multitudinous seas incarnadine,
> Making the green one red.

The last two lines say the same thing. One in resounding Latinate words, the last in simpler Anglo-Saxon derived words, possibly for the groundlings who without a grammar school education wouldn't understand words like 'incarnadine'. But the words are for hearing. Out of the polysyllables roars the image of tumultuous waves across vast oceans, crimsoned with blood, rolling round the world. After this rhetoric and intensity comes Anglo-Saxon bluntness like a dowsing of cold water as the awful literalness of his action strikes Macbeth.

While Shakespeare was writing *The Tempest*, his last play, the King James Bible was published. And just as Shakespeare's verbal daring has profoundly influenced our language so the Authorised Bible has affected the way we use our words today. It used only 8000 of them, plain fare after Shakespeare's cornucopia. But the two strands of plainness and richness are as evident in modern writing as they were in the seventeenth century. Writers like Joyce, Henry Miller, Burgess, Faulkner write with verbal splendour. So did Dickens and Hardy and Lawrence. Whereas Hemingway and Raymond Carver reflect the spare, commonword style of Bunyan and the King James Bible.

It must be evident from the words I've used so far that contemporary English is in fact a mix of plain and polished. When I speak of 'vast oceans' I'm using an Anglo-Saxon word, 'vast', reintroduced into the language by Shakespeare, and 'ocean', a Greek word meaning 'swift'. 'Tumultuous' and 'penultimate' are Latin, 'blood' is Anglo-Saxon, and 'crimson' derives from an Arabic word for the cochineal beetle from whose crushed carapace the colour is made.

Of course, instead of 'incarnadine' (Latin), the English lexicon offers 'scarlet' (Persian), as well as 'crimson' (Arabic) and 'red' (Anglo-Saxon), 'vermilion' (Latin), 'carmine' (Arabic), 'damask' (Syrian). And so on. Not only does this list encapsulate, summarise, demonstrate, show and exemplify the rich alternatives our dictionaries offer but it also embodies the varied history of the English and England. As a trading and seafaring nation we imported red silks from Persia and dyes from Arabia; we were invaded by small Germanic tribes, Angles, Saxons and Jutes whose language overwhelmed native Celtic; the Anglo-Saxon of Alfred borrowed Danish words from the Vikings to extend its range but was itself swept along, 500 years later, with a flood of Latin words brought over by the Normans; our imperial adventure gave us 'juggernaut', 'bungalow' and 'jungle' from India, 'voodoo', 'juke-box' and 'bananas' from Africa; and, during recent times, in another example of reverse colonisation the Americans sent us 'antagonise', 'placate', 'canyon', 'bonanza' and a thousand other usages.

This richness of vocabulary has its seductive dangers for the writer and the reader. Hoping to impress, some writers use long words and ornate sentences and confuse the reader with obfuscatory phrasing. 'Obfuscate' is a Latin word meaning 'to darken'. In this instance to cloud plain sense with a barrage of words. Obfuscation is everywhere. And it is the enemy of plain English. Its other name is 'jargon'. It is used by car salesmen whose second-hand cars are now 'pre-enjoyed' or 'experienced'. It is used by the military who destroy jungles with napalm and claim the tactic is part of a 'pacification programme'. It is used by local councils who don't employ dustbin men any more only 'refuse collectors', and by employers who now 'terminate contracts by mutual agreement' instead of giving their 'manual operatives' the sack. What do 'downsize' and 'rationalisation' really mean? When does a 'strike' become 'a withdrawal of labour'? If a hospital death is 'therapeutic misadventure' do we actually die anymore? Death is now banned? Why do we 'utilise' not 'use'? 'Initiate' not 'begin'? 'Terminate' not 'end'?

Because as teachers, doctors, councillors, solicitors, politicians, businessmen, soldiers, we hide from responsibility behind a camouflage of words. Or we so bemuse people they are blinded to the truth and persuaded that what is an obscene 'massacre' is only a harmless 'clean-up operation' and can be ignored.

This clouding of the truth goes hand-in-hand with woolliness or verbal inflation. One word becomes two, then three, then many; 'now' inflates into 'at this moment in time', 'I know' converts to 'it has come to my attention that'. Stifling citizen protest with words is a bureaucratic tactic but all word users are guilty, including creative writers. Ernest Hemingway advised us all to be alert and turn on our automatic 'crap detector' before starting to write. Crapulent expression is pervasive!!

George Orwell, that champion of plain English, mocked the pretension and hypocrisy of those who use words to intimidate and exclude people from their club of special users. He takes the beautiful words of Ecclesiastes from the King James Bible and converts them into what the Americans call gobbledygook. They read like this:

I returned, and saw under the sun, that the race is not to the swift, nor the battle to the strong, neither yet bread to the wise, nor yet riches to men of understanding, nor yet favour to men of skill; but time and chance happeneth to them all. (Ecclesiastes 9 v11–12)

Objective consideration of contemporary phenomena compels the conclusion that success or failure in competitive activities exhibits no tendency to be commensurate with innate capacity, but that a considerable element of the unpredictable must invariably be taken into account. ('Politics and the English Language')

What this jargon ('prattle' in Latin) does is emasculate words. The spectacle, drama and sinewy rhythm of the phrase 'the race is not to the swift, nor the battle to the strong' vanishes into the woolliness of 'objective consideration of contemporary phenomena'. Vibrant text is reduced to the sterility of the textbook. Similarly, the emotive force of 'strike' is enfeebled when it is turned into a committee of words, 'a withdrawal of labour'. My dictionary says if I strike, I 'give up work to secure higher wages'. That's what the word denotes. But my experience of the word tells me it also means violence, confrontation of the picket line, the drama of hard-eyed bosses locking out grim-faced workers, fear and hate and bloodymindedness. These are what the word connotes or suggests, and behind every word there is a web of suggestion and association which gives it its richness and as some say its texture. Think of what 'rose' suggests. What images, ideas, feelings do you associate with that word?

Words, then, are not innocent. They are emotionally loaded and full of attitude. 'Slim' is OK but is 'thin' or 'skinny'? What about 'anorexic'? 'Perspiration' is OK – just. But is 'sweat'? Not for ladies, surely! Words are ideologically biased. Dale Spender in her book, *Man Made Language*, argues that words themselves are gender partisan and sustain patriarchal (male) authority. 'Man' is privileged by being the word to represent all mankind, women included. The words 'pen' and 'pencil', the instruments of writing itself, derive from a Latin word meaning penis. History suggests that writing was always regarded as a male activity. The first English dictionary, published in 1604, was intended for 'Ladies...and any other unskillful persons'. Reading a few pages of Janet Mills' book, *Womanwords*, will make you realise how misogynistic English word usage has been in the past. And if you think all this has changed in our liberal, post-feminist period then read Joanna Russ' book, *How To Suppress Women's Writing*, for a sobering account of contemporary anti-woman words.

So, use a dictionary and a thesaurus. Adopt Hemingway's attitude. 'All my life,' he wrote, 'I've looked at words as though I was seeing them for the first time.' Words should be relished and enjoyed. It is sloppy, ignorant handling that ruins them. On BBC Radio 4 I've just heard a sculptor describing how his most recent exhibit, 'a lattice work of struts and bars' almost fills the gallery. 'It *inundates*' the space, he claimed. Any dictionary would have told him that the word derives from the Latin 'inundare' to drown in waves and a lattice work sculpture could hardly drown anything let alone space. As writers we need to be alive to the private lives of words and respect them or we just get messy and vacuous and banal. The critic listening to the sculptor said he was 'totally overwhelmed' by the exhibit: which he would have been had the gallery space indeed been inundated. 'Overwhelmed' is complete enough without the unnecessary adverb, 'totally'. More verbal inflation followed when the critic closed the conversation by saying how much he had enjoyed their 'ongoing dialogue'. Or was it 'conversation'. Or 'chat'? Or 'talk'? Or just plain old 'dialogue'? Zap this sort of stuff with your crap detector – NOW. Listen to any current affairs or news programme any day on the media and you'll gather a hundred examples of word abuse and misuse. Do this and sharpen your word sense. Or join the Royal Society for the Protection of Words.

Words, of course, being sociable travel in groups or sentences. Some sentences are simple affairs. Others are more complicated and they join with one another to work in tandem. While the grander types, which want to create an impression, however false, are more complicated, having a number of interrelating clauses and phrases, and a longer chassis. Good writers vary both the length and internal shape of their sentences to create particular effects. Because we don't think in complete sentences some early experimental (Modernist) writers like Dorothy Richardson, James Joyce and Virginia Woolf have used sentences many pages long, often without punctuation.

At the other extreme, because we don't talk in complete sentences either, unless we're being formal, some writers, such as Roddy Doyle, have written novels composed almost entirely of short sentences and sentence fragments, like Dublin street talk.

When you write you have to decide who are your readers and which are the best vocabulary and sentence structures for your purpose. Clipped, staccato fragments? Or flowing elegant phrases with parenthetical insertions? Either way you have to be sensitive to the rhythms of individual words and phrases. Read a lot of other writers. Listen carefully to what's read out in your workshop. Decide if what you need is *Hoicking him by the oxters, his enemy swung him widdershins* OR *His adversary gripped him by the armpits and swung him anti-clockwise.* Or whether *I'm suffering from a temporary financial inconvenience* is more appropriate than *I'm skint.* Or whether it should be *His gaff's the poshest in the manor* OR *His is the most upmarket house on the estate.* Now think about the issues that these examples illustrate. Are some too wordy and jargon-ridden? Is it a matter of context where language use depends on who you are addressing, in what place and at what time, and on what impression you want to give?

When words get together they have a party. Tempo and pace, rhythms and resonance, music to a beat. English words are accentuated or stressed. Writers craftily arrange these stresses in patterns to create distinctive rhythms or metres. You can find out more about metrics in Chapter 7. For starters try these lines from Alexander Pope's *Essay on Criticism*:

> When Ajax heaves some rock's vast weight to throw,
> The line too labours and the words move slow.

Pope was showing how a writer can retard a line and make it mimic the matter, feel as slow and laborious as if lifting a great weight. Consider the part Anglo-Saxon monosyllables play in creating this effect. By reading the lines aloud and listening to the sounds of the words you can work out other techniques the poet is using. Try it. Here are the next two lines:

Not so, when swift Camilla scours the plain,
Flies o'er the unbending corn, and skims along the main.

How quick the sounds flow and even accelerate at the end of the couplet.

Now read the first paragraph of Thomas Hardy's novel *Under the Greenwood Tree*. It evokes the sound of the wind blowing through the branches. Try paragraph five of D. H. Lawrence's *The Rainbow*. Read the opening two or three paragraphs of Katherine Mansfield's short story 'At the Bay' or almost any page of Faulkner's *Absalom Absalom* and you'll see what rhythmic movement good writers get out of prose. At the moment I am reading, among others, Pete Davies. Here are two of his sentences.

The journos tap-tapped on their portables in the press box, the keys rustled and clacked, a sound like the scurry and whisper of mice. The man from *The Times* sipped liquor from a hip flask, and passed it along.

You could call these rhythms organic, that is, punctuation and vocabulary reflect or mimic sense. The onomatopoeia of 'tap-tapped on their portables', the comma after 'flask' to emphasise the man's movement. Try and recognise this kind of sound when you read it. Don't try too hard in your writing. It's easy to overwrite.

When sound and beat meet you hear music. And some writers play with the music of words and compose a melody out of language. Read W. H. Auden's poem, 'Seascape', for examples of verbal music. You'll hear softly breathed sounds, liquid vowels, languid diphthongs, the guttural growlings of the sea, tumbling pace, sharp breaking and lines so lazy they drowse the reader with their long, slow, assonantal syllables. Read Swinburne for melody, Tennyson's poem 'Break, break, break' for elegiac motion, Hopkins' sonnet, 'Spring', for the ringing freshness of bird song.

The Bible is where it all started, opening with the words, 'In the beginning was the Word'. More accurately, the word was the beginning. Because until words came nothing was identified and named. What words do is bring into being by separating one thing from another, night from day, sky from earth, trees from animal, dog from cat, and confirm and shape what our eyes see, ears hear.

Words also create in another way. Singly and in groups they evoke images, pictures in the head. The more vivid those pictures, the more telling the writing. One way of creating arresting images is through metaphor. For an excellent discussion of metaphor read Nigel Lewis' *The Book of Babel*. The word means to transform and is at the heart of language. When the Anglo-Saxons called the sea the 'swan's road', they were using metaphor, comparing one thing with another and creating a new image. Norwegians called the sea 'blue moor', the Icelanders, the 'whale's way'. They were high on metaphor just like the early explorers, who described sea-horses, duck-billed platypuses, hog's back hills and El Dorado, the land of gold. We think metaphors. We talk metaphors. The best ones give a startling freshness to the world around us. Or rather they give *back* to the world the freshness that woolliness and tired metaphors, known as clichés, have stolen.

Workshop Writing

The workshops that follow are about word play, about how words work and how you can make them work in new and exhilarating ways.

1   Naming Names

Workshop 1
A   Each member of the group writes down all his or her names, including nicknames and pet names used in the family, if you like. Using these letters, try to make yourself a pen name. Try to use every letter, that is, make anagrams, but add or miss out one or two if necessary, for example, Justin Moth (John Smith). If nothing successful results from just your

own names, add another family name, such as your mother's maiden name, until you find what you like.

B   Imagine what kind of book would be written under this pen name. List a few titles. Justin Moth might have written *Chrysalis to Cradle, The English Lepidoptera* (2 vols) or *Candle in the Dark.*

C   Invent names of characters from one of these books and incidents involving them. For example, Estrella lives on an island. She is about to leave home for the first time. Why? Her mother says she will keep her room empty till she returns. Estrella buys a candle. She gives it to her mother who places it on the windowsill of Estrella's room and lights it every night. Write a similar summary.

D   Between the workshops, collect from a dictionary and thesaurus words such as *wax, tallow, wick, flicker, snuffout,* or phrases such as *hold a farthing candle to the sun*. Light and observe a candle, perfumed, perhaps. Touch the wax, both when it's molten and when set. Write a maximum of 100 words in any form you like using images/ideas from this experience.

Workshop 2

A   Each member of the group presents an object from the first workshop, for example, the candle, and reads out the short piece of writing.

B   Individually, or in pairs, produce a plot summary, scenario, monologue, narrative incident, or image, based on the name of a person, animal, object or place.

C   Extend later by finding a photograph or painting containing a thing, person or animal you connect with this name and begin again from this new stimulus, for example, a Rembrandt painting of a candlelit figure.

2   Flint

This is a workshop to keep things and words as closely linked as possible. The object of the following activities is to base the imagined in the real, using accurate descriptions of the sort written by scientists, reporters or detectives and to blend these with the imagination of the poet or the fiction writer.

A   Find a substance which is common where you live. Collect interesting specimens of its various shapes, sizes, colours. Look at it closely, touch, smell and if appropriate taste it. Then find words for what you are experiencing. The choice of objects is wide open, natural or artificial will do. One of my favourites is flint. It comes in many shapes. It was used as a weapon by our ancestors. It is also a tool and an ornament. Crushed flint whitens pottery but destroys the lungs of the millers so it has to be ground in water. It is harder than steel and when it breaks it forms a very sharp edge. If you strike it with iron pyrites, you can make fire. It is compact, almost opaque, usually dark grey or brown inside, chalky white outside.

Flint is a kind of chalcedony, or quartz-like sand. It is extremely common. Best of all it can look like Henry Moore sculptures, and resemble headless torsos, bones, limbs, snakes, birds, fish, and sometimes, from different angles, several of these. It rings when you strike it and it is rough outside, smooth inside.

B   Research the substance you choose, using encyclopaedias, scientific guides, photographs, sketches, tapes, videos. Collect technical terms and the names of different varieties. These can be checked in a dictionary.

C   Try writing a poem, piece of prose or monologue, describing the substance and/or exploring an image it suggests. Perhaps find another shape you can relate to the first. If your object has suggested a bird or a snake, then write a dialogue between the two. Begin with factual description and a limited number of words. Soon you'll find you need metaphors. Or think of the Uncle Remus stories about Brer Rabbit and Brer Fox and write a fable about an animal or human. Or try an imagist poem, in the manner of HD's 'Whirl up, sea!'

3   Naming Shells

Like most flora and fauna, shells have colloquial names like razor, as well as scientific names like *ensis siliqua*. Both are metaphors. Razor may take some explaining to modern shavers, but Sweeney Todd might help. *Ensis siliqua* is sword of sand or silicon sword.

A   Start off by collecting a carrier bagful of shells. I get most of mine from Wales. A favourite spot is Abermenai Point on Anglesey, opposite the mainland town of Caernarvon. The tide rushes past depositing all sorts between there and Newborough. On the mainland just south of Harlech is Shell Island which lives up to its name. Llandanwg nearby has a very clean beach and St Tanwg's church is almost buried in the dunes. There's a meadow, Y Maes, and a small café-shop with a fine exhibition of scallops, turret-, slipper- and necklace shells, Arctic cyrinas, smooth venus and gem pimplets, opelets, cloak anemones and beadlets among others.

B   Using a torch and a magnifying glass, study some of the shells closely. Find names for what you see. A close-up view of razor shells reveals growth layers like tree rings, or finger-nails. They could be cast-offs from the hand of some giant spirit of the shore. Invent some similar origin or explanation for your shells. Choose a form – prose, verse or monologue/ dialogue – and let your creations speak.

4   Johnny Two: An Unsolved Mystery

Have you ever heard of a man called Johnny Two? If, like me, you're addicted to newspapers, you'll know how they try to arouse our curiosity. They trade in the bizarre with titles like 'Man bites dog, falls 200 feet and walks away'; 'Woman on diet of geranium petals'. There's nothing much about who these people are, why they did what they did, or what happened next, and no follow-up. Not usually. But in November 1988 the *Guardian* printed a six-inch double column account with photo of a mysterious stowaway discovered on a Cypriot cargo boat six days out of Felixstowe. The *Johnny Two* sailed to East Africa and back but the Home Office refused to let the man land so he repeated the trip, a five-month journey of 40 000 miles. He refused to speak. He lived on fresh fruit and vegetables and drank only water, except for two or three beers. No one had a clue who he was but they called him Johnny Two.

Then, surprise. In January 1989 a five-column-inch follow-up. The Home Office has relented. The man is in hospital where psychiatrists are trying to persuade him to talk. But nothing since, unless I've missed it. Anyone with information?

A   Is he a traumatised amnesiac, a vegan fanatic, some kind of existentialist mystic, a criminal on the run or a political refugee whose life is in danger if his enemies track him down? In the photo, Johnny's long face is framed by hair. He stares expressionless. Try writing an internal monologue showing through the mind and senses of Johnny his view of life. What is his real name? How does he use words? Is he trained in some occupation? Invent some technical terms he might use.

B   Now do a view from the outside. You can be a crew member, an immigration officer or a psychiatrist. Choose words to describe Johnny and arrange them in the kinds of sentences your speaker would use, for example, log, letter home, interview notes.

C   Assume Johnny speaks a language you have never heard before. Create the sound and written form of this language. Does it have simple, short words or polysyllables like Inuit or Australian aborigine? Invent 50 words of Johnny's. Use repetition at some point. Provide a translation, not necessarily word for word.

5   Feeling What You Say

The activities in this workshop attempt to conceptualise from your sense experience. It's hard to find precise words for what you see, hear, smell, touch or taste. It's harder still to be original. You can't know what anyone else's senses tell them but you do know some people are colour-blind, tone-deaf, or just blind and deaf.

A   Close your eyes and touch as many objects you are familiar with as possible. Begin with your face and hair and move on to things around you. Try to distinguish opposite sensations without naming them. Then find words to convey the degrees of smooth, rough, flat, embossed, raised, humped, hard, soft, and so on. Then group these words, for instance into soft and flat, hard and raised, smooth and round. Now look up the lists under 'concave' and 'convex' in the thesaurus.

B   Use a magnifying glass and a mirror to do the same thing for sight. Focus on the back of your hand, especially skin pores and hair, veins and bone structures. Then move on to other objects. Proceed as before to the thesaurus and write down spectrums of words conveying visual features. Some of these will overlap touch, for example, 'round', 'concave'.

C   With your eyes closed again, smell herbs, spices, and various fruits and vegetables. Try to find opposites like 'strong' and 'subtle', 'sweet' and 'bitter'. Look up thesaurus lists under 'pungency' and 'fragrance'.

D   Arrange small quantities of familiar food and drink within reach so that you can taste them without looking at them or smelling them, for example, on spoons. Smell first, then taste. Again, find clear categories such as 'salt', 'sweet'. Look up thesaurus lists under 'sourness' and 'sweetness'.

E   Set a timer or an alarm for a short period such as five minutes. Close your eyes and listen. Distinguish sounds and find words for them. Look up 'silence', 'loudness', 'faintness' in the thesaurus. Again you'll find categories overlap each other, for example, 'faint' is used for sound and sight, and possibly taste.

6   Simple and Elaborated

This is a workshop on verbal texture; plain stitch and decoration and the implications behind such different styles.

A   Consider this passage from David Jones' book *In Parenthesis*, a personal account of trench fighting in the First World War.

> Saturate, littered, rusted coilings, metallic rustlings, thin ribbon-metal chafing – rasp low for some tension freed; by rat or wind, disturbed. Smooth-rippled discs gleamed, where gaping craters, their brimming waters, made mirror for the sky procession – bear up before the moon incongruous souvenirs. Margarine tins sail derelict, where little

eddies quivered, wind caught, their sharp-jagged twisted lids wrenched back.

This is dense, metaphoric, verbally ornate writing. Is it over-done? Russell Hoban in Chapter 10 of his novel *Turtle Diary* has his narrator Neaera H argue that verbal richness is an indulgence. She cites Hopkins' poem 'The Windhover' (kestrel) as a 'mannered' poem. She prefers the frog's jumping of Basho's haiku (3-line Japanese poem) to Hopkins' kestrel hovering. For her the frog has 'more falcon in it than Hopkins's bird simply because it has more of *things-as-they- are...*'

For Neaera too many words hide not reveal the essential nature of natural objects. You could argue that David Jones has overwhelmed his subject. He has beautified the brutal, bedazzled the reader with verbal magic and taken our eyes off the realities of trench life. Would a simpler more direct style work better? Take time to consider this question. Are *you* writing for show or for real?

Consider too the fact that both Hopkins and Jones were Welshmen. In Welsh poetry there is a tradition of verbal extravagance and exultation, passion, hwyl. Shouldn't we take such cultural and historical factors into account before passing judgement?

B   Select a simple image – a cat stretching, a baby yawning, a fish swimming, butterfly resting. Now try writing a simple Basho-like poem about it. You should try and capture the essential quality of the subject, the thing-as-it-isness!! In contrast write a David Jones-style treatment of the same subject trying to be as accurate about the object as possible. You will need to use metaphor, graphic verbs and enriched adjectives.

7   Adjectives and Verbs

This workshop, or workshops, considers sample passages and considers the effect of particular types of words. Any good prose extracts will do but I've chosen pieces from Thomas Mann, Ellen Glasgow and Virginia Woolf.

A   Write about sunsets, night skies, storms and haunted houses and adjectives will come swarming. They can be great attention seekers and very invasive. In unguarded writing they lead to swollen prose, a condition known to professionals as adjectivitis. So be on your guard, don't be fooled by verbal dazzle. Every word, adjective or otherwise, should work its passage and not be freeloading. Here is a passage from the third page of Thomas Mann's short novel *Death in Venice*, describing one of Aschenbach's moments of fantasising:

> Desire projected itself visually: his fancy, not quite yet lulled since morning, imaged the marvels and terrors of the manifold earth. He saw. He beheld a landscape, a tropical marshland, beneath a reeking sky, steaming, monstrous, rank – a kind of primeval wilderness-world of islands, morasses, and alluvial channels. Hairy palm-trunks rose near and far out of lush brakes of fern, out of bottoms of crass vegetation, fat, swollen, thick with incredible bloom. There were trees, mis-shapen as a dream, that dropped their naked roots through the air into the ground or into water that was stagnant and shadowy and glassy-green, where mammoth, milk-white blossoms floated, and strange big-shouldered birds with curious bills stood gazing sidewise without sound or stir.

Discuss with your partner or group the effect of the adjectives in this writing. Sometimes they come in a tumble three or four together. Why? There are some long sentences here. Why?

A   Imagine a character like Aschenbach who has visionary moments, episodes of rich mental fabulation. Write a passage describing such an episode.

B   Read the opening page of Virginia Woolf's short story 'Kew Gardens'. This is closely observed, sensory writing. Imagine some exoticism place or a moment when your senses are heightened and everything seems extraordinarily real, immediate and intense. Try writing a passage of prose evoking the exoticism of a moment of intense awareness. For a model read the opening of Woolf's novel *The Waves*.

C   Read the opening page of Ellen Glasgow's novel *Barren Ground*. Identify the adjectives in the second paragraph and decide what the first dozen have in common. Account for the contrast with another group of adjectives in the same paragraph.

D Of course, no piece of writing depends on any one type of word, whether adjective, verb or noun, for its effects. In good writing words work as a team. Read the third paragraph of Ellen Glasgow's novel and after discussion with your group write notes on how the nouns and verbs and adjectives work together to create the central image of storminess. Notice the surge and drive of the sentences. How is this momentum achieved? What's its point? Imagine a turbulent or tranquil scene. Write a prose passage that captures, through verbs and adjectives especially, the essential quality of the experience.

Other passages to consider are: the account of the storm in Thomas Hardy's *Far from the Madding Crowd* and the opening two pages of 'At the Bay', a short story by Katherine Mansfield.

8   There's Life in the Old Phrase Yet

Overuse has turned many a good metaphor into a dead metaphor or a cliché. A phrase like 'exploring all the avenues' has long lost the force of any comparison with tree-lined streets. No real rocks are in sight when you leave 'no stone unturned' and 'geared towards' does not raise any pictures of cogwheels. But every cliché began as a freshening and imaginative idea, only for the rest of us to ruin it for the creator. For a survey of clichéland dip into Nigel Rees' book, *The Joy of Cliché*. Take care from now on. If you don't, you are sure to find yourself using dead metaphors.

A   The media use more clichés than most and they're not all quoted from PR handouts and press releases. Take two daily papers, one tabloid, one broadsheet. Record about five minutes each of a radio phone-in and a TV talk show.

B   From these sources collect words and phrases you've heard many times, such as 'tackling a problem', 'a golden handshake', 'getting the sack', 'dogged by misfortune', 'a different kettle of fish', 'an uphill struggle'.

C   Study these examples for any signs of live metaphor. Can you recognise any of the original freshness in the images? You'll need a dictionary to check the origins of words like 'tackle'. Visualise the fish kettle, the sack, the gold, the dog, and so on.

D   Try using some of these phrases and others in a piece of writing. It doesn't matter what form the writing takes. Here are some suggestions:

1 A poem about a fatal motorbike accident in the colloquial talk of the frightened but stimulated spectators, with puns like 'they were dead right'. Think up your own situations.

2 A prose piece called *An Old Words Home* in which clichés live out their days together. Try and use as many clichés as possible.

3 A surreal dialogue in which the speakers explore the possibilities of a phrase like 'a different kettle of fish', for example:

> A: Was it a gas kettle?
> B: No, electric.
> A: Did it have a spout?
> B: No, it was oblong.
> A: And what kind of fish was it?
> B: Halibut.

4 Sentences of clichés, for example, 'The nuts and bolts may take some time to settle, once the dust has cleared they will eventually be ironed out'. Try and create the longest multiple cliché you can.

5 Try recycling clichés. Make a list of ten then alter each one to freshen it up. 'White as a sheet' becomes 'As light as a sheet in the breeze'.

9   Sounds and Visuals, Words and Images

Don't underestimate the following activities. They may seem trivial, but they loosen up your mind and allow you to draw on the unconscious mass of images all of us experience in dreams at night or during the day. Your choices, apparently at random, may release feelings and memories which can lead to powerful writing, if you can control them. Use them when you're short of inspiration or when you need a new direction in a piece you've been working on for some time. They also help a group get to know each other.

Word association

Play this in pairs or groups. A person begins with any word. The next responds without stopping to think, and so on back and forth or round the group. Record or write down the sequence. It's better if you don't know each other too well otherwise in-jokes and private conversations affect the choices.

Found

If you've taken Rorschach's test, you know how the optical part of the human brain is programmed to find meanings where none were intended. So you can see faces in the cracks on a wall, maps in stains on a ceiling, mountain ranges in banks of cloud, ploughs in the stars and misty landscapes in condensation on a window. The verbal part of the brain, the left hemisphere if you are right-handed, tries to make sense of words and letters even when they aren't being used for normal communication. Try these activities:

1   Buy or make about ten dice, with a letter on each face. If you're making them, mix vowels and mostly common consonants, but include all the letters of the alphabet. Shake the dice onto a table and form words. Make your own rules, for example you don't have to use every letter, or you can shake one die again. Have a dictionary nearby to check unfamiliar combinations of letters. Link the result- ing words into phrases. Make images and develop them into haiku or short sentences.

2   Open a dictionary at random. Touch a word. Write it down. Repeat as often as you like until you have a bank of, say, 50 words. Begin to link them, adding 'and', 'but', 'the', 'with' and similar words.

Cut ups

According to William Burroughs, Brion Gysin, the American painter, used to take a familiar text, such as a prayer, cut it into quarters and shift the position of each quarter. New meanings then emerged.

Burroughs himself wrote a piece called 'Minutes to Go' from cut ups. One of his novel titles, *Cities of the Red Night*, sounds as if it came by chance, but that was just a starting point. The novel is clearly more than just a random collection of words.

You could find a text of your own. It could be some of your own writing, a legal document, a list of rules, anything you like. Cut it into four and follow Gysin's example. If that doesn't work, try another method of your own. For example, cut sentences into single words, pairs, threes, and so on up to groups of six. Keep doing that until all the words have been used. Then mix them up and make a new order.

The Humument: a treated text

Tom Phillips, the painter, wanted to use words in his work so he devised this project which has lasted three decades and produced two illustrated books and the libretto of an opera. In 1966 he chose the first book he found for sale at threepence (1.25p), and in the evening when his conscious mind was tired he opened a page at random and selected a few words. Then he inked out or painted over the unused words, so each page became a text. Later, he grouped them under topics like art, marriage, and so on.

If this idea appeals to you select an old book and try something similar.

10   Word Patterns

These activities are fun. Try them on your own or as warm-ups for workshops.

Anagrams

Anagrams are widely used in crosswords. They improve your awareness of word formation. You don't have to stick too rigidly to the originals. Add or omit the odd letter. AIM LET POOR CHILL and HIM NOT REAL CHEAT are exact anagrams of Michael Portillo and Michael Atherton, but A NORMAL ALCAN CAN FOR A CAREER or NO CAREER FAME FOR FRAZE or FROM NORMAL ALCAN CAN CRAZE are loose anagrams of Ermal Cleon Fraze, the inventor of the ring pull.

Nonagram

One person takes a nine-letter word and arranges the letters in three rows, thus:

    SMA
    GRA
    NON

The rest of the group see only the jumbled letters. You have to make as many words as you can of four letters or more as well as finding the original nine-letter word or words. Each word must contain the letter in the centre, in this case R. You can only use each letter as many times as it appears, thus A and N twice. No foreign words, no abbreviations, no plurals, no third person singular verbs and no proper names. All the words must be in a nominated dictionary.

You learn some unusual words doing nonagrams, such as 'dengue', 'eyas', 'galdragon', 'gobang', 'moya', 'nephalist', 'piaffe', and 'poon' (see the *Concise OED*).

You could just as well pick them direct but nonagrams are more fun because you invent them and then confirm they exist, even if you didn't know what they mean or never have a chance to use them.

It's surprising, too, how many unused combinations of letters there are, such as 'smargon', 'gramason', 'rangonas', and 'monnag'. When you've collected enough try writing a nonsense poem. You might like to look at 'Jabberwocky' by Lewis Carroll for inspiration.

Palindromes

These are pieces of writing which read the same backwards or forwards, for example, RATS LIVE ON NO EVIL STAR, which is a perfect palindrome, or NAOMI, SEX AT NOON TAXES, I

MOAN, which needs different lengths of word. Anagrams and nonagrams are good training for palindromes.

Lipograms

In this case, a selected letter or word is omitted from a piece of writing. A lipogram is more than a game. The French writer Georges Perec wrote a novel without using the commonest letter, E. In French this letter is pronounced *eux* which means 'them'. Perec said 'them' referred to his parents. His father was killed in the army in 1940. His mother disappeared to Auschwitz near the end of the Second World War. Perec called his novel *La Disparition*, The Disappearance. According to his biographer, Perec cured a writing block by writing lipograms.

Try writing a piece of prose omitting the use of a common letter. The commoner the letter is, the greater the challenge. Start modestly writing only 50 words or five sentences to begin with.

Perec later wrote *Les Revenantes*, The Returners, using E and A but omitting I, O, and U. You could try a piece omitting E and one other vowel. Perec also wrote a palindrome 1000 words long.

Reconstruction

To do this you need a small group, if everyone is to get a turn. Each person chooses a line or two from a favourite author. The piece should not be too well known. It may include rhyme and should contain a memorable image, as:

> Though wise men at their end know dark is right,
> Because their words had forked no lightning they
> Do not go gentle into that good night.

This stanza has 26 words and is about the maximum length possible. Everyone needs a sheet of unruled paper and a pair of scissors. Someone reads or spells out the words in any order but the right one. The rest write down the words, cut them up and try to reassemble them in the original order. Reconstruction reveals the difficulty of combining randomly presented words. It also produces alternative arrangements. Some of these may actually seem improvements on the original.

Concrete poetry

Writers have used typographic effects for centuries. George Herbert's 'Easter Wings' and Lewis Carroll's 'Mouse Tail' are typical examples. More recently writers have experimented with concrete poetry using letters and words as abstract sounds or visuals, just as *musique concrète* used sound of any kind. Bob Cobbings' sound poems, Ian Hamilton Finlay's words on glass and Edwin Morgan's 'The Computer's First Christmas Card' are examples.

Try playing with the visual qualities of words. Type, paint or write the letters of words into shapes which suggest their meanings. Look at the poems of e. e. cummings for typographical inventiveness.

Writing On

Naming People, Places and Things

- Check out some of the names Dickens used. Pecksniff, Uriah Heep, Fagin. The names are indicative. Collect some photographs of people or groups of people like a board of directors or football team or formation dancing team and give them some appropriate names.

- Collect nicknames from your workshop group and explain their possible origins.

- Imagine a gang of teenage kids, girls, football supporters. Give them names. Read Damon Runyon's stories in *Guys and Dolls* for expressive possibilities. Create names for members of some in-crowd or clique or select group – fashion models, society hostesses, golfers, W.I. committee, an all-woman rock band for example.

- Browse through the telephone directory and pick out some likely names. *Goldfinger* was born this way. Write a brief profile of your selection.

- From newspapers and magazines select some full portraits and add names based on a physical feature of the person represented or an animal they remind you of.

- Commercial names are a problem. Vauxhall Novas don't sell in Spanish-speaking South America because the word means 'won't go'. Invent names for a new environment-friendly car, a computer game featuring whales, a theme park for Star Trek fans, and so on.

- Adding names to an early draft can produce surprising results. Take this example, used by John Moat:

  > It was a farming country of scattered houses with associated buildings. A typical longhouse on the corner of a minor road faced east with a long drive approaching the front door, little used. A large meadow occupies the corner. A ditch and tall trees, bushes and undergrowth border the meadow.

  The description is factual, the details are concrete but something is missing. Now contrast this version:

  > Through the binoculars the farm lay pink and white. The long drive to the front door was empty. Baxter's Meadow with its dead elms was clearly visible at the corner of the lane. It was Doggett's Farm, for sure.

- It's not just the proper nouns which make the difference. There's more colour and the exact species of tree adds precision. More things are named. Describe a place you know well using proper names where appropriate.

Plain or Fancy

- Some adjectives have been overused and lost their original force to become bland, portmanteau words. Consider *awful, terrible, horrible, wonderful*. Discover their original meanings from a good etymological dictionary. Now collect at least ten common adjectives which have been overworked to the point of exhaustion. Is it ever justified to use such wishy washy words?

- Imagine the world has lost all its colour. Everything is monochrome. Describe any outdoor scene, using adjectives appropriately.

- Verbs give force and energy to writing. The generalised verb 'walked' can transform into 'shuffled', 'ambled', 'strode', 'limped', 'strolled' and so on. Such words create images which are precise and telling. Of course it is possible to be over-specific and write prose so clogged with image it stops dead in its tracks. The point to remember is that spare writing will suit one purpose and enriched writing another. Leaness is most telling after a glut. You decide. Writers who have mimicked Dylan Thomas at his adjectival best have just grown wordy. Marvel at the opening of *Under Milk Wood* but tread the same line with caution. Imagine some accelerated action punctuated with suspended motion – an acrobat or trapeze artist at work, a golfer on the tee, a grey-hound at a race – in a short piece try and capture the dynamics of motion, acceleration and arrest.

- Think of the cliché 'poetry in motion'. Select a good example of such motion and write a richly sensory, cliché-free description of your chosen subject. Look at Enobarbus' description of Cleopatra and her barge in Shakespeare's *Antony and Cleopatra*.

Lists

- I've always been fascinated by lists, the ritual of registers in school, Derby winners, chemical elements, stars and con-stellations, rivers, mountains. Make your own interest lists.

- Invent the names of the first ten artists and titles on Top of the Pops in December 2010. Give this topic some thought. Use your imagination but remember that some careers are long and include revivals.

- Similarly, create the ten best-selling works of fiction, with their authors, for the year 2015.

- Find new names for the months to reflect new influences on our lives, perhaps commercial, so February becomes

Valentine, March, Materna, for Mothering Sunday, and December, Expender; or to suit climate, like those used after the French Revolution, Brumaire, misty, for November, and so on.

- Find a street plan. Make a list of names which could be people, such as Rosemary Lane, Peter Street. Do the same with a 1:25000 Ordnance Survey map. It's important to use this scale because there are many more interesting names. The South Pennines Leisure Map is particularly rich. Gorple, Harry Side, Dick Delf Hill, Gut Royd Farm, Liberty Rush Bed and Great Jumps are just a sample. Using traditional rhythms, for example rhyming couplets or haiku, write verses from these lists. You will find the ambiguities of language allow layers of meaning to develop. Alternatively, one of the names may inspire a poem, in the way Adlestrop did Edward Thomas.

- Find a guide to birds, trees or flowers and make a list of names you like the sound of. As well as general guides, lists of local flora and fauna are useful. Find these at nature reserves or tourist information centres. Some examples are dunnock, yaffle, nightjar, dowitcher and greenshank; noble fir, warty birch, crack willow, and western hemlock; golden samphire, fat duckweed, viviparous fescue, common dodder, stinking goosefoot and henbane. Combine these names into pieces of writing. Don't just play with sounds. Look up origins and think about sense. This research could add a dimension to your knowledge of your locality. You may even include a geological analysis of the rock strata, as William Carlos Williams did in *Paterson*.

Making New Words

- Collect prefixes such as re-, un-, con-, dis-and suffixes such as -ful, -ive, -ation. Perm these with roots to make new combinations you like the sound or sense of, for example, 'dis-termin-ation', 'under-tract-able'. Collect other inventions such as 'undertaking', on the motorway, or 'over-stand', Benjamin Zephaniah's variation on understand. Produce a piece of writing which uses these new words, perhaps along these lines: 'The superfused transtortionist interformed periculously high above the subnet'.

- In German new words are formed by combining existing words, so vacuum cleaner is dustsucker. Make a list of manmade objects and find new names for them, such as sitwalker (bicycle) or thinkbox (computer).

- Paul Auster's character Stillman was so worried by words that he picked up broken objects on the streets of New York and gave them names. Walk about where you live. Find broken or lost objects and name them. Auster doesn't go into detail so the names can be borrowed or invented.

Inventing a Language

- There are occasions when writers need not just new words but a new language. Russell Hoban's *Riddley Walker* is an example. James Joyce was particularly interested in this activity. So was Anthony Burgess. Devise about twenty new letters. Make words with them. Write a short poem.

- Science fiction is particularly rich in invented terms and languages. Bruce Sterling (*Shismatrix*) and William Gibson (*Neuromancer*) wrote the first cyberpunk novels. Try selected reading from these writers, or from Philip K. Dick, and write some short cyberpunk pieces.

- Write a poem in which refugees from earth have landed on another planet and are trying to explain the effects of global warming to the inhabitants in a mixture of English and the language of the locals. See Craig Raine's *A Martian Sends A Postcard Home* and Edwin Morgan's 'The First Men on Mercury'.

- Write an incident using English words but try to make the reader understand that some or all of the characters are actually speaking another language and cannot understand English. See the play *Translations* by Brian Friel and Chapter 7 of *For Whom The Bell Tolls* by Ernest Hemingway.

- Write a paragraph of a story set in a place you know well which has been changed by economic or ecological disaster. Introduce some new words. Use them to let the reader guess what they mean, like William Gibson's 'simstim' constructs or Russell Hoban's 'sarvering gallack sea' (sovereign galaxies).

Argots

- Within our common hoard of words there exist 'niche' vocabularies, such as technical languages associated with professions and crafts or sports and recreation. Try collecting some special words/terms/phrases from other members of your group and produce a number of short glossaries. Subjects could include oil painting, plumbing, ballroom dancing, sailing, campanology, photography, the Internet, first-aid, rugby, computing, welding, caving and a host of others.

- Some vocabularies are defined by class and region. Collect some local words from your own area. Try writing a short dialect piece in which a character recounts an anecdote from their past. You could base it on someone you know.

- Most subgroups (fans, gangs, sects, cults, etc.) develop their own distinctive vocabularies. Can you think of reasons why this should be so? Many of them are like secret codes such as Cockney back slang and argybargy, the secret language of Keith Waterhouse's book *There Is a Happy Land*. Try writing a rap or street ballad using slang.

- For examples of street talk and the languages of outsiders or subcultures read James Kelman and Irvine Welsh, Hubert Selby Jnr or Alice Walker. Try writing a piece that aims for street realism. For example, a teenage addict talking to a counsellor, a street gang member interviewed by a social researcher, a football fan describing his typical Saturday rituals to a reporter.

- Try writing a character sketch in the language of an estate agent, in music terminology, in hip-hop or acid house argot. Think of other examples.

- Read extracts from the work of such cop writers as Ed McBain. Or from the underworld writings of Derek Raymond. Or from the novels of James Ellroy set in the 1940s and 1950s. Savour their use of special vocabularies or slangs. Using their slang try writing some dialogue involving characters who are Travellers or residents in a 'cardboard city' or Geordies or poachers. You may have to do some 'field' research to guarantee accuracy.

- Copywriters use words in witty and inventive ways. I know of a 'canine beautician'!!! called 'Shampoodle and Setter'. Collect some examples of lively language from billboards, TV ads, magazines. Try and invent some of your own slogans and catchphrases for an anti-noise or anti-betting or anti-car campaign. Or for a pro-betting or pro-exercise or pro-church-going or pro-foxhunting campaign. Imagine a new product or service is coming on the market and devise 25 words of copy for a magazine ad.

Stimulating the Senses

- Go somewhere quiet at night, outdoors if possible. Keep still and listen until you hear something. Or imagine an amnesiac awakening to sense experience, perhaps after an accident. Write down sense words. Begin with sounds, such as 'creak', 'rustle', 'hum', 'buzz', 'wail', 'shriek'. Then go on to the other senses. Write the opening paragraph of a story in which the narrator has lost his or her memory. See 'Coma and Metamorphosis One' in Iain Banks' *The Bridge*.

- For this task you will need a wine list or column in a magazine which tries to describe colour, taste and aroma, using words like 'fresh', 'zingy', 'bouncy' and 'fruity', and magazines featuring and advertising fashion and cars, cooking columns or flowery restaurant menus. Collect adjectives and nouns from these sources. Divide the words into favourable (euphemistic) and unfavourable (pejorative) such as 'sumptuous', 'full-flavoured', 'luscious', 'bland', 'over-spiced', 'sickly sweet', 'salt', 'savoury'. Note any neutral words and ones which compare the food, drink or products with human or other living beings, for example 'light-hearted', 'full-bodied', 'unassuming', 'bold', 'sturdy'. Describe a meal followed by a car journey. The narrator is a gourmet and motor enthusiast. Include dialogue. Or describe the same incident from the point of view of the food eaten, the wine drunk or the car driven.

No Ideas but in Things

- William Carlos Williams meant by this that an object is its own symbol and doesn't have to mean or stand for anything. Surface, what you see, is enough. That is why so much depends on the red wheelbarrow in his poem by the same name. Description in the manner of the painter's still life is the writer's way of keeping words close to things. E. L. Doctorow, the American novelist, wrote that, 'Good writing is supposed to evoke sensation in the reader – not the fact that it is raining, but the feeling of being rained upon.' Collect dozens of small objects made of wood, metal, stone, plastic, paper, glass, china, and keep them in a shoe box. Take out two or three at random. Simply describe the object in as few precise words as possible. Use words which convey sense experience.

- Invent an explanation for their presence in the same place at the same time.

- Expand by adding characters and make the objects minor or major details in the plot of a story, for example clues in a murder or robbery.

Avoiding the Abstract

- Don't use too many abstract nouns. In fact, use hardly any. *Show* the idea in action. Don't *tell* readers. Let them guess. It makes them feel good if they can work it out for themselves. Here's a short exercise to practise showing. Make a list of abstract nouns such as hope, fear, joy, impatience, shame. For each idea find – an image, a line of speech. For example, for hope the images might be a packed bag, an airline ticket and a sombrero, together on a doormat. The dialogue might be, 'I'll phone when I arrive. I promise.' Write a sequence of images mingled with fragments of direct speech which embody the abstraction of your choice.

- Sometimes the abstraction and the concrete word work well with each other. Thomas Hardy's poem 'Heredity' explores the idea of family characteristics. He sees, 'trait and trace ... leaping from place to place / Over oblivion', the homely leapfrog image explaining evolution. 'Hope had grown grey hairs', wrote Gerard Manley Hopkins in his poem, 'The Wreck of the Deutschland', 'Hope had mourning on'. Try selecting some personifying phrases like this for selected abstract words and build them into short poems.

Chancing It

- Turn on a radio. When you hear speech write down some words and phrases. Change stations at least every thirty seconds. Write a piece using these words.

- Cut words from newspapers and magazines. Use phrases as well as single words. Look out for bizarre words and images, for example SUPER TRAIN TALKS or OLIVE LAKE FEARED. Fill an envelope with these words. Shake out a handful and arrange them into statements, questions, images, dialogues.

- Create an image from three words chosen by free association, such as button, coat, thread. 'Threadbare coat unbuttoned, she strode through the crowd.' Practise with a partner and take it in turns to select a word and challenge the other to write down as many associated words that come to mind within ten seconds. Use the new vocabulary to write a few lines.

Word Games

- If the first letter of each line of a poem spells a word you have written an acrostic. Write an acrostic spelling such words as 'love' or 'water'.

- HEH is an acronym for Healthy Eating in Hull, a fictitious health education campaign. Invent some acronyms of your own.

- An antonym is a word of opposite meaning to another. Rewrite adverts substituting antonyms wherever possible.

- 'Current' and 'currant' are homophones: words sounding the same but spelt differently. Write sentences using homophones to play on their multiple senses.

- Construct your own personal alphabet along the traditional lines of children's books where A is for apple, and so on. Writing one or two lines per letter devise a pollution alphabet, a food and wine one, a love one, a war one or anything else.

- Americans say, 'I am going to visit *with* you'. The British talk about being 'different *from*' and 'different *to*'. These little words are prepositions. They combine with verbs to produce dozens of different meanings. I can look down, up, through, into, under, with, by, along, beside, back. Select some verbs – see, put, think, talk, sleep. Perm them with prepositions like up, down, over, under, across. List unusual combinations like think DOWN and work them into a poem.

- Write a poem using only prepositions, conjunctions and adverbs. If this doesn't work allow yourself one noun and two verbs.

- Select a common object like a feather or a comb. Write some riddling lines like, 'all teeth and no bite' (comb) or 'curled like a new moon' (feather) and challenge your partner to guess the object. You can do the same for an abstract idea and it's a game that works well with two competing teams.

- One person in a group thinks of a celebrity, historic or fictional person. The rest have to guess the identity by asking, 'If this person were a piece of furniture, fruit, drink, picture, piece of music, what piece of furniture, fruit or whatever would they be?'

- Select some obscure words from the *Oxford English Dictionary*. For example, GRAIP. Others in the group write possible definitions/origins. Is GRAIP, 'a ceremonial fish spear used in fertility dances to the sea god Anyannuin' or 'the slimy deposit left after the first scraping of leather hides in a tannery' or 'an old Swedish word for a three-pronged fork used to lift dung or potatoes'? Check in the dictionary to find out which one of these three is correct. Gather in all definitions including the right one and leave the group to guess the real meaning.

- This activity celebrates fortunate errors, Freudian slips and useful accidents of every sort. Elizabeth Bishop wrote a poem called 'The Man-Moth', a printing error for mammoth, about a human insect which rises from the subway and lies spread-eagled across the face of a skyscraper. Find new words by removing a letter, usually a consonant, from existing words, so native becomes naïve, shoe hoe, table able. Then substitute the new word in phrases like, 'paddling a naive canoe', 'a lucky horsehoe', 'a game of able tennis'. Graham Rawle combines such phrases with surreal visuals in the *Guardian* every Saturday, for example, 'Dan enjoyed a drink but was starting to develop a bee belly', beside a photo of a fat man with a striped stomach.

- Mrs Malaprop in Sheridan's play, *The Rivals*, talked about 'allegories on the banks of the Nile'. Common errors today include: 'He can't sell his house because of the mining subsidy', 'The president has lost any credulity he ever had, after his latest error'. Collect words of similar sound but different sense and invent a character to use them.

Variations on a Theme

- Write a poem in the clipped speech of telegrams. End each line with STOP. Try to develop a relationship between two or more people. See 'Telegram' by Carol Ann Duffy.

- Tell a story using headlines. Find a subject treated controversially by the press, for example, anti-motorway or animal rights protesters. See Joyce's *Ulysses* which contains a section set in a newspaper office where the paragraphs are short and each has a headline.

- Breughel's painting *Flemish Proverbs* is the model for this activity. Begin with a saying, such as 'Time waits for nobody'. One writer began his piece, 'Time and nobody were great friends'. It was called Time Travels. Write a series of short pieces and try to group them, using a common setting or time.

- Try writing some original proverbs. Focus on some familiar objects such as a watch, pair of scissors, feather, key, mirror, eye or hand and use each as an inspiration for your proverb.

- In his extraordinary book *Exercises in Style* Raymond Queneau, the French novelist, demonstrates how you can treat the same incident in a hundred different ways. He imagines a bus arriving at a stop and the passengers pushing to get on. During the scuffling a man's coat button gets ripped loose. In a series of separate vignettes he writes an olfactory version of these events, a metaphoric version, and an onomatopoeic one, a retrograde, present tense and asides version. Also a version in grand opera language, headlines and mathematical terms. Try selecting a small incident in your life and write it up in a variety of styles. Here are some suggestions. In *permutations*, that is in groups each made up of 2, 3, 4 and 5 letter words. In *anagrams*. In *geometrical/botanic/anatomical* terms. In words without E. In *monosyllables*. In *disc jockey chat* or *hip-hop* or *blurb* language. You can think of other possibilities.

Booklist

Auden, W. H., *Selected Poems* (Faber, London, 1979).
Auster, P., *New York Trilogy* (Faber, London, 1988).
Ayto, J. & Simpson, J., *The Oxford Dictionary of Modern Slang* (OUP, Oxford, 1992).

Banks, I., *The Bridge* (Macmillan, London, 1986).

Bishop, E., *Complete Poems* (Chatto, London, 1991).

Burroughs, W., *Cities of the Red Night* (Penguin, Harmondsworth, 1982).

Carlos Williams, W., *Collected Poems* (Penguin, Harmondsworth, 1989).

Carlos Williams, W., *Paterson* (Penguin, Harmondsworth, 1990).

Carroll, L., *Alice through the Looking Glass* (Penguin, Harmondsworth, 1984).

Davies, P., *All Played Out. The Full Story of Italia '90* (Heinemann, London, 1990).

Dick, Philip, K., *Do Androids Dream Of Electric Sheep?* (Panther, London, 1972).

Doyle, R., *The Barrytown Trilogy* (Secker & Warburg, London, 1992).

Duffy, C. A., *Selling Manhattan* (Anvil, London, 1987).

Ellroy, J., *White Jazz* (Century Publishing, London, 1992).

Fairfax, J. & Moat, J., *The Way To Write* (Elm Tree Books, London, 1981).

Faulkner, W., *Absalom, Absalom!* (Vintage, London, 1995).

Friel, B., *Translations* (Faber, London, 1981).

Gibson, W., *Neuromancer* (Gollancz, London, 1984).

Glasgow, E., *Barren Ground* (Virago, London, 1986).

Hardy, T., *Under The Greenwood Tree* (Macmillan, London, 1974).

Hardy, T., *Selected Shorter Poems*, ed. J. Wain (Macmillan, London, 1988).

Hemingway, E., *For Whom The Bell Tolls* (Cape, London, 1992).

Herbert, G., *Complete English Poems*, ed. J. Tobin (Penguin, Harmondsworth, 1992).

Hoban, R., *Turtle Diary* (Picador, London, 1977).

Hoban, R., *Riddley Walker* (Cape, London, 1980).

Hopkins, G. M., *Poems*, ed. G. Gardner (OUP, Oxford, 1970).

Jones, D., *In Parenthesis* (Faber, London, 1969).

Jones, D. (ed.), *Imagist Poetry* (Penguin, Harmondsworth, 1972).

Joyce, J., *Ulysses* (The Bodley Head, London, 1960).

Joyce, J., *Finnegans Wake* (Faber, London, 1975).

Kane, P., *The Hitch-hiker's Guide to the Electronic Highway* (MIS Press, New York, 1994).

Kelman, J., *Not, Not While the Giro and Other Stories* (Minerva, London, 1989).

Lawrence, D. H., *The Rainbow* (Penguin, Harmondsworth, 1969).

Lewis, N., *The Book of Babel* (Penguin, Harmondsworth, 1995).

Mann, T., *Death in Venice* (Penguin, Harmondsworth, 1988).

Mansfield, K., 'At the Bay,' in *Undiscovered Country*, ed. I. A. Gordon (Longman, London, 1974).

McBain, E., *The Ed McBain Omnibus* (Mandarin, London, 1993).

Mills, J., *Womanwords* (Virago, London, 1991).

Morgan, E., *Collected Poems 1949–87* (Carcanet, Manchester, 1990).

Orwell, G., 'Politics and the English Language' in *The Collected Essays, Journalism and Letters*, vol. 4 (Penguin, Harmondsworth, 1978).

Perec, G., *A Void*, trans. G. Adair (Harvill, London, 1994).

Phillips, T., *A Humument* (Thames & Hudson, London, 1980).

Pope, A., *Poetical Works*, ed. H. Davis (OUP, Oxford, 1978).

Queneau, R., *Exercises in Style*, trans. B. Wright (Calder, London, 1979).

Raine, C., *A Martian Sends A Postcard Home* (OUP, Oxford, 1979).

Raymond, D., *How the Dead Live* (Sphere Books, London, 1988).

Rees, N., *The Joy of Cliché* (Futura, London, 1985).

Richardson, D., *Miriam* (Virago, London, 1979).

Runyon, D., *From First To Last* (Penguin, Harmondsworth, 1990).

Runyon, D., *Guys And Dolls* (Penguin, Harmondsworth, 1993).

Russ, J., *How to Suppress Women's Writing* (Women's Press, London, 1984).

Salinger, J. D., *The Catcher in the Rye* (Hamish Hamilton, London, 1951).

Selby, H. Jnr, *Last Exit to Brooklyn* (Paladin, London, 1987).

Sheridan, R. B., *The Rivals* (OUP, Oxford, 1968).

Skelton, R., *The Practice of Poetry* (Heinemann, London, 1971).

Solt, M. E. (ed.), *Concrete Poetry. A World View* (Indiana UP, Indiana, 1970).

Spender, D., *Man Made Language* (Pandora, London, 1990).

Spiegl, F., *Keep Taking The Tabloids* (Pan, London, 1983).

Sterling, B., *Shismatrix* (Ace, London, 1986).

Sterling, B., *Mirrorshades: An Anthology Of Cyberpunk* (Paladin, London, 1988).

Tennyson, A., *Poems*, ed. W. Williams (Penguin, Harmondsworth, 1984).

Thomas, D., *Collected Poems* (Dent, London, 1952).

Thomas, D., *Under Milk Wood* (Dent, London, 1991).

Welsh, I., *Trainspotting* (Secker & Warburg, London, 1993).

Welsh, I., *Acid House* (Vintage, London, 1995).

Waterhouse, K., *Waterhouse On Newspaper Style* (Viking, London, 1981).

Waterhouse, K., *There Is a Happy Land* (Sceptre, London, 1992).

Woolf, V., 'Kew Gardens' in *The Penguin Book of Short Stories*, ed. C. Dolley (Penguin, Harmondsworth, 1967).
Woolf, V., *The Waves* (Penguin, Harmondsworth, 1992).

4 Writing the Self

Ailsa Cox

As we reach the end of a frenetic century, our world is largely shaped through nostalgia. Postmodern culture regenerates images from the past, apparently having exhausted new possibilities. The children of the 'Woodstock generation' turn into New Age hippies in the nineties. At the time of writing, Star Wars toys (*c.* 1980) are being featured in *The Face*. No matter how young you are, you're a part of history.

What all this does is compartmentalise the past. We talk about 'the sixties' or 'the twenties' as if they were the same for everyone. Each decade is given its own iconography – bobbed hair and the Charleston for the 'roaring twenties', mini-skirts and the Beatles for the 'swinging sixties'. Autobiography demonstrates a diversity of experience which stretches far beyond these familiar stereotypes. It gives a voice to those who have been marginalised within both history and literature.

This is particularly true of women, whose writing has traditionally remained private, in the form of diaries and letters. Dorothy Wordsworth's *Journal* is far less well known than her famous brother's poetry, which often incorporated images drawn directly from her observations. In the past, women who published their work tended to use a male pseudonym, like George Eliot, or to emphasise their respectability through their married status, like Mrs Gaskell. Nowadays, the taboos against women's writing are not quite so obvious, but female experience is still frequently devalued.

Writing down your own experience is a way of opening up the human dimensions of history. In her preface to *That's How*

It Was, Maureen Duffy speaks of writing about her working-class background within 'a precise historical moment' that links the private self with wider social issues. This is something outside the history books. Similarly, no amount of factual reportage can communicate the experience of being held hostage with the poetic force of Brian Keenan's *An Evil Cradling*. No fictional account would have quite the same power. He was there, locked in a Lebanese cell, and while reading about it, we are there too.

Autobiography has been an instrument of black consciousness in America since the time of Harriet E. Wilson and other former slaves. These are the testimonies of 'ordinary' people, rather than the famous lives who are the subject of most commercially published autobiography. The writers proclaim their own individuality in the midst of a society which tries to limit their potential according to race. They also celebrate the vitality of an undervalued culture. So they are speaking both on their own behalf and for a social group. Their work actively encourages others to pick up the pen.

The tradition of autobiography as empowerment has been a feature of the worker writer movement, in both Britain and the USA. Many community projects bypass the literary establishment altogether by producing their own publications; and, following the impact of DIY punk graphics and desk top publishing, there has also been a growth in small circulation magazines and fanzines. The tastes and attitudes of young people are often belittled by their elders or, like rave culture, perceived as a threat. By speaking for yourself, you're fighting against these misrepresentations.

Autobiography compels through its authenticity. But any literary text is a construct, shaped for its potential readership. Memory itself is selective. In Alice Munro's short story, 'Princess Ida', the young narrator hears contradictory versions of her grandmother's character, depending on which of her relatives is actually telling the tale. Munro often uses her fiction in this way, to illustrate the subjectivity of our perceptions of the past. Memories turn into stories in our heads. Some details are forgotten, while others grow in significance, as we ourselves change and develop. Not only is the passage of time a fictionalising process; the demands of oral storytelling will, inevitably, lead to some re-editing. The same will be true of writing on the page. Many highly accomplished autobiographers – V. S. Pritchett, Maya Angelou, Michael Powell – include in their work passages of dialogue which can scarcely represent verbatim memories.

Postmodern critics highlight this interrelationship between fiction and autobiography, disputing the opposition between 'truth' and 'fiction'. The very term, 'autobiography', was only invented at the start of the nineteenth century, at a time of increased belief in individual liberty and faith in human progress. In our own time, 'finding yourself' has become a major preoccupation. With the decline of religious certainty, there has been a tendency to look for a meaning in life through individual self-expression. Postmodernists would argue that there IS no meaning. There is no 'real me', waiting to be discovered; no such thing as a 'true story'. The self becomes a series of performances, rather than a fixed identity; autobiography turns into another type of fiction.

In practice, however, autobiography and fiction do require different approaches to what may well be the same basic material. Mary McCarthy's *Memories of a Catholic Girlhood* constantly questions the reliability of her own memory, as well as drawing attention to fictive devices, such as the running together of separate incidents. But her admissions only serve to underline her commitment to some kind of historical accuracy. The autobiographer is undertaking a search for some kind of verifiable truth, however provisional. She can tease her audience or offer conflicting realities, but she must at least be aware of this particular relationship with the reader. Weak writing is often flawed by a confusion between autobiographical and fictional form.

At the early stages of writing, it is best not to become obsessed with these broader technical issues. Writing about personal experience offers the opportunity to concentrate on language and imagery, rather than the mechanics of plot. We all tell stories in our daily conversations and each family has its fund of private legend. Where the family listener is sympathetic the blank page is mute and can be uniquely terrifying.

Autobiography eases the transition between speech and written language, helping you to find your own distinctive voice. It enables you to draw on the resources of the unconscious mind, which will fuel your conscious use of craft. Autobiography is not just for new writers. When Virginia Woolf felt blocked in her professional writing, she turned to reminiscences of her own childhood in *A Sketch Of The Past*. Throughout her life, she kept a personal journal as a sort of creative practice yard.

More recently, Primo Levi's *If This Is A Man*, Maxine Hong Kingston's *The Woman Warrior* and Wole Soyinka's *Ake* have all become contemporary classics. These writers have not chosen autobiography because they lacked the imagination to make things up. They've done so because they have something urgent to say from their lived experience. Levi was a survivor from the concentration camps. Hong Kingston writes about Chinese culture in America, and Soyinka about colonial Nigeria. In speaking for themselves, they are conscious of the many others who have not had the chance to be heard.

Workshop Writing

The purpose of these workshops is to experiment with language and imagery, by exploring personal experience. They are also designed to help you find your own voice. The earlier workshops focus on memory, while some of the later ones concentrate more on immediate observation and on harnessing the resources of the unconscious. Although they describe prose writing, most can be adapted for work with scripts or poetry. The first workshop is an introductory session; the others can be run in any order.

1   Seven

The door is not closed on our childhood when we become adults. People suffering from Alzheimer's disease, at the very end of their lives, often re-enact scenes from their earliest days. Proust's narrator, Marcel, in *Remembrance of Things Past*, is transported back through time simply by tasting, once again, a particular sort of cake. This workshop aims to recapture childhood perceptions through the use of sense impressions. It also helps to develop a personal voice, by connecting speech with writing. As an audience for oral storytelling, the workshop builds confidence in new writers, emphasising that there is something of interest in everyone's life story.

A   Everyone in the group is asked to remember when they were roughly seven years old. The exact age doesn't matter. We are thinking of a stage when the world still seems new and strange, but when babyhood is far behind.

Going through the five senses – sight, hearing, touch, smell, taste – jot down one particular sound, texture, and so on that brings that time back to you. It can be pleasant or unpleasant: the taste of new bread or of cod liver oil. A few words are all that you need at this stage, just enough to jog your memory. Some people will relate to one sense more strongly than the others. It doesn't matter if you have to leave one out.

B   The group then shares the sense impressions on their individual lists, describing not only the details of texture, taste and so forth, but the associations they bring with them. Sometimes the sense impressions will connect with one another. The smell of sliced green apples might lead on to the taste of the pie, which, in turn, conjures up a Sunday morning and the noise of suburban lawnmowers. Other lists will be more fragmented. One of the pleasures of this type of workshop is discovering the wide range of personal experience. That diversity is reflected in different ways of tackling the exercise.

C   As everyone explains what they've put down, they will inevitably put their sense impressions into context, shaping their anecdotes into stories. A student once recalled the smell of the canal, which reminded him of having to carry a large pane of glass through Salford for his father. Just by describing the feel of the glass, he was communicating some of the terror of being seven years old, at the illogical mercy of adults. In itself, this was a small incident, but he kept his listeners enthralled.

The aim, at this point, is to relax and talk freely. The conversation may generate more memories, as varieties of experience interconnect. For instance, one group I worked with shared herbal remedies from both 1920s Manchester and the West Indies in the 1950s. Most people will not need too much prodding to share their memories, although a chairperson may well be needed to subdue dominating individuals or encourage quieter members. As in all autobiographical exercises, tact is essential. Do not make assumptions – for instance, that everyone has grown up with two parents.

Very occasionally, someone's memories will be so painful, that they become upset. This doesn't necessarily mean that the workshop is a negative experience for them, but no one should be forced to spill their secrets to a room full of people they may only just have met. While being as supportive as you can, remember this is not a therapy group. Keep the focus on practicalities rather than self-analysis. It goes without saying that whatever you learn about others within a writers' workshop should remain confidential.

D   The workshop members now transfer their storytelling onto paper, working as quickly as possible, while the memories are still fresh. The writing should be as simple and direct as possible. The sense impressions don't have to be worked into the piece systematically, but the writing should always be rooted in the physical perceptions of a seven year old. The reader should be taken into someone else's world through the use of sensuous detail. Don't strain after a plot, but let the storytelling develop as it did through speech. Virginia Woolf writes about 'moments of being', flashes of supreme awareness that stand out from day-to-day existence. For her, it is typified by a memory of listening to waves breaking beyond the nursery window. It's this subjective sense of the past that we're attempting to recapture.

E   The results can be polished outside the workshop. Once you start writing autobiographically, you may find it difficult to stop, as you unwind a whole chain of memories, each one reminding you of something else. Few of us remember chronologically, and you don't have to write that way either. The facts of time and place are less important than the quality of the experience.

F   Some workshop members will write in the present tense, using the language of a child. Roddy Doyle adopts this voice for his novel *Paddy Clarke, Ha Ha Ha*. Others will write as their adult selves, looking back, as in Janet Frame's *To the Island*; they may even use the more detached, third person narration of J. G. Ballard's *Empire of the Sun*. It is up to the individual to find their own way, by trusting their instincts rather than following a preconceived formula. The one rule that may be necessary is to write through specifics, rather than generalising. In other words, avoid too many 'woulds'. Rather than 'on Sunday we would....' write about a particular Sunday, even if you have to roll several incidents into one.

2   Fifteen

This workshop extends the approach of the previous exercise, with the aim of completing an autobiographical short story.

A   This time, the group is asked to go back to the time when they were fifteen years old. For some, this will be a very short journey; but a year is a long time, when you're a teenager. Tastes and habits change almost overnight. As with the previous exercise, the age is chosen to represent a period of transition. At fifteen, you're on the border between childhood and maturity. You're striving to establish a distinct identity, while remaining acutely conscious of your peers.

You're asked to make a note of three things – something you wore, an expression you used and a piece of music familiar from that time. The clothing could be school uniform, an item of fashion or the wellies you wore in the farmyard. It doesn't have to be anything remarkable; men often find they were dressed in much the same way then as now. The expression could be youthful slang, like 'fab' or 'wicked', the chants from football matches, a catchphrase ('Beam me up Scottie') or dialect. Many fifteen year olds identify passionately with a particular kind of pop music. If this is not you, you may remember a hymn in church or school, or theme music from TV. Once again, remember, there is no such thing as a wrong answer. Don't worry if you can't come up with something for each category. You can also adapt the age range, if thirteen or sixteen feels sharper than fifteen.

B   You now have up to three details which, for you, symbolise a particular time. With a partner discuss what lies behind those symbols. Did you have an argument with parents or school about the way you dressed? A student told me recently how he and his friends copied the invented language of *A Clockwork Orange*. In the film *Heavenly Creatures*, set in New Zealand in the fifties, teenage girls' fantasies are set to the tunes of 'the world's greatest tenor', Mario Lanza. For a teenager in the nineties, the songs of Kurt Cobain might be more relevant.

When you talk to your partner, you're finding out not just what they did when you were younger, but what it felt like to be young at that particular time. Within these parameters, the conversation should be informal. You're opening one another up, rather than firing questions. There may be interesting similarities and discrepancies between partners from different backgrounds. Some may have spent their lives within a particular subculture, while others were already tied down by responsibilities in the home or workplace.

C   We now step back a little from the purely personal, placing private experience in an historical context. To your list of symbols, add something that was in the news when you were fifteen. You might not have been that interested at the time. One student still had her diary from 1939; Evelyn's partygoing was well documented, while the outbreak of war almost passed her by. Did your news item have any impact on your life? Where were you on the night of the moon landing, or the day Margaret Thatcher resigned?

D   Next, describe something that happened to you when you were about fifteen. It doesn't have to be anything earthshattering; Friday night at the youth club is fine, so long as you turn the many Friday nights into one, writing specifically rather than generalising. You can use any of the symbols you've been talking about, or none. You can make reference to the wider world, or forget your news item completely.

Use the language of speech. It is alive and ever-changing, and expresses your personality more distinctly than formalised 'Queen's English'. If you've been doing some work on teenage slang, you might want to explore the language further, by writing your piece as a monologue. Or you might want to introduce snatches of dialogue. Other characters might become as important as your own younger self. In George Lucas's autobiographical film, *American Graffiti*, the attention is on a group of friends, rather than one individual.

E   Bring your work back to the group as a whole after you've worked at it outside the workshop. As you shape reminiscence into story, you begin using the fictive devices discussed in Chapters 5 and 6. You will inevitably condense and simplify. The workshop should not concern itself with what is true or false. Does the story sound authentic? Is it a convincing picture of life at fifteen? The reader will believe almost anything, if you make it vivid; the supernatural elements in Stephen King's horror story, 'Carrie', work because the world of his sixteen-year-old heroine seems so true-to-life.

3   Family Gatherings

This workshop switches the attention from yourself to the other people in your life. You should interpret 'family' broadly, to include friends and neighbours, as well as blood relations. You could even adapt the exercise to cover events outside the family, such as farewell parties and reunions. What matters is that you're dealing with a network of people, who are interrelated socially.

Big occasions like weddings, funerals and Christmas celebrations put everyone on public display. This is why films like *Four Weddings and a Funeral* have found so much comic potential in these social rituals. There may also be deeper tensions at work, like those at the Christmas dance in James Joyce's story 'The Dead'. Whatever tone you adopt, this is an opportunity to look closely at characters and their relationships to one another.

A   Visualise a family gathering, like one of those above. Remember everybody who's there. You'll know them in varying degrees of intimacy; some you'll know very well, others you'll never have seen before. You could put them all around a table, in church pews or in an imaginary group photo. Write about them in as much detail as you can, focusing on their behaviour together.

Families can be extremely complicated, especially now divorce is so common. At a wedding, there might be several sets of parents and grandparents. Ex-spouses size up one another's new partners. You might feel most interested in the people you know least well – the black sheep of the family, or the legendary uncle from America (see Alice Munro's 'Princess Ida'). How do such characters match up to their image within the family?

Joyce, in 'The Dead', captures the predictability of family festivals; for 30 years the Misses Morkan have served a goose dinner at their party and, we suspect, there has always been a resident drunk, like Freddy Malins, who is kept in control on this occasion. Keep your characters within their setting; build up the atmosphere; what's eaten or drunk, the speeches that are made, the music and games. Describe the setting – someone's house, perhaps, or a pub.

B   You should now have a mass of material, possibly an amalgam of several New Year's Eves, christenings or whatever. Choose a character who particularly interests you, and develop what you already have into a more detailed character sketch. What are they doing, when you visualise them in that setting? You can now go beyond the original brief, to include more background detail, or even bring in other stories about your family member. What was their place within the family? How did other people see them, and how did they appear to you?

4   Return of the Native

Both this workshop, which focuses again on memory, and the next, which suggests ways of tackling the present, make use of a sense of place through descriptive exercises.

A human presence often seems to speak through a physical setting, whether it's the house you live in or, like Dorothy Wordsworth's Grasmere, a landscape. The places you once knew are not just physical reality, but part of your own interior landscape. Even the sound of an address can conjure up a whole mood. 'The yellow house at 2427 Blaisdell Avenue', with its 'small and brownish rooms' seems a fit setting for the beatings Mary McCarthy receives in *Memories of a Catholic Girlhood*.

A   Imagine you are revisiting a place you once knew. It could be the street you grew up in, or a holiday beach. Choose a fairly limited area – one hillside, rather than the whole of Wales! What matters is that you haven't been back for at least two years. Write a description of the place, not as it might be now, but as it was, with as much physical detail as possible. If it is a building, it should be deserted. You can introduce people into a landscape, so long as they're part of the background, rather than the focus of your writing.

B   Use your description as the beginning of an autobiographical piece, describing your memories of this place. Think of yourself as an explorer, investigating strange surroundings. Put other people into this place, and watch their behaviour. You can even observe your younger self. Don't forget that weather, lighting and temperature are all part of the atmosphere. This descriptive piece can be developed into a longer narrative, either by yourself or, as an experiment in fiction, by another workshop member. Jeff Torrington's autobiographical novel *Swing Hammer Swing!* takes you straight into the Glasgow of the sixties, while Amos Oz's *Elsewhere, Perhaps* opens with the line, 'You see before you the kibbutz of Metsudat Ram'.

5   A Room of My Own

The plot and characters of George Perec's novel, *Life, A User's Manual*, are expressed entirely through physical descriptions of the apartments within a huge residential block in Paris. Describe your own room – either a room you use now or one from your past. You won't be able to include absolutely every item in it, and so you will find yourself selecting items that have special significance to you. You might describe the story behind something that was handed down to you, or describe your misadventures while putting up the shelves.

Do you share a room, or do others come barging into your own space? Have they left evidence of themselves behind – children's toys, or cups that they have drunk from? Is your room a mess, or obsessively tidy? What can you see from the window? As in Workshop 3, an element of detachment should temper your description. You want your reader to be able to step into this room, and imagine the kind of person who lives there.

6   Journeys

How do we describe our lives when we're in the middle of them? Movement's all around us; the present turns into the past before you've time to write it down. Journeys, like old-fashioned stories, have beginnings, middles and ends. In writing, they offer a means of structuring experience.

There's been a huge boom in travel writing recently, which is often a form of autobiography. Bill Bryson's *The Lost Continent* is a search for the small town America he remembers from boyhood. Amryl Johnson returns to Trinidad for *Sequins on a Ragged Hem*. Moving in the other direction, a group of American students I once worked with described their arrival in Britain, coping with our peculiar 'phones and working out that those big black cars are taxis. You don't have to cross the Atlantic to come up with worthwhile material. For this workshop we'll concentrate on a much shorter journey.

A   Take a notebook on your journey into the workshop. Think of it as a sketchbook, or as a camera, with words instead of images. Make rough notes along the way. If this journey is part of your normal routine, you may not have taken much notice of your surroundings. What's typical on this day, and what's different? How is your environment changing? Do you go past buildings that are being put up or knocked down? Is the season changing? If you travel on public transport, watch the passengers; if you're in a car, watch the other drivers while you're waiting at the lights. (Obviously, don't write while you're actually driving!) You should have a mass of random impressions.

B   In the workshop, recreate a moment within your journey. It could be departure, arrival or the time the train spent stuck outside the station. You will need to select from your notes, developing fragmented images into a much fuller picture. Keep a sense of flux; this exercise is all about movement through time and space. Try writing in the present tense, using the short, chopped sentences you might find in a diary. What you lose grammatically, you may gain in immediacy. Derek Jarman's journals convey the urgency of someone living with HIV through brief paragraphs and snatched half-sentences.

7 Through the Looking Glass

Dreams are a direct line into the unconscious. Graham Greene claimed that several of his novels had their origins in images from dreams. In all of your writing, whether it's strictly auto-biographical or a political thriller like most of Greene's work, or any other kind of genre, you should trust your irrational side. Let your unconscious surprise both yourself and your readers.

A   Keep paper and pen by your bed. When you wake up, jot down your dream as quickly as you can. Dreams have a knack of disappearing once the day begins.

B   Write down your dream in more detail. You might try using the third person rather than 'I'. This will keep some kind of distance between yourself and the material, which may otherwise be so close to you that you can't see it clearly. During the dream itself, you may have that same odd sense of detachment, which makes *Alice in Wonderland* so convincingly dream-like. Write as simply and exactly as you can, allowing the details to speak for themselves. You may well choose the present tense, as a way of bringing immediacy to your account.

Dreams are, almost by definition, fragmented and illogical. Just get down what you can. Some people swear they never dream. Or you may find that because you're doing this exercise you suddenly stop dreaming. If this is so, and if you really can't remember any dream ever, try making up your own nightmare by acting out (on paper at least) your phobia.

Most of us can think of something which sends shudders down our spine, whether it is spiders, lifts or the theme music to *The Archers*. Use this as your nightmare, again writing in the third person and the present tense, reporting as simply as possible. If you have neither nightmares, dreams, nor phobias, you are unnaturally sane.

C   In small groups, read your dreams to one another. Resist the temptation to psychoanalyse. Treat this material as pure invention. You're looking for strong images, which could be made still clearer or developed further. Horror and fantasy fiction often seem to derive their power from private nightmares; think of Edgar Allen Poe's tales of premature burial.

Writers whose style is laboured or self-conscious often find this kind of exercise helps them to 'let go'.

8   Changes

For this workshop, we'll stay with Graham Greene, whose advice was to write autobiographically, but always change one thing. That is one way to make the transition from auto-biographical to fictional writing, which will be dealt with in more detail in the next chapter.

A   Think of something that changed your life. It could be something as superficially trivial as a new haircut. It could be a chance meeting or moving house. Make some rough notes, trying to locate the precise moment of change, and to relive what it felt like from the inside.

B   Now make your change. Alter a setting, or switch char-acters, while keeping to a first person narrative. This idea developed out of a workshop, which centred round a descrip-tion of a party. One writer found it impossible to get to grips with her piece until she wrote from the point of view of some-one of the opposite sex, rather than through a character exactly like herself.

C   You are now on the road to fiction. One alteration may well lead to another. Don't specify the changes you've made during initial feedback from the workshop. Later on, a general discussion will be helpful. What difference did your change make to the story? How did it affect the rest of the material? Could the members of the workshop tell what you had invented? And does it really matter any more?

Writing On

Once you've started to write autobiographically, each piece of work can be used to generate another, especially if you've some kind of audience. The feedback from a workshop or from your own friends and family can lead you still more deeply into the past. They will want to know more, and they will ask questions you might not have thought of.

Even if you're writing in complete isolation, the process of writing down your memories is self-perpetuating. Have a look at your old diaries and letters. Some of the books listed at the end of this chapter may offer points of contact with your own experience. Reading an anthology like Liz Heron's *Truth, Dare or Promise – Girls Growing up in the Fifties*, might prompt you to write something on your own girlhood. Football fans might find inspiration in Nick Hornby's *Fever Pitch*.

It's all a question of keeping the ball rolling. The suggestions below offer a range of stimuli which can be adapted for group work or individual use. Bear in mind everything that has been said in the workshop sections about writing with immediacy, through as much physical detail as you can manage.

Tape Recorders

- You can make use of oral story-telling, as well as written testimony. The tape recorder you use should be as unobtrusive as possible, even if this means sacrificing sound quality. Something with a built-in microphone is best. Try interviewing one another, developing the session as a conversation rather than an interrogation. Avoid asking questions that invite a simple yes or no; this lesson would also apply if you were using the tape recorder to gather family history. The advantage of this kind of activity is that the speaker is using her own language. Many people are much livelier oral storytellers than they are writers. The disadvantage is that transcribing is extremely time-consuming, at a ratio of roughly three hours writing to an hour of tape. You will then need to edit the material, cutting out some repetitions while retaining the speech patterns of the individual. One or two 'know what I mean?'s are enough. It's probably best to let someone else do this work of transcribing and editing, because it is so hard to 'hear' yourself. You can then take up the story by writing down your experiences for yourself.

Maps

- Make a map of your world when you were five, ten, thirteen... This will bear no resemblance to ordnance survey; it will be a rough diagram of the places that mattered, in relation to one another. Janet Frame describes 'my place', a secret place among the fallen trees, which could not have been far from her house, yet which seems like another world. When I was a child, the canal and railway line were as far as I was allowed to go. Beyond them, I imagined somewhere dangerous and exotic, like the 'here be dragons' marked at the edge of the known world in medieval maps. Write a piece about the imaginative and actual territory of your childhood world. Say how you preserved it from intruders. Describe how that world faded or collapsed. Can you pinpoint the period or incident when this happened?

- How do the different worlds of our lives relate? In *Lost in Translation*, Eva Hoffman chronicles the transition between her early life in Poland and moving to the US. Even the move from home to going to school means a huge expansion in your mental territory. Make a plan of a street where you used to live. Who lived in the houses? Who ran the shops? Plot out your own life. Use the idea of a journey, like Bunyan's *Pilgrim's Progress*, with your own 'Slough of Despond' and 'Celestial Cities'. Chart the key moments in your life, like stops along the subway. The journey doesn't have to be a straight line. You could take all kinds of turnings, or even double back.

- Think of other ways to show your life in diagrams. A family tree is the obvious one, with plenty of space to flesh out the names. What else has made you what you are, apart from your family heritage? Show yourself at the intersection of all these influences – friends, education, religious or political beliefs. Where do those beliefs come from? Describe a time when you were at a crossroads in your life.

Rites of Passage

- Write about moments of decision and important relationships – early friendships or a teacher who influenced you. Try to capture these experiences as they were felt from the inside.

- Describe:

  Your first day at school.
  Your first job.
  Learning to ride a bike/swim/drive.
  Your first football match.
  Your first disco.
  Leaving home.
  First ride in a plane.

- Describe any experience when it was new to you. Express both your fears and your excitement. Write about the last time, too – the day you left school, or walked out of the job. If you've come to Britain from another country, or moved around within the UK, write about leaving one place and arriving in another.

- Many a back cover promises, 'This book will change your life'. But what actually changes your life? Write about moments of change, both as they were to you then and as you see them with hindsight.

- Some periods in your life could be painful to write about. Both Janet Frame and Susanne Kaysen have given accounts of their time in mental institutions. Buchi Emecheta's autobiography is called, for good reason, *Head Above Water*. The act of writing is itself a sign of survival. Try writing about a painful period/episode/relationship in your life. Only do this if you feel you can face up to the experience. Read Blake Morrison's *And When Did You Last See Your Father?* It's a sensitive and moving account of a son's relationship with his father. He comes to terms with his father's terminal illness by recovering his childhood past and setting memories alongside the painful present. Maybe this is a technique you could use.

Photographs

- Family snapshots can be very productive, both in work-shops and for individual writing. Doris Lessing starts with two photographs, when she writes about her mother in her memoir, 'Impertinent Daughters'. One shows her as 'a large, round-faced girl, full of ... confidence', the other as a 'lean, severe old thing, bravely looking out from a world of disappointment'. Lessing fills in the gap between the two with a mixture of family history and imaginative speculation. Try doing the same with two contrasting photographs of yourself or someone you know well.

- Photographs often conceal as much as they reveal. Even the most amateur snapshot is posed, while studio photographers are masters of artifice. Early in this century, families about to enter the workhouse often dressed up for one last picture together. At first glance, they appear to be living in prosperous circumstances. When you look at photographs of yourself, how much do you recognise? Was that well-scrubbed schoolboy really you? What was happening just before, or after, the photo was taken? Write down your impressions.

- One workshop I ran decided to use family photos in a different way, by swapping them around. The fictional characters that resulted were surprisingly different to the auto-biographical versions. Try this in your group.

Family Portraits

- In *Portrait of an Invisible Man* the American writer, Paul Auster, wrote about losing his father. He gathered together fragments of memory –

  The size of his hands.
  Their calluses.
  Eating the skin off the top of hot chocolate.
  Tea with lemon.

  Make your own list of things that remind you of a family member. Use them to create a family portrait.

- Hugo Williams deals with the memory of his father by building a poetry collection around the things he wrote in his letters home from boarding school. Write a letter to your parents, your children, a brother or sister.

- How did you fit into the family? Were you the baby, or the oldest, the one who looked after the others? Did your parents wish you were a girl or a boy? Were you an only child, or one amongst many? Who brought you up? Jackie Kay is another directly autobiographical poet, in her collection, *The Adoption Papers*. Model a poem on some of her writings in this collection.

Language

- Everybody has a private vocabulary, which they may not even be fully aware of. Some expressions are handed down through generations; you might suddenly hear yourself repeating something to your own children that was often said to you. My own mother's 'Patience is a Virtue' often crosses my lips. Alice Munro's *A Royal Beating*, takes just such a family saying as the beginning of a story. Outside the home, Muriel Spark's Miss Jean Brodie characterises her favourite pupils as the 'crème de la crème'. Dialect words can be equally evocative; in Manchester, if something is easy, we say that it's 'bobbins' – a leftover from the defunct cotton industry. A brainstorming session should bring to light many other examples of family sayings, dialect words or expressions like Miss Jean Brodie's which have taken on a personal meaning. Write a sketch/fragment triggered by an evocative word from your past.

Rules and Taboos

- Jamaica Kincaid's 'Girl' is discussed in Chapter 5. It's a good example of the way in which our lives are bounded by rules, both spoken and implied. In my own story, 'Be a Good Girl', I made use of a family taboo against using the toilet when out visiting relations. Draw up a list of five rules from your childhood; compare them with those of other workshop members. For better, or worse, institutions all have rules. Draw on your experience of family, school, the workplace, hospital, church or prison and describe some of the *unspoken* rules that influenced your life.

- What happened when you broke the rules? Mary McCarthy describes the awful guilt of a forbidden sip of water before her first Holy Communion. But she also manages to manipulate the rules of her Catholic school by claiming to have lost her faith. Have you ever told a lie? Were you found out? Write about the incident and its aftermath.

- At the beginning of one of her autobiographical books, *I Know Why the Caged Bird Sings*, Maya Angelou describes the embarrassment at wetting herself in public. Recall an embarrassing moment from your own life and either write about it in Angelou style, or imagine you are trying to explain it all away to an adult. Write the dialogue.

Music and Film

- Music has already been mentioned in Workshop 2. Why not bring the actual music into the workshop? You could even put together your own *Desert Island Discs*. Terence Davies' autobiographical films, *Distant Voices, Still Lives* and *The Long Day Closes*, marry images of working-class life in the fifties with a range of sound references, including the BBC shipping forecast, pub singalongs and snatches of soundtrack from Hollywood films. Think about the first film you ever saw, and the place you saw it in. What was your favourite TV programme, ten years ago? Merge these particular memories into a piece of writing.

Food

- Food is always good to write about, because it brings together so many of the senses. It is also an important part of our culture, whether it's fish and chips, spiced dal or jerk chicken. Recipes don't have to be boring lists of instructions; you can begin by describing how you learnt about this dish and the personal associations that it brings with it, as well as telling the reader what it looks and tastes like. Not all meals are pleasurable, of course; you could write about school dinners or wartime rationing.

- In your workshop, compare lists of the sweets you used to eat when you were a child. You can also compare childhood games and playground rhymes. Individually, remember a special toy, and what it meant to you. Create a verbal collage of images and memories. Include snatches of songs, fragments of ads, sweet names, jokes, skipping rhymes and so on.

Diaries

- If you take your writing seriously, you will become more analytical about your work, as time goes on. You will learn to edit, to redraft and to perfect your style. All of that is important, but if your conscious mind intrudes too early your writing will lose the energy of the unexpected. This is where keeping a journal, as suggested in Chapter 2, comes in handy. Use it as a place where you can write without censoring yourself or stopping to polish a phrase. You need never show this writing to anybody else. You can do exactly what you like with it. You don't have to fill it in as a daily chore, or record every single thing you do. It's there for your raw material, for ideas, thoughts, images and dreams. Diaries serve another purpose, by recording a life as it develops. The result may stand up on its own, like Derek Jarman's journals. Or you might go back to it later, as source material for something else. Germaine Greer incorporates parts of her notebooks in her memoir, *Daddy, We Hardly Knew You*. Some of them go back twenty years. If you have any old diaries, expand one or two of the entries that interest you into the present day, adding new insights or developing them further.

Booklist

Angelou, M., *I Know Why the Caged Bird Sings* (Virago, London, 1994).
Auster, P., 'Portrait of an Invisible Man' in *The Invention of Solitude* (Faber, London, 1988).

Ballard, J. G., *Empire of The Sun* (Granada, London, 1985).

Bryson, B., *Lost Continent* (Secker & Warburg, London, 1994).

Bunyan, J., *The Pilgrim's Progress* (OUP, Oxford, 1984).

Burgess, A., *Clockwork Orange* (Penguin, Harmondsworth, 1986).

Carroll, L., *Alice's Adventures in Wonderland. Through the Looking Glass* (Wordsworth Classics, Herts, 1993).

Doyle, R., *Paddy Clarke, Ha Ha Ha* (Minerva, London, 1994).

Duffy, M., *That's How It Was* (Virago, London, 1983).

Emecheta, B., *Head Above Water* (Heinemann, London, 1994).

The Face, no. 75 (London, December 1994).

Frame, J., *To The Island. The Envoy From Mirror City. An Angel At My Table* (Paladin, London, 1984).

Greene, G., *A Sort of Life* (Bodley Head, London, 1971).

Greer, G., *Daddy, We Hardly Knew You* (Penguin, Harmondsworth, 1990).

Heron, L. (ed.), *Truth, Dare or Promise* (Virago, London, 1992).

Hoffman, E., *Lost in Translation* (Minerva, London, 1995).

Hong Kingston, M., *The Woman Warrior* (Picador, London, 1981).

Hornby, N., *Fever Pitch* (Gollancz, London, 1992).

Jarman, D., *Modern Nature* (Vintage, London, 1992).

Johnson, A., *Sequins on a Ragged Hem* (Virago, London, 1988).

Joyce, J., 'The Dead', in *Dubliners* (Flamingo, London, 1994).

Kay, J., *The Adoption Papers* (Bloodaxe, Newcastle-upon-Tyne, 1994).

Kaysen, S., *Girl, Interrupted* (Virago, London, 1995).

Keenan, B., *An Evil Cradling* (Hutchinson, London, 1992).

King, S., *Carrie* (New England Library, London, 1992).

Lessing, D., 'Impertinent Daughters' in *Granta 14, Autobiography* (London, Winter 1984).

Levi, P., *If This is a Man/Truce* (Abacus, London, 1995).

McCarthy, M., *Memories of a Catholic Girlhood* (Penguin, Harmondsworth, 1975).

Morrison, B., *And When Did You Last See Your Father?* (Penguin, Harmondsworth, 1994).

Munro, A., *The Beggar Maid* (Penguin, Harmondsworth, 1980).

Munro, A. 'Princess Ida' in *Lives of Girls and Women* (Penguin, Harmondsworth, 1993).

Oz, A., *Elsewhere, Perhaps* (Flamingo, London, 1989).

Perec, G., *Life, a User's Manual* (HarperCollins, London, 1992).

Poe, E. A., *Selected Tales* (OUP, World Classics, Oxford, 1980).

Powell, M., *A Life in Movies* (Methuen, London, 1987).

Pritchett, V. S., *A Cab at the Door/Midnight Oil* (Penguin, Harmondsworth, 1986).

Proust, M., *Remembrance of Things Past*, vol. 1 (Penguin, Harmonds-worth, 1989).

Soyinka, W., *Ake/Isara* (Minerva, London, 1995).

Spark, M., *The Prime of Miss Jean Brodie* (Penguin, Harmondsworth, 1965).

Torrington, J., *Swing Hammer Swing* (Secker & Warburg, London, 1993).

Williams, H., *Writing Home* (OUP, Oxford, 1985).

Wilson, H. E., *Our Nig* (Vintage, London, 1993).

Woolf, V., *Moments of Being* (Hogarth Press, London, 1976).

Woolf, V., *A Writer's Diary* (Grafton, London, 1978).

Wordsworth, D., *The Grasmere Journals* (OUP, Oxford, 1993).

5 The Short Story

John Singleton

Some writers think all prose, including autobiography, is fiction. Writing about self is really *alibiography* they say – stories invented to explain (away?), rationalise, excuse, justify and disguise the truth. The same writers would also doubt whether there is any such thing as truth. For them there are at best versions of the truth, partial glimpses perhaps, no more. Fictions. John Barth, the American novelist, sums this up. 'The mother of all fiction,' he writes, 'is surely our common sense that our lives are stories – more exactly that each of our lives is a story-in-progress whereof each of us is perforce the central, if not necessarily, the dominant, character.'

In writing about the self our unconscious censoring and the deficiencies of memory mean we have to fictionalise to some degree anyway, if only to make sense of a mass of confusing and fragmentary recollections. We invent dialogue for ourselves, rearrange chronology, try metaphor and assonance and rhythms to heighten emotion and dramatise, telescope events, eliminate extraneous detail, focus on key moments, images, ad infinitum. The whole tale is a careful crafting deploying a wide range of narrative tactics and effects.

Despite this, autobiographic writing differs significantly from fiction. Even though the personal past may be the source for both kinds of writing and new writers tend to go there for their early fictional material, the short story does not depend on memory, the recall and accurate description of past times. Autobiography only *translates* the past, the short story *transforms* it.

The vital force in this re-creative process is the imagination. According to Rose Tremain the writer's task is, 're-imagining reality'. Re-imagining, she says, 'implies some measure of forgetting. The actual or factual has to lose definition, become fluid, before imagination can begin its task of reconstruction. Data from the research area of the book will remain data. It will be imaginatively inert.' As with historical data, about which Rose Tremain is writing, so with the writer's own history, it is no more than data till kindled by the imagination.

Graham Swift, author of *Waterland*, in an essay on the nature of storytelling considers the advice often given to new writers, namely to write *only what you know*. 'I could not agree with anything less. My maxim would be for God's sake write about what you don't know! For how else will you bring your imagination into play? How else will you *discover* or *explore* anything?' If we rely on our own experience as material for our stories, what happens, asks Swift, once our limited stock runs out? 'One of the fundamental aims of fiction,' he argues, 'is to enable us to enter, imaginatively, experiences other than our own.'

Writing to discover suggests that when we start as writers we are in the dark so to speak, about to travel the unknown, and we should let imagination illuminate the way. As L. P. Hartley wrote, at the beginning of his novel *The Go-Between*, 'The past is another country. They do things differently there.' Whether this is an accurate metaphor or not it does suggest that the important thing about writing fiction is not arriving at a destination (ending) nor having a map beforehand (plot), but the travelling itself. For new writers the comfort is that we can surrender to the force of the imagination and let the brain take the strain. Paul Klee, the German expressionist painter, used to describe his first sketchings as taking his pencil for a walk. That's a useful and stress-free way to start a short story – just take your pen for a walk.

Here we may have another useful distinction between these two ways of writing – autobiography and fiction. The first describes the self as already known, or explains the self as presently understood. While fiction on the other hand explores the self as yet hidden, in the dark. It's like *déjà vu*. Something secret hitherto is revealed which you sense you've known unconsciously all the time. It's come from a strange land, like the captain's secret sharer in Joseph Conrad's short story of the same name.

Dreams offer a useful analogy. Their symbolic language and dislocated narrative structure have been widely interpreted as a secret code disguising profound truths about the interior landscape of our lives. In a similar way our fictions, more coherent than dreams, less resistant to interpretation but coded nevertheless, explore and reveal something about our real selves. To some writers this suggests there is some unconscious creative process that works autonomously in our lives, all they have to do is get in contact, surf the psychic freeway. So they access the unconscious by automatic writing or by using dream images and sequences as the starting point/ material for fiction. For E. L. Doctorow, the American novelist, writing is about travelling blind. Of his recent book, *The Waterworks*, he has said, 'I wrote the book crucially because I knew nothing about it (the country west of the Hudson river). That's how writers write: by trying to find out what it is they are writing.' Or as E. M. Forster famously asked, 'How do I know what I think until I see what I say?'

It is not this deeper sense of self in fiction that John Braine in his book *Writing a Novel* warns the would-be novelist against, but the idea of seeing fiction as autobiography in a thin disguise. 'The function of the novel isn't self-expression,' he argues, 'it isn't to sort your life out: it isn't to change society. Above all it isn't about you. You must use your experience, direct or indirect, but only as the purposes of the story dictate...You have to get rid of yourself.' And let something else take over?

For John Braine then fiction may be based on real people, real events. *Based on* but not mirror images of them. In stories the characters we create are usually collages of actual people, composite figures. They start from the real, from what excites the imagination, and what emerges is a new person. The relationship of direct personal experience to fiction is like that of a cake to the cupboard. What's in the cupboard is in the cake but in the end they aren't anything alike.

But whether you start writing a short story by trawling the unconscious for ideas/images or whether you take personal experience and transform it, either way you need to craft the imagined, cook the raw. Fortunately writers are not on their own in the business of shaping the material of fiction. From birth to death we are surrounded by stories and story-tellers. Families are full of them and at get-togethers the tales circulate, told and retold singly and collaboratively. All the traumas, tragedies and taboos, all the crises, conspiracies and coincidences of daily life enriched by retelling. This is where our sense of story and narrative first develops and it's enhanced and developed in pub and club, café, bistro and office, locker room and launderette. It was by sitting under his mum's kitchen table that Sid Chaplin, a writer of Durham mining life, learnt his storytelling art. He hid there in the evening listening to the gossip and local tales and all the narrative banter of neighbours and friends dropping in for a chat. These community tales and voices found their way into his adult fiction, and were the mainstay of all his writing.

Family and locality and the wider culture of our nation sustain our individual sense of story. Our culture gives us a voice, language, and ways of 'speaking', written and oral stories. They are like templates, helping us shape our own narrative of self and family and community. As writers this is one way we enter the culture; it's a sort of self-initiation, a finding and defining of one's place there. A number of contemporary writers have gone to traditional narratives and consciously reworked them. Robert Coover, a contemporary American writer, has face-lifted the folk tale to expose the artifice and convention of such writing and thereby the illusory ground of all fiction, as well as exploring contemporary psychological realities. Fabulists like Angela Carter have imaginatively adapted fairy stories to entertain, to explore through symbolic narrative the hidden world of the unconscious and to feminise what are often presented as very male narratives. A writer who challenges gender stereotyping and the sexism of the Brothers Grimm's tales and creates female characters who are enterprising and independent reminds us that our political and moral views influence the shape of a short story as much as our concerns about form, structure and style.

But even in matters of form and style we cannot escape our cultural moorings. Many writers and commentators argue that there is a basic pattern to the short story, a kind of universal shape. A short story, it is argued, evolves through a number of stages, sometimes described passively as – beginning, middle and end; sometimes more dynamically as – situation, complication, crisis/dilemma, resolution. In other words the status quo is upset, disturbance follows but then, after some effort, equilibrium is restored. Chekhov, one of the greatest masters of short fiction, likened his stories to tortoises; they were all middle he thought. Whether middle or muddle these are the underlying contours of short fiction in our eurocentric culture, helpful blueprints from which to build fiction of our own.

Stories from other cultures, Amerindian for instance, however do not follow these same contour lines. Here's a hypothetical example. Three Indians are returning from a hunting trip. One falls down a deep hole and is seen by a bear who closes in to attack him. What happens next? Well this is classic beginning and middle, complication and crisis stuff. A European resolution of this situation would have his two companions turn, bravely fight off the bear or divert it cunningly and devise an ingenious method of getting the fallen comrade out of the hole so they can escape before the angry bear returns. Here is drama – tension, suspense and relief. Crisis – they've almost got him out but the rope breaks. One of the two rescuers lures the bear away with the fresh meat. This is food desperately needed for the tribe. Dilemma – should he waste it on a bear? Meanwhile his companion decides to put the fallen man out of his misery and save him from the horror of being eaten alive. And so on. You can think of other possibilities, variations on this pattern. Indeed that's what short story writing is about – working out the possibilities, the variations and resolving the dilemma or crisis.

But not if you are an Amerindian. How would this story be told outside the tepee? It would have a very different shape. Why? Work out some possibilities. What the European versions focus on is the importance of the individual and the virtues of courage, resourcefulness, enterprise, co-operation, the division of labour and the conquest of nature. These are the qualities and values of an entrepreneurial, capitalist culture that celebrates progress and profit and which still dominates our thinking today and apparently the way we structure our fiction. After all both our fiction and our scientific materialist world are about solving problems and defeating the savage, unpredictable nature of our condition.

More recent fiction has challenged these contours. Post-modern writing has tried to expose the conventions, the workings of fiction itself, so the reader is no longer under the enchantment of story, no longer hidebound by formal conventions and the cultural constraints of narrative. The new reader and new writer can move in a far braver world free to experiment with form and structure. Some short fiction over the last two decades has been highly innovative. Traditional notions of structure and pattern have given way to cyclical and dual narratives, fractured and dislocated narratives, cross-genre forms and intertextual writing, multiple, open and alternative endings, cyberspace writing where duration and location are non-existent and even consciousness is open to question. These and other radical ideas for writing fiction will be explored in the next chapter.

Workshop Writing

This section describes seven workshops on writing short fiction. They are arranged in a sequence and tackle the problems of getting started, finding material, plotting and shaping narratives, openings, point-of-view, creating characters, and monologues.

1   Telling Tales

The aim of this workshop is to build up a collection of tales based on those told and retold within families and, through group discussion, develop selections from this 'raw' material into short stories.

A   For the first stage it's helpful to work in pairs. With your partner you swap at least two stories told within your family, each partner writing down the story as they hear it. This initial recording is important and should be done quickly by sketching in ideas, images and so on rather than by making a verbatim translation. The recording should be done on loose paper and be legible. If possible at this early stage give each anecdote/incident a working title or titles, both partners making suitable suggestions. This helps focus the events and the possible theme of any story emerging from this raw material. As you can see from the final workshop in this chapter, focusing the story and keeping the narrative on track is one of the major problems all fiction writers have to resolve. Now retell the two stories so that both of you remember them well.

B   In this second stage the partners share their tales with the whole group. A large group could be divided into two smaller ones of eight people if this is more comfortable. Each partner now TELLS one of the stories she has just heard and the other partner then comments on the accuracy of the version especially noting any additions or omissions. Most of us like to embellish stories we hear. This is how tales grow and develop. It is how we learn to create stories. While this is going on the rest of the group should listen carefully and WRITE down any examples of storytelling technique. These may include repetition for emphasis, metaphor, dialogue, use of local idiom, description of place or character, contrast, pace, particularising detail, use of imagery – indeed anything that enlivens the narrative. The idea here is to make people aware of the many possible ways of crafting a story. The only better way of developing awareness like this is to read short stories, one a day at least!

Once every pair has recounted their tales the group should discuss and share examples of technique and each member add new ideas to their list as and when they hear them discussed. This way everyone compiles their own master list.

C   In the third stage in this workshop one of the tales is selected for more intensive working by the whole group. The idea here is to develop a *storyline*, by summarising up to a maximum of six basic scenes and putting them in sequence. This is the first step towards creating a story. From now on the story is referred to by its title. Someone needs to write a list of these scenes on a board and each member of the group should make their own copy.

Next each of the scenes is also developed from suggestions by the group. The only requirement now is that one new character has to be added to the storyline. By now the group are into script conferencing, that messy but fruitful collaboration typical of soap-opera scripting where the writing team regularly brainstorm new ideas for the show. Suggestions will include adding physical description, dialogue, interior monologue (thoughts), new characters, a narrative voice, that is someone to 'tell' the story. What gets produced is also the equivalent of the *storyboard* used in film and video production, and the visually expressive in the group should draw it in strip cartoon form on the board. Any one of these developments always creates discussion and argument, a kind of creative bubbling out of which good writing emerges.

D   After this demo of narrative inventiveness the last part of the workshop should be about everyone starting to write their own story. Each person selects any one of the tales heard and first of all does a storyline, then converts it into a storyboard and finally begins a short story from it. To be cooked in time for the next workshop.

2   Recycling

In this workshop members explore wonder tales – myths, fairy and folk tales, fables, legends and sagas. The aim is to develop further a sense of how traditional stories are crafted and to free up the imagination by writing fabula: tales of the wondrous and the fantastic.

It's easy to assume that fantastic stories are merely escapist. In fact such tales deal with the stuff of ordinary life: family jealousies and rivalries, taboos, betrayals and deceits, love and possessiveness, domestic violence, guilt and forgiveness, revenge, hate and punishment, survival and fidelity, generosity, friendliness and sacrifice – the whole works. It doesn't take long for the workshop to reveal the relevance of these old tales to our own experience. A brief look at Marina Warner's book, *From the Beast to the Blonde*, a history of the fairy story, or *The Uses of Enchantment*, Bruno Bettelheim's classic account of the psychological reality of fairy tales like *Cinderella* and *Little Red Riding Hood*, will surprise and delight you.

Writing in a fabulous vein and drawing on traditional material not only unlocks the imagination, it also offers the contemporary writer a prototype narrative structure, a base from which to chance the imaginative arm.

A   The workshop could start with an exchange of stories, members telling versions of tales from their own repertoire. This gives everyone a sense of their richness and diversity, acclimatises everybody to the experience of the 'wonder' tale, gets you into the feel and idea of performing and 'voicing' narrative. The first stage of the workshop then is to look at these basic narrative patterns by examining a well-known fairy tale or myth or legend. Take for example either *Hansel and Gretel* or *Jack and the Beanstalk* or *Sir Gawain and the Green Knight* and discuss their features. Do they follow the pattern of complication, crisis, resolution? How is suspense created and sustained? What techniques are used? Repetition? Digression? Parallel-plot? Caricature? This discussion can take place in the whole group or in small circles or with partners.

B   However arranged, this settling-into-the-theme process should be followed up/continued by working in pairs and considering other tales. Each pair should make a list in journals of the narrative techniques they have identified in each tale.

C   Either on your own or in collaboration with your partner take a well-known traditional tale or myth and rework it. A modernised version of *Orpheus and Eurydice*? Or *Snow White*? Or *Cinderella*? Or *Bluebeard*? Or *Beauty and the Beast*? For more ideas see the Writing On section below.

Prior to the workshop you could read some modern wonder tales such as Jamaica Kincaid's *My Mother* or her story 'What I Have Been Doing Lately' or Alison Fell's *The Shining Mountain* or a fable from Suniti Namjoshi's collection *Feminist Fables* and compare them with traditional ones. Your reflections should be entered in your journal.

Traditional stories are the ancestors of many of our contemporary tales. Philip K. Dick, the science fiction writer, wrote a story called 'The Cookie Lady'. Each day on his way home from school a small boy stops off at an old lady's house, enticed there by the cookies she offers him. While he eats them he reads to her something from his school books and each time he does so she begins to feel young. After finishing the reading and the cookies the boy is always tired and eager to go home. His mother is uneasy at these visits and finally says they must stop. She agrees to one final visit. When the old lady hears this news she is upset and cooks him extra sweet cookies this last time. While he reads she holds his arm, her eyes closed. Energy and life suffuse her, she is elated. The boy is exhausted and leaves, struggling up the street against a strong wind. In front of her mirror the 'old lady' dances with joy: she is young, her skin wrinkleless, her flesh plump. Anxiously the mother waits for her son's return. She hears a noise. It's only a piece of spent rag flapping exhaustedly against the wooden door.

Whether Philip K. Dick had *Hansel and Gretel* in mind when he wrote 'The Cookie Lady' I don't know but it haunts his story like a ghost. Other writers have deliberately modelled their fiction on fables, myths and fairy stories and have recast them and modernised them. Read any of the stories in Angela Carter's collection *The Bloody Chamber*, or some from Robert Coover's book, *Pricksongs and Descants*. What they are doing is what all writers do, they have sifted the treasury of past stories and recycled them.

3   The Raw and the Cooked

This workshop considers personal experience as a basis for writing stories and explores ways of crafting (cooking) the facts of our lives and the lives of others – neighbours, relatives, friends and people in newspapers – into fiction.

To make successful fiction out of the direct material of their lives writers have to achieve what is called distance, detachment, a measure of objectivity. Stay too close to familiar experience and you lose a clear perspective on events and leave no room for the imagination to do its work.

In this workshop I have used an idea from one of my students. Janet told me about an image of a wasted landscape. She traced it back to a recent cliff walk she and her husband had taken while on holiday. It was late evening, nearly dark and the moon was up. They'd left the lights of the town twinkling below and were following a track leading inland. Suddenly the moon emerged from behind a scarf of cloud and revealed, spread before them, the desolate and bleached landscape of the salt flats.

You can see that in retelling this account I am already using a number of fictional techniques!!!

Janet wondered how she could make a short story out of this mix of memory and strong image. We decided to workshop the experience.

A   First we looked for *contrast* – the stuff of the dramatic. We found it readily enough: the lifeless, monochrome landscape of the flats next to the jaunty lights and bustle of the town. The talkative man, the quiet woman.

B   We looked for *conflict*. What if the husband wants to go on into the flats and the wife does not? Will she desist? Will he insist? Perhaps because he wants to intimidate his wife for some reason; get his own back for her humiliation of him in their recent row? *Dilemma* here for the wife. She fears the dark, a fear perhaps based on some trauma from childhood. This conflicts with her desire to preserve the delicate truce between her husband and herself tacitly agreed on since the row that afternoon. He pretends it's the beauty of the place that drives him on.

C   The next stage is about shaping and structuring. About looking at possibilities. Asking the *what if* question. What if they enter this strange place and something unexpected happens which realigns their relationship? What could that be? They get lost? What happens then? How is the crisis *resolved*? We are on our way, a storyline is emerging.

Janet was surprised that this image of the salt flats made such a strong impression on her. Here were two worlds. One with twinkling lights, a place of human warmth and contact and movement. One grey salt banks, alien and cold and desolate. These would be the two poles of the story holding it together.

In workshopping like this it's important to keep on asking questions, keep on testing out possible scenarios. Different kinds of queries begin to surface. Did these opposites reflect the so far unacknowledged and unresolved contrasts (conflicts) in Janet's own life? She too lived in two worlds – home and children, college and study. Home was safe. College was strange and sometimes a discomforting place where she felt she was on a threshold and being urged to cross it against her will. If so then the story about having to go into the dark, though not autobiographic in any literal sense, was about self at a deeper level.

In Janet's real life the walk ended at the salt flats and the two returned to the hotel. But in the story as it grew out of workshop discussion our imaginations had the man and woman, still tender from their row, entering an unknown and unpredictable territory. The imagination supplied the fantastic moonlit landscape, the idea of getting lost, and the childhood trauma.

D Teasing out the contrasts and dilemmas internal to the character and external in the situation, speculating on motives and identifying possible themes helped shape this material into fiction. Group members now need to select a storyline and write. Do you want to explore the theme of female independence? In which case the story could be told from the point of view of the female character, could be written in the first person voice and could show the woman taking control of the situation and making the decisions. If it is to be about marital power games it might best be written in the third person and neither partner dominates events.

It could also be a story about the dangerous illusion of romantic love as symbolised in moonlight reflections on still summer seas, and how it conceals dark truths. In this version a stylised sentimental view of the sea at night could contrast with a much bleaker, more 'real' image of the salt flats. Setting and locational description act as metaphors for the central theme of the story and the language of the whole piece then becomes critical. The moon appears at first the moon of popular song but as the story progresses it becomes a harsher, colder object reflecting the change in mood and tone of the piece.

E The material for this kind of workshopping is inexhaustible. The brainstorming treatment can transform autobiographic material, newspaper headlines, obituaries, photographs, single images, phrases overheard on the bus, chance remarks at a dinner-party or in a pub or anywhere. Material can be brainstormed with a partner. Each pair gets the same starting point and twenty minutes to come up with a storyline which follows the pattern of complication, dilemma/ crisis and resolution. These are shared with the group and then everyone chooses a storyline that appeals and writes the story itself.

4   The Time Bomb

Jimmy McGovern, TV scriptwriter and creator of the crime series, *Cracker*, always asks of any story, 'Where's the bomb?' For unless there's an explosion in people's lives there's going to be no drama, nothing and no one at risk and nothing to hold the viewing reader.

And all explosions have fall-out. Part of the writer's task is to explore the possible reverberations of the metaphoric bomb that he or she has dropped. Many writers claim that it is the after-effects they are most interested in. And there are different kinds of bomb. Like the one ticking waiting to explode, the time bomb. When Angel Clare discovers on the eve of his wedding that his beloved Tess is already married the long delayed explosion of this bombshell blows them all apart, he to Brazil, she to the cruelties of Flintcomb Ash.

To continue this metaphor perhaps too far, any good writer will lay the fuse and light it so it burns slowly for the reader to watch helplessly as it crackles slowly but not too loudly towards the unwitting victim. In one sense this is only a restatement of that classic requirement of the short story that it should start in a settled world, an equilibrium that is soon to be upset, even blown apart.

A   In this workshop the idea is to take some real life situations where a 'bomb' was dropped or exploded. Partners swap such stories, ones they've heard from family or neighbours or friends. Each pair selects just one account and creates a storyline using half a dozen scenes. The idea is to arrange these scenes so the maximum degree of suspense is created by using a 'slow burning fuse' and delaying the 'explosion'. Of course if you lay landmines in the story, a number of hidden danger spots, you can have characters nearly step on them time and again without actually setting them off and wounding. This is a favourite device in TV soaps, the secret from the past that is always in danger of being revealed.

B   Here's a situation. An ad appears in a local newspaper. Someone wants to sell an unused wedding dress. No bomb there. Yet. Try devising a number of storylines using this ad as your starting point. Don't start from where a character notices the ad in the For Sale column. Why not? Don't write the story of how the owner's fiancé dumped her at the altar. Why not? Each pair of you should get about five storylines going with suitable explosive effects. Use 'The Wedding Dress' as your title and try writing a story based on any one of your versions.

Here's one version. As a surprise gift a mother buys the dress for her daughter who is about to be married. It's a bargain and it means they can have a white wedding in the family. The daughter and her fiancé, who runs The Apothecary, a hypnotherapy centre, want an alternative ritual in the ruins of a local abbey. From the Council's Leisure Services Department they at last get permission to use the area and they are ready to tell her mother of their plans.

In another version the seller is also the dressmaker. She makes a dress each year. She sews, into the skirts, bird motifs which traditionally bring bad luck to the wearer. She is always in black herself!!!!!

5   Point of View

Who 'tells' a story is as important as *what* is told, and both determine *how* it is told. *Paddy Clarke. Ha Ha Ha*, Roddy Doyle's 1993 Booker Prize-winning novel, is 'told' as if by a ten-year-old boy; events and the world are thus seen from his point of view. If his mum were to tell the story the effect would be very different. It wouldn't then be a book about childhood and growing up in a Dublin suburb; more one about marital relationships perhaps, or one woman's fight for independence in the context of Irish working-class Catholicism. If Roddy Doyle had invented a detached storyteller such as a geriatric

Catholic priest it would be another story. And if he himself were to tell the story as a neutral and invisible writer it would be as different again. From his position as god-like author Doyle would be able to tell the story from many different points of view, Paddy's, his mum's, his dad's, his best mate's, anyone in Dublin. This would give a more rounded sense of experience than could be perceived by any one character. But compared with a tale straight from the character's mouth the all-round approach could lose immediacy and conviction.

A writer wanting both particular voice and a broader sweep could write as a detached third person author but explore things from a central character's point-of-view using interior monologue as a way of achieving the convincing intimacy of the 'voiced' narrative.

A   This workshop is on ventriloquy – throwing your voice so it sounds like other people. Start by rewriting the opening sentences of selected published stories from different points of view. Do some demo sentences as a whole group then work in pairs on other openings. What kind of differences do the alterations make to the story?

B   Alternatively the whole group could work on a common situation. Imagine that A wants to talk to another family member B, about a topic B wants to avoid. The setting is domestic. Each character is doing some chore. The scene should be treated from four different points of view. All the group should start with third person, omniscient author, then try successively, participant narrator A, then B, then silent observer point of view. Share examples with partners or the whole group and discuss the effects each option makes to the story.

C   Imagine a wife is telling her dinner party the story of how she and her husband capsized in a river while canoeing on their recent holiday in France. Imagine there are four guests at table. Maybe there is more than one teller of the tale. Maybe the thoughts of the guests reveal other possibilities in the story. Maybe the actual events are recreated by the author as it were. Maybe the whole evening's conversation is being recounted second-hand next day in the form of a telephone conversation by one of the guests to her friend, or perhaps written as a letter. Here there is a multiplicity of tellers and voices all interweaving. To what effect?

D   As a follow-up to this workshop try reading James Joyce for an example of the subtle and telling use of fictional voices. Read 'Eveline' in *Dubliners*. It's worth trying out this difficult Joycean technique of merging what is thought and never said with what is said and never thought. He is mimicking his character but at the same time making us aware of the impersonation. We hear the character's voice but it's reported and mixed with the Joyce voice in a parody of the original. It's as if the character doesn't have a voice of her own, outside the author, independent and strong. This is precisely the person Joyce wants to create, a woman enfeebled by dependence and lack of imagination. Imagine a character who has to make a 'big' decision, settle on some new departure or direction in their lives, and write a piece modelled on the Joyce story.

6   Character Building

All stories are about people, and creating characters to care about is the biggest challenge writers face. Writers learn the skills of creating characters first by studying how other writers do it and then by trying it for themselves. Though this workshop looks at how William Trevor creates the character of Mrs Abigail in his novel *Children of Dynmouth*, you will be able to think of other extracts just as good.

A   The workshop begins with a general discussion about people we know and how we measure their character/temperament/personality. What clues reveal an individual's traits? What does body language tell us? Appearance? Men and women behave differently. Are their differences fundamental or superficial? What do we mean by the real person within? And so on.

B   Working with your partner, examine the Trevor extract (p. 46) and discuss with each other what impression the character of Mrs Abigail makes on you. Trevor uses the same mimicking technique as Joyce, described above (see Workshop 5, Point of View). Consider the following questions. Where is the language Trevor's and where Mrs Abigail's? What's the point of drifting from author's voice to character's? Why does each of the three sentences in para. 2 start with the words, '*She made*...'? Mrs Abigail is described as a '*slight woman, with soft grey hair*'. Think of the significance of the word *slight* here. Dialogue and reported speech though are also features of this presentation and it's worth noting the timing and sequencing of them and how they interleave. At the same time that he reveals something of Mrs Abigail Trevor is giving the reader information about two other characters. Compare all this with Commander Abigail's profile on page 49. He is presented mainly through physical description and reported speech in a subversive and comic sketch of the man.

C   After some partner discussion the group as a whole should pool ideas about Trevor's technique. To complete the workshop think of a couple you know only vaguely and write a piece introducing two characters based on them. Try using some of Trevor's techniques. Or turn to the Writing On section of this chapter and select any relevant task from there.

7   Trouble Shooting

After writing your first few short stories it's worth taking stock and talking. Every new writer meets the same problems, and discussion is the first step to a solution. It also spreads the pain and leads to a greater understanding of how and why fiction works. Here are some common problems/questions about the crafting of short fiction.

I don't know what to write about

Be honest! Is this an avoidance tactic? Are you frightened of white space and the possibility of failure? Maybe you feel you should be writing something heavy, serious. You've made a mountain to climb already. Forget the big theme! Forget the dramatic moment. Stories grow out of the ordinary and the everyday. They don't have to start with the extraordinary.

Writing doesn't have to be *about* anything either. Essays are *about* something, feature articles are *about* something and so are entries in an encyclopaedia. But fiction starts elsewhere. See below. In fact what you are writing may not be clear until you write. Michelangelo used to say the sculptural form was inside the marble not his head. Only in hammering away did his subject emerge, the body out of the marble tomb, like Lazarus.

So, start with an image, a snatch of conversation, a headline, a personal incident, a chance phrase. Don't worry about plot at first. Let the story find its own way. Just write. Relax. You can change it all tomorrow. If you need a plot/storyline as a guide stop after a while and consider where your pen has taken you. Work out a scenario. Follow it and see if it takes you in an interesting direction.

As one writer in my class put it – don't walk blind through the world. Notice, observe, eye and ear everything around you. Keep up with current events, new ideas in science, advances in technology, follow public debate on the big 'issues'. Get angry.

I don't know where to start
Start in the head, think a bit, write a bit. Pen talks to the head, head to the pen. Writing is this kind of conversation, two-way traffic.

Never start at the beginning. Start in the middle. It's much easier. Write the beginning later if necessary. Once on a roll don't stop.

Start from an object. Marina Warner finds writing from paintings a stimulus. Try this. Look at the surrealists like Magritte, fabulists like Chagall or narrative painters like the Pre-Raphaelites. Take one example of such work and use it as a stimulus. Use photographs and other pictures. Italo Calvino was inspired by Tarot cards. They fired his imagination with their strange and haunting imagery. Rework existing stories. Jean Rhys took a minor character, Mrs Rochester, from Charlotte Brontë's *Jane Eyre* and made her the centre of her novel *The Wide Sargasso Sea*. Tom Stoppard did the same for Rosencrantz and Guildenstern. Try writing the story of some neglected or forgotten figure from another well-known story. Take a poem and turn the events behind it into prose fiction.

I don't know where to end or how to end

End with an image, a reversal or reiteration of the opening image. Use a framing device. If you have shaped your story on the complication/crisis/dilemma/resolution model then endings are less of a problem. If you can't see an ending it may mean there is no discernible pattern to your narrative and that the story is not well enough focused (see below). In this case you need to think hard about the material and restructure. Leave it for a week or two and return fresh to the problem. Or talk to someone whose judgement you trust. Get an outside, more objective view.

If, however, your story is deliberately shapeless so it acts like a metaphor for the pointlessness of life as you see it then you can end anywhere, mid-sentence if you like.

The story's getting out of hand

This is a warning sign. You may be enjoying the writing too much. Indulging. It's OK for a first draft, to keep on trucking, but you may have a hard time getting back on track later. Or it may be your waffle detector at work. If you feel the story is going off road STOP. Look at the map. Are you advancing the story or simply embellishing? Kind of treading water till you hit on a good idea? Both of these are well-recognised stages in the compositional process. See them for what they are but don't be deceived. Learn to edit and murder your children. See Chapter 11 below.

I can't write dialogue

This is partially a matter of developing a good ear by listening to actual dialogue – in pub, shop, bank queue, at the party or the club, in the playground, the chip shop and the street, behind the counter, on the till or the terrace. Tune yourself to the rhythms of speech by eavesdropping on casual chat. Try writing it down afterwards. Read good writers and see how they use dialogue. Look at James Kelman or James Joyce or Jeanette Winterson or Alice Walker. Select an admired short story. Take any scene and extend it into more dialogue.

Test your dialogue. Read it aloud. Ask someone to listen and comment. Skip small talk that may sound natural but which adds nothing to your story. Avoid additives like *she exclaimed with surprise* and *he roared angrily*. They are just stage-directions for fiction.

These are only some of the problems all story writers encounter. No doubt your own group can describe others and devise ways of dealing with them. These can be written up into advice notes for upcoming writers. For instance what answers would you give to these questions: *How can I be original? How can I stop my stories being boring? What is the right order for my scenes? I can't think up plots. What do I do? All my characters seem the same. Like me. How can I make them different? How can a male writer create convincing female characters? Or a female convincing males? How much research do I have to do?*

The group could devise a rota. Each week someone has to write a commentary on a specific problem and recommend one example of good practice for new writers to follow.

Writing On

This section describes in summary form ideas for further developing your work. Some of the suggestions can be developed in workshops and all of them can be used to stimulate your own independent writing.

Portraits and Keyhole Sketches

- Observe another person but secretly from a distance. Imagine you're on surveillance. The subject may be in a garden, swimming pool, on the beach, a train, at an art gallery, a meeting, sports venue or anywhere. Note down or tape-record the subject's physical features, dress, mannerisms, gestures, language. What do your observations tell you about the temperament/personality of your subject? Shape this raw material into a profile/pen-portrait of him or her. As well as creating a visual image/impression try and get under the skin like a good portraitist does and reveal the real person hidden or part hidden beneath.

- Painters often make sketches, quick, impressionistic depictions of their subject preliminary to working on the final portrait, landscape or other subject. Or they may make more considered representations of people and objects. These are sometimes called *studies* and are often the basis for later larger works. Try writing some quick sketches of people, 5–10 lines. Or some studies of an imaginary 'sitter' – a person in a deck chair, child asleep in a bed, man watching television, woman talking to dog, boy lounging, girl making-up and so on.

- Look at a copy of one of Rembrandt's self-portraits. The 1658 painting in the Kunsthistorisches Museum in Vienna is frequently reproduced. It powerfully suggests the enfeeblement of age – the slack fleshiness of the face, the looseness of the skin, the fatigue and resignation in the eyes. WRITE an honest self-portrait.

Monologues

- The notion of a sitter holding themselves up for scrutiny by painter or photographer is an interesting comment on vanity, narcissism, egotism. And an idea for a short story! Paul Durcan in his book, *Give Me Your Hand*, has written a number of character studies/portraits based on paintings in the National Gallery. He uses the painting as a *point of departure* for exploring the real person beneath the public surface of paint and show. Write a monologue in which the sitter addresses his/her mother or father, wife or husband, lover, brother or sister. Or addresses the painter.

- Among the greatest of portrait painters were the Dutch masters – Frans Hals, Paul Rubens and Rembrandt. You'll find examples of their work in any good art history book. Select one portrait picture. Recreate the portrayed person through *interior* monologue. Creating a convincing historical character is an imaginative challenge. Remember these sitters were actual people. You are resurrecting them, giving them flesh and blood, desires and hopes. For period authenticity use some of the clues in the picture – dress, furniture, food, posture. Other examples: *The Scream* by Edward

Munch, *Pope Innocent X* by Velasquez, *Portrait of the Artist's Mother* by James Whistler, *The Kitchen Maid* by Vermeer or Cezanne's portrait of his wife. Other inspirational artists: Andrew Wyeth, Egon Schiele, Edward Hopper, Francis Bacon, Lucien Freud, Pablo Picasso.

- Ian McEwan's story 'Conversations with a Cupboard Man', is a monologue with an inferred listener, the social worker. Try writing a monologue with a silent observer or listener. Another story, 'Butterflies', in the same collection, is written in the first person but is not a monologue. Read the story and write a scene with the same character but set in the town library.

Point of View

- In both the McEwan stories a narrator/teller has a distinctive *voice*. This is reflected in the style of speaking, the vocabulary used, the sentence shapes. Try writing an anecdote/episode in a distinctive voice. Model your writing on Jayne Anne Phillips' one-page story 'Mamasita' from *The Secret Self 1*, an anthology of short stories edited by Hermione Lee.

- Write a harangue. Read Jamaica Kincaid's one-page story, 'Girl'. A mother is giving her daughter some advice about how to behave in the world of men. The past equivalent is the etiquette and conduct books written for young women in the eighteenth and nineteenth century and like them 'Girl' is really about social control and female identity. Such books no longer exist but there still survive powerful dos and don'ts controlling and defining both men and women. So try a one-sided, Kincaid-type piece in which a mother/father lectures a son/daughter. Concentrate on getting the voice spot on. Capture the inflections and indications of class, regional speech, generation and gender if you can.

- Point of view is related to voice. Authors may adopt voices or persona and become an additional 'presence' in the narrative, or they may take over and 'body-snatch' one of their characters, or they may create a distinctive narrator.

Imagine someone telling the story who has multiple person-
alities; a very unreliable narrator! Write a story in different
voices but all centred in the one personality.

Dialogue

- When it comes to dialogue writers should have ears like
  magnets, according to Eudora Welty. She saw writers as
  eavesdroppers, tuning in to other people's conversations.
  She thought certain elements in talk become attracted to
  the listening writer in whose imagination they become mag-
  netised, highly charged with significance, and thus find
  their way into fiction. As trial runs write some naturalistic
  dialogues. Start with scraps overheard and develop for
  about half a page. Only use two voices but try and indicate
  by inference age, gender, class, occupation, region and so
  on. If things go well it'll grow into a short story.

- Practise writing dialogue with two characters, strangers
  perhaps, who come from very different backgrounds and
  differ in age and sexual orientation.

- Everyone of us knows that while we are saying one thing we
  often have thoughts (reflections and images) running in a
  very different direction. Write a passage of dialogue in
  which the thoughts of one or both the characters occasionally break onto the page.

- Listen to the radio and concentrate on a particular voice –
  that of a presenter or someone interviewed. Visualise the
  person and make notes on their appearance/temperament/
  mannerisms. Place him/her in a crisis situation and see how
  they react.

- It's interesting to record voices from your family, play them
  back in the workshop and see what kind of verbal portraits
  other members create from the recordings. How accurate
  are they? Produce photographs of the 'voices' and compare
  with workshop versions.

- These portraits can be fleshed out. Workshop one of them.
  Suggest weaknesses, dislikes and likes, obsessions and

preoccupations. Give the emerging character one major fault/flaw – such as jealousy, indecisiveness, self-import-ance, narrow-mindedness, timidity. Imagine the character in a room or house and make the fault a reason for him/her leaving there for good. Reveal subtly through spoken words details of the situation and the character's feelings about leaving. The group could workshop other scenarios. The possibilities are limitless.

Starting

- Look at the photographs of Cartier Bresson, the studio por-traits, the street scenes and other shots. He described him-self as a painter of the moment. Take any one of his *moments* and WRITE a vignette – a short self-contained evocation – based on the photo. The writing should be *based on* the Bresson image and not just an inventory of what's in the photograph. Be imaginative. Bresson used black and white. Introduce colour, snatches – *moments* – of dialogue, a fleet-ing thought.

- There are Bresson images around us all the time. You only have to look for them and they happen. They'll happen next time you walk down a street, beside a canal, in a park; wander in a market, carboot sale, department store; sit in a church. Write cameos (framed image) of such *moments*. Many short stories begin with images momentarily caught.

- Writers borrow camera techniques from the cinema. Films frequently open with long distance or pan shot. This is followed by mid-shot and close-up. Try writing the opening of a story that starts in this broad way and narrows down to a particular image. It's a useful trick to imagine you are the eye of the movie camera, framing the scene, scanning the terrain of someone's life or a landscape and then homing in on some telling detail.

- Make a list of minor unexpected moments in your recent life – a disliked neighbour comes round to borrow a cup of milk; you are locked out of the house; an injured stray cat arrives on your doorstep; the phone rings at two o'clock in the morning and there's no one at the other end; you arrive home with someone else's shopping; you run out of petrol driving across moorland at night. Select any one to kickstart a story.

- People are contradictory, even the most consistent person-alities, and people are sometimes unpredictable, even the most reliable. Imagine a person whose own life is governed by routine and who is a stickler for rules. Something happens, something small that alters him or her and makes them behave out of character. Use this possibility as the starting point for a short story. This seems like a complica-tion/crisis/resolution pattern in the making! Behaving *out of character* is what makes the lives of both fictional and real people compelling viewing. Struggling to behave *in character* is also an interesting prospect. Trying to behave out of character but not quite making it is another intriguing poss-ibility for fiction.

- Think of a piece of past advice that has stayed in your mind. Do you still believe it? Did the advisor live up to his/her own advice? Has it affected/directed, blighted/brightened your life since? Adapt this material for a short story.

- Imagine a character who lives in a fantasy world like Billy in *Billy Liar*, the novel by Keith Waterhouse. Like the woman in an episode of *The Bill* who, convinced she was Barbara Stanwyck, the movie star, not only spoke and looked like her but acted out scenarios from her films. Those who dream like this either draw others into their fantasy or are isolated by it. How do you explain such behaviour? Your story might explore motivation here. Create a character who doesn't know where actuality ends and fantasy begins.

- Find a newspaper story focusing on some perplexing or strange event. Look at the News in Brief section. Recently there was a story published about a solicitor, an Iranian, who doused her clothes in petrol and set herself alight in the main square of Teheran as a protest against the Islamic government. Use this event as the start or end of a story. Like many writers you'll find newspapers a rich source of inspiration.

- Sometimes unusual and provocative titles release the imagination and set you off on the story trail. Here are some examples – *Uhms and Errs, SFX, Mr No-one, Alias, The Boy Who Lost His Shadow, The Death of Time, Footsteps, Lemons, Zero Plus Zero, Etcetera*. With a small group brainstorm some titles of your own. Improvise some suitable story-lines. Chose one that appeals and develop a story proper.

- Raymond Carver, the American short-story writer and poet, wrote his prose in a spare, flat style. Try reading some from *Cathedral*. Write a Carver-like story of no more than 500 words.

Recycling

- Reworking and recycling well-worn tales and narrative motifs is part of the writing process. Writing is a matter of rewriting. Try adapting a popular tale for our times: for example *Molly Whuppie, Tattercoats, Beauty and the Beast*.

- Write a creation myth or myth of origin. Here are a few titles: *How Earth Was Born, How Death Came into the World, How the Leopard Got Her Spots. How Atoms ... Electricity ... Television ... Pollution ...* any household utensil, *Came into the World. How Babies ... Stones ... Anger ... Fire ... Gravity ... Dreams ... Words ... Fossils ...* etc. etc., *Came into the World. Why Moon Was Born. Why Accidents Happen* etc. etc.

- Write a modern monster myth: *A Minotaur in Manhattan, Apollyon on the M6, Grendel in the Docklands*. Ted Hughes' story, 'The Iron Man', is an inspirational example. Rework the Frankenstein story, the Cyclops tale.

- Write a modern fable or fairy tale. As a helpful guide read 'The Snow Child' or 'The Werewolf' in Angela Carter's collection *The Bloody Chamber*.

- Write a talismanic tale. By this I mean a story based on some magical object – such as a feather, a thimble, pebble or key. In a group you can improvise story-lines and select the best for developing into a full-length piece.

- Collaborative tales are rewarding to write. Take a group of six or so where each member supplies a stage of the story. Start with this: 'Everyone said the world was in a mess. So all the animals, except one, met to sort things out.' Each contributor adds one or two paragraphs or longer section if agreed at regular intervals, say every week until the story is complete.

- Similarly a group could devise over a period of time a book-let of tales, a cycle of stories centred on the exploits of some fabulous character. He or she or it could be modelled on the trickster figure of Anancy in the Trinidadian and West African folk stories or on Loki, the scoundrel from tales of the Nordic gods.

Setting

- In some fiction creating a sense of place is as important as creating characters. Setting and locational descriptions establish the reality of a fictional world, give the reader a sense of authenticity, but they also carry some of the thematic weight of the story. 'The Prussian Officer', by D. H. Lawrence, opens with a troop of soldiers on a route march in the oppressive summer heat. It ends with the exhausted soldier catching a final glimpse of some distant icy peaks. The heat-shimmering fields of the valley and blue purity of the mountains embody the emotional and psycho-logical extremes of the story. Imagine a house – gothic or modern – or a room – contemporary or in past time. Write a story in which either room or house figures as the central motif.

- Imagine a landscape or seascape or townscape, or a sub-terranean or extraterrestrial location. Open and close a story with a description of one of these imagined places.

- During the 1830s and 1840s the artist Turner painted a series of remarkable seascapes. Look at some reproductions of them. Write a response. Imagine you are a lone mariner or someone on a cliff top. Describe what you are seeing.

- *Invisible Cities* is a novel by Italo Calvino in which he created some fabled places. Read sections *Cities & The Sky 1* or *Hidden Cities 4*. Recreate your own imagined spaces. Experiment with titles like *Invisible Parks* or *Invisible Rivers* or *Invisible Seas* or *Invisible Mansions* or *Invisible Streets* or *Invisible Empires* or *Invisible Resorts* or *Invisible Art Galleries* and so on. These should be short pieces – 200 words maximum. Try writing a number so they form a sequence.

- Settings often reflect the state of mind, mood or emotional condition of a character or even how the author feels about human existence. Try creating a setting that reflects one of the following – loneliness, joy, despair, resignation, celebration, tranquillity, anxiety, guilt, triumph, failure, grief, relief.

- Read some of the landscape descriptions in Cormac McCarthy's novel, *All The Pretty Horses*. Write in a similar manner about an area you know well.

Booklist

Braine, J., *Writing a Novel* (Methuen, London, 1974).

Bettelheim, B., *The Uses of Enchantment* (Penguin, Harmondsworth, 1991).

Brontë, C., *Jane Eyre* (Dent, London, 1983).

Calvino, I., *Invisible Cities* (Picador, London, 1974).

Carter, A., *The Bloody Chamber* (Penguin, Harmondsworth, 1981).

Carver, R., *Cathedral* (Collins, London, 1984).

Carver, R., *Stories* (Picador, London, 1985).

Coover, R., *Pricksongs and Descants* (Minerva, London, 1991).

Dick, Philip K., 'The Cookie Lady,' in *Second Variety* (Grafton, London, 1990).

Doctorow, E. L., *The Waterworks* (Macmillan, London, 1994).

Doyle, R., *Paddy Clarke. Ha Ha Ha* (Minerva, London, 1993).

Durcan, P., *Give Me Your Hand* (Macmillan, London, 1994).

Eco, U., *The Name of the Rose* (Picador, London, 1984).

Fell, A., 'The Shining Mountain,' in *Close Company*, ed. C. Park & C. Heaton (Virago, London, 1988).

Hartley, L. P., *The Go-Between* (Penguin, Harmondsworth, 1990).

Hughes, T., *The Iron Man* (Faber, London, 1989).

Joyce, J., *Dubliners* (Penguin, Harmondsworth, 1991).

Kincaid, J., 'Girl,' in *Wayward Girls & Wicked Women*, ed. A. Carter (Virago, London, 1992).

Kincaid, J., 'My Mother', in *Close Company*, ed. C. Park & C. Heaton (Virago, London, 1988).

Kincaid, J., 'What I Have Been Doing Lately,' in *The Secret Self 2*, ed. H. Lee (Dent, London, 1987).

Lawrence, D. H., 'The Prussian Officer', in *The Prussian Officer and Other Stories* (Penguin, Harmondsworth, 1992).

Lee, H. (ed.), *The Secret Self 1* (Dent, London, 1991).

MacCarthy, C., *All the Pretty Horses* (Picador, London, 1993).

McEwan, I., *First Love, Last Rites* (Picador, London, 1976).

Namjoshi, S., *Feminist Fables* (Sheba, London, 1984).

Phillips, J. A., 'Mamasita', in *The Secret Self 1*, ed. H. Lee (Dent, London, 1987).

Swift, G., 'Postscriptive Therapy', in *The Agony and the Ego*, ed. C. Boylan (Penguin, Harmondsworth, 1993).

Rhys, J., *The Wide Sargasso Sea* (Penguin, Harmondsworth, 1983).

Tremain, R., 'The First Mystery,' in *The Agony and the Ego*, ed. C. Boylan (Penguin, Harmondsworth, 1993).

Trevor, W., *The Children of Dynmouth* (Penguin, Harmondsworth, 1985).

Warner, M., *From The Beast to the Blonde* (Chatto & Windus, London, 1994).

Waterhouse, K., *Billy Liar* (Penguin, Harmondsworth, 1970).

Welty, E., *One Writer's Beginnings* (Faber & Faber, London, 1985).

6 Innovative Fiction and the Novel

ELIZABETH BAINES

'Technology ... to a very real extent that's what we *are.*' These are the words of William Gibson, author of the cyberpunk novels *Neuromancer* and *Virtual Light,* contributing to a recent TV documentary about the fundamental changes taking place in our society. It was William Gibson who coined the word 'cyberspace', and thus conjured up the concept of a 'space', hitherto unknown, reached through computers, but arrived at beyond them: a new dimension where we all can connect.

If our view of ourselves and our world radically changes, then it might be expected that the stories we tell about ourselves will also change, and the way that we tell them.

During the twentieth century there's been a melting-pot feel about Western fiction, and in many ways it's an exciting time to be writing now: the old rules have been erased, it seems, and to some extent everyone, including the new writer, is free to make his or her own. Writers have consciously rejected what have been seen as the naïve certainties and manipulative arrogance of nineteenth-century fiction – the omniscient, all-knowing (and thus colonial and patriarchal) author, the attachment to realism, the well-rounded character (that 'famous fraud', according to Craig Raine), the crisis-resolution linear plot based on the triumph of the individual over adversity.

Writing in the early years of the century, Franz Kafka extended the possibilities of what might be accepted as a short story. While having the tone of myth, his fables, parables, essay-style pieces and sketches – some of them only half a page long – are also highly personal and idiosyncratic. The result is enigmatic and unsettling – a kind of hybrid, like the

129

heirloom pet, half-cat, half-lamb, which the narrator refuses to explain in his story 'A Crossbreed'. These stories confound conventional expectations, question the very concept of identity and the nature of existence.

Novels written in the sixties out of the altered states of consciousness induced by drugs provide a further affront to the realist tradition. William Burroughs' classic *Naked Lunch* is a challenging mix of hallucinatory vision, the satirically visionary, and chatty and erudite notes to the reader inserted slapbang in the middle of the text. There is reflexive commentary on the text itself: 'I do not presume to impose "story" "plot" "continuity." ... You can cut into *Naked Lunch* at any intersection point...' Here we have something of the idea of a novel as flexible, open to interpretation and manipulation by the reader. Some novelists have taken this to extremes. The innovatory British novelist B. S. Johnson famously produced a novel in bits in a box – readers are said to have responded enthusiastically to his interactive invitation by stealing its sections piece by piece from the bookshop shelves! In recent years the definition of a novel has widened considerably: Vikram Seth's first novel *The Golden Gate* is a novel entirely in verse, as is the recent *History: The Home Movie* by Craig Raine. There has been the rise of the graphic novel, with its most serious expression in Art Spiegelman's moving book about the Holocaust, *Maus*.

As has been pointed out by sceptical commentators on 'postmodernism', much of this is not actually new. B. S. Johnson's wonderfully high-spirited and satirical novels with their non-verbal elements and typographical experiments ('replication' of pages of ledgers, blank spaces for silence, the words of inarticulate characters stretched out painfully across the page) and the playful, illustrated novels of contemporary Glaswegian Alasdair Gray are in an old, if interrupted, tradition. We can point to Laurence Sterne's eighteenth-century *Tristram Shandy*, with its wild narrative jumps, discursive asides and blacked-out and marbled pages. The *novel*, as the very term suggests, has always been associated with news and novelty. In the sixteenth century it was a term used for topical tales of everyday life, as distinct from formulaic and courtly romances. Here in the West magic realism – with its heady blend of hard-nosed realism and fantasy – has been embraced as an aspect of postmodernism, but Isabel Allende, South-American author of *The House of the Spirits*, has commented that in her part of the world they've always written and told tales in that way.

Still, there is this sense now in the West that things are different from how they've ever been before. Mass communication has altered our vision. The world is multiple. There are many, many viewpoints, and they're not even stable, as the shifting, cross-cultural novels of Salman Rushdie portray. Much recent fiction has been concerned with point of view, in particular with points of view which previously have received scant airing in Western literature. The rejection of omniscience has led to what I call a literature of *voices*: the ventriloquism of the short stories of American Grace Paley, with their cast of mostly working-class characters of various ethnic origin, all 'speaking for themselves', the project of British writers like Glaswegian James Kelman and Manchester-based Livi Michael to make working-class vernacular acceptable codes for literature, and working-class experience a fit subject. Livi Michael uses the 'democracy' of multiple viewpoint: the mind of each character is entered with equal intimacy. Jane Rogers has also experimented with viewpoint to explore reality: *Mr Wroe's Virgins* consists of four alternating first-person narrations of the same series of events. Feminist writers keen to assert the female viewpoint have found various stratagems: Emma Tennant has retold familiar stories such as Faust from a feminist perspective, Sarah Maitland has done the same with classical myths, and there are Angela Carter's reworkings of European fairytales. Margaret Atwood has subverted traditionally masculinist genres – the outback 'quest', the thriller, the sci-fi dystopia – to explore the social condition of women. There has been a concern with reassessing the past and its effect on the present, and novels like Michèle Roberts' *Daughters of the House* make constant use of flashback to this end.

All of this is thrilling for the new writer. The old hierarchies are under question and the orthodox forms in Western literature are undergoing mutation and cross-fertilisation; there is a sense that our own voices, our own perspectives matter, and that we are free to invent forms which can convey them.

There has been a concern to expose the constructed nature of both history (for example, Graham Swift's *Waterland* and Toni Morrison's *Beloved*) and fiction itself. The now classic *The French Lieutenant's Woman* by John Fowles exposed brilliantly both the arbitrary and culturally-dictated nature of the narrative choices made by the Victorian novelist in particular and novelists in general. Coming up to the final pages, Fowles discusses for the reader the possible ways to end his story of a Victorian fallen woman and the gentleman who becomes involved with her. Perhaps he could give us more than one, he says. The trouble is, though, he points out, the ending he places *last* will seem like the *real* ending, such is the power of endings. Then with a dazzling stroke he subverts his own argument. The final ending fulfils both Victorian social codes of propriety *and* our contemporary ideas about the emancipation of women. But the ending which *precedes* it has a different, potentially stronger resonance: it fulfils the romantic terms of the Victorian novel which, even while exposing it, Fowles has created so effectively, putting us under its spell. Ultimately, the ending of this novel is 'open' – the alternative possibilities and their respective implications go on reverberating in our minds – quite unlike the closure, or straightforward resolution, of traditional story-telling, where the ending primes us in no uncertain terms what to think or feel.

Maybe, in spite of everything, we still want the traditional enchantment of story? It's a point to keep in mind. Many of the exercises that follow will encourage innovation, but one or two are designed to test out how far you can go with your innovations and keep readers engaged. Of course, innovators shouldn't expect to be immediately understood, and many of the writers I've mentioned didn't find it easy to publish their work to begin with, or to stay consistently in print. Innovators keen to publish in the present climate could be in for a battle. In the last few years, British publishing has become largely dominated by a few major commercial corporations. While one effect of this is that an unprecedented number of titles is now being published each year, including an unprecedented number of first novels, another is that in general the publisher's eye is firmly on saleability. In the universities we might be talking about postmodernism, but in the High Street the blockbuster rules the day. I strongly suggest that before embarking on a novel you research the market or search your heart carefully: the novel is a gregarious form, and there are not many who write them who *really* don't care about having them published.

There's this thing about the novel: wherever I go and get chatting to casual strangers – taxi-drivers, fellow rail passengers, my dentist once when he had my mouth jammed open – and reveal that I'm a novelist, I get this reaction: *'I've* always thought of writing a novel...' and then they start on the plot. Sometimes it's their life-story, sometimes it's the Jeffrey Archer-type job that will bring in a million. But there's always this sense of the novel as a magic door at the interface between imagination and reality, and once you go through things will never be the same. And so it is, and so it won't. The novel has power, the novel *matters*, as Salman Rushdie has so devastatingly found.

Workshop Writing

The writer is traditionally pictured as a lonely soul, tortured yet somehow specially blessed, labouring in a garret, painfully yet transcendentally, and always oh so romantically. It's a picture that serves to preserve the mystique about the process of writing which has daunted many an aspirant writer and, I believe, silenced a good few. This section is intended to knock flat that myth and show that, while most of us undoubtedly need good periods of peace and quiet, especially for longer pieces, the most innovative and individual fiction can emerge from group writing activities. The workshops are designed to encourage the process of mutual inspiration as well as mutual feedback and support. They begin with some suggestions for getting going, and move on to practice and experimentation in *point of view and narrative voice, structuring, postmodernist techniques versus convention, genre* and tackling *longer fiction.*

1   Igniting the Spark

Here's my main advice right at the beginning: STOP THINK-
ING ABOUT HOW IT OUGHT TO BE DONE. JUST DO IT.
The first stage of writing is merely a matter of getting in touch
with your instincts, freeing up, getting the antennae tuned. It's
the process of what's traditionally called 'inspiration', that
word so haloed in mystique. In fact there's nothing mystical
about it at all (though it might feel like it when you get fired
up!); there are some completely practical ways of arranging for
it to happen. Here are three:

Workshop 1   Consequences

Most of us played Consequences as children, which makes it
highly appropriate: a major part of writing is getting in touch
with that childlike, playful and instinctual part of yourself.

A   Here is a version practised by the Surrealists and which,
for reasons which will become clear, they called *Exquisite
Corpse*. Each group member takes a loose A4 sheet of paper
and writes across the top the titles of seven columns, as
follows:

Adjective/Adjective/Noun/Adverb/Verb/Adjective/Noun

These titles of course constitute the grammatical components
of a sentence.

B   Next each member writes five adjectives – whatever
comes into his or her head – one under the other in the first
column. The completed column is then folded under out of
sight – the paper being folded vertically – and the sheet passed
on for the next column to be filled in by the next person.

C   What emerge when the sheets are finally unfolded are
some amazing sentences (prepositions and pronouns can be
added at the last minute for sense) – weird, surreal, comical
and lyrical. Members take it in turns to read out the choicest
ones on the sheet with which they ended up. It can be an
inspiring experience to hear words you contributed – even
seemingly 'ordinary' ones – suddenly cast in an unexpected
light via juxtaposition with someone else's, and it is a good

way of getting over those initial inhibitions about 'fine writing' and choosing your words carefully. Needless to say, this exercise is excellent for getting a group feeling going – so necessary for later, critical discussion – and for establishing a mode of mutual and shared creativity. In groups I've worked with, substantial full-length pieces of fiction have sometimes come out of the sparks engendered by initial exercises like this.

D   At this point (i.e. with the experience *behind* them), the group will probably feel ready to discuss some of the issues involved: issues of 'chance' in the process of writing, the issue of shared creativity, and so on. Some groups are fascinated to find that without any communication during the game, different people have come up with similar motifs, and want to discuss the implications of this. This is the point at which I usually suggest that members keep a journal, to record their thoughts after their writing experiences, as well as ideas for writing.

E   The exercise can be taken a stage further. You can try rearranging the sentences on your sheet to create the basis of something more meaningful or more interesting – whole sentences or parts of them. You could even cut or rip up your sheets horizontally, separating the sentences, everyone putting them into a bag, and the bag being given a good shake before each person takes out a random five with which to do the same exercise in rearrangement. Jettison what doesn't seem to fit or work and add anything that occurs to you to improve the piece. Already you are launched on the process of rewriting, and this reshuffling, cutting and adding is precisely the editing process you will need to be trained to use in any longer piece of fiction. This stage is generally more cerebral, there's the chance to sit back and consider – but there's still a fair bit of 'inspiration' involved: it's important to keep the antennae out for new 'chance' connections and new ideas that might pop up. The novelist William Burroughs has practised a kind of reversal of this two-stage intuitive-to-cerebral process: cutting up the pages already written, throwing the pieces up in the air and allowing the arrangement in which they land to influence his final edit.

What all this shows is that writing can be as much of a game as you let it, you can be as much in control (or out of it) as you like at any stage, and there's always room for playing about a bit more. Get rid of the idea that there's only one right way to tell a story, and you'll feel immensely free and empowered!

Workshop 2   Tell a story round the room

A   One sentence each round the room several times – no pausing to think, you've just got to go. This can produce some complex and hilarious stories in absolutely no time: it's exhilarating to find how quickly a story can be conjured up out of seemingly nowhere, how little it matters if bits of it are mad or muddled (you can edit those out – in this instance forget them!). And once again it's quite fascinating to see the different directions other people can take your ideas – another lesson in the multiple possibilities in structuring or developing any story.

Workshop 3   Magic box

A   This exercise is based on the Surrealist notion of the 'Found Object'. The leader or one member of the group brings in a box of objects, some weird and wonderful, some quite mundane. The other group members know nothing of the contents beforehand. They are told that they will be asked to choose something from the box and write about it. They are instructed not simply to describe the object (though they can), but to write whatever the object triggers in their heads. The box is opened, and handed round. Each member has about five seconds to decide upon an object, take it out, and *begin writing straight away* (no sitting thinking). They write for at least five minutes, more if they want to.

B   After everyone has finished, the pieces can be read aloud to the rest of the group. I've never done this without the result that everyone is astounded at what comes out, some of it seemingly unrelated to the objects which triggered it. People are usually keen by this point to discuss the creative processes that went on: How much of what was written 'came from' the object, and how much was already there inside the writers' heads? Did the object trigger the unconscious in the way the Surrealists believed such 'found' objects did?

C Later, the piece can be edited or developed in the way outlined above.

This exercise has great practical use for your writing in general: many published writers speak of the usefulness of developing a receptiveness to things 'out there' to trigger off their internal world, and on a longer piece of fiction it's one of the ways in which you can keep going, keep reigniting your ideas.

Many writers, including me, often begin the idea of a whole novel with only a single image; and the objects in this exercise have the potential to operate in this way: a metaphor or symbol for the theme of a whole work, like the 'antique' glass paperweight in George Orwell's *Nineteen Eighty-Four*, which symbolises the lost individuality of the characters, frozen into the past by a repressive regime, or the coloured marble of the title of Margaret Atwood's *Cat's Eye*, standing for, among other things, the watchful integrity of the lonely, bullied main character. Such an image can recur throughout, with changing implications, or as in *Nineteen Eighty-Four*, can occur just once or twice, but strikingly, and still provide a pivot for the novel's theme. I had known for years that I wanted to write a novel about high technology childbirth and its moral and social implications, but couldn't see a way of doing it or how it could make a novel until one day I went for a walk and came across a hedge full of wild roses. For some reason I couldn't fathom, that hedge of roses really struck me – I could feel connections buzzing in my subconscious. For days I was obsessed with the image of roses, though I still didn't know why. And then it all started to come together: roses – Sleeping Beauty – Snow White – a woman trapped in a glass case – a woman strapped down on a hospital bed: and there I had it: a reworked fairy tale. Then the image went on proliferating: thorns/spindles/hypodermic needles; hundred-year sleep/modern drugs/women cut off by socio-medical ideology from choice and full engagement in the world of life and work – well, I was off! And none of it happened until I let it come in 'sideways' – subconsciously as it were, and responded to that image signal.

Exercises of this sort, in which pressure is put on you to *keep writing* and avoid thinking too hard are very valuable in developing your confidence in your own instincts. It's also essential training for the writer of a novel, who really does have to keep going.

2   Many Ways to Tell a Story: Point of View and Narrative Voice

In Chapter 5 we have seen how the same story could be told from a variety of points of view – any one or more of the protagonists, the omniscient narrator, or a silent observer. There are further subtleties of difference in the way we could choose to tell it. Begin this workshop by considering what they are. Prepare beforehand with reference to novels and stories.

Point of view
The point of view of a single character could be conveyed in different ways.

First person ('I').   You could have the character tell their own story in their own words. There are various ways of doing this. Your character-narrator's view of things may be *reliable*, intended to be taken seriously and on trust by the reader, or *unreliable*, where we are meant to see through her self-deceptions or naïvety, as in the early pages of Samuel Richardson's eighteenth-century novel *Pamela* or in Emma Tennant's contemporary pastiche *The Adventures of Robina*. In the latter case, the reader is aware of an authorial tone – usually ironical – underlying the voice of the character. There are variations in the kind of tone which first-person narration can convey. Novels like Charlotte Brontë's *Jane Eyre* or Daphne du Maurier's *Rebecca* use the detached tone of recollection long after the event, which allows for commentary and reflection. A mode favoured by many contemporary novelists (the start of Margaret Atwood's *Surfacing* being a good example) is that of first-person present-tense narration, producing an illusion of events related as they happen and a tone of immediacy and urgency. There is 'stream of consciousness' – thoughts and memories streaming out one after the other, as in the sublime monologue by the character Molly Bloom at the end of James Joyce's *Ulysses*. First person narration is of course the basis of the letter and the diary novel forms.

Third person ('he' or 'she'). Another way of telling a story from a character's point of view is to use the intimate third person: that is, to stay very much inside her head, recording her intimate thoughts and sensations and still to some extent using her tone of voice. This is one of the most flexible narrative voices, allowing you to see your character objectively at the same time as providing a convincing sense of her inner life, and allowing you to relate things which may be important or useful to the build-up of the story, but which the character cannot know. Many modern novels use this approach with varying degrees of distance and intimacy; Fay Weldon's third-person narration gets right inside the fears and longings of her female characters, yet she is also able to view them with considerable irony. Graham Greene used what might be considered, technically, an omniscient third person narration, but it's really more of a shifting intimate third person: in *The Power and the Glory*, for instance, he slips into the minds of both protagonists in turn – the outlawed priest and the lieutenant who's hunting him down – creating a powerful dramatic tension between their conflicting motives. Stream of consciousness can be achieved via intimate third person narration, as can be seen by a look at Virginia Woolf's *To the Lighthouse*.

Second person ('you'). This is difficult to sustain over a longer piece, but potentially striking in short doses. It can be used in several ways. The narrative voice may be that of one protagonist addressing another – imagine Emily Brontë's *Wuthering Heights* recast: the ghost of Kathy addresses that of Heathcliff – or that of an observer-narrator addressing one of the protagonists. It could be employed in the sense of 'one'– in which case it's really a kind of disguised though somewhat universalised first person – as in this extract from the short story 'Things Being Natural' by Nigel Pickard: *You've had an argument and then you've taken a wrong turn, and now you are travelling along a road in a part of the city you don't recognise. There is silence in the car like smoke...It gets into your eyes and throat, rendering you speechless...* Look at the beginning of Iain Banks' novel *Complicity* for another example of second person narration.

As we've already seen, a story can be told from the points of view of more than one character, and the tensions and ironies built up between the contrasting points of view can be strong, powerfully replacing the need for authorial comment. A famous example is William Faulkner's *The Sound and the Fury*, a story which begins with the confused view of an 'idiot' and is gradually made clear through the perspectives of his brothers. An interesting reversal of this technique is Jane Rogers' *Mr Wroe's Virgins*, about a group of young women taken as followers by a nineteenth-century prophet. Here the same story is related several times over by the different characters, portraying strikingly different versions of reality, and proving significantly the different possibilities for any story. In works like the American Louise Erdrich's *The Beet Queen*, different characters take up the story at progressive points of its development.

Tense

The tense in which a story is told can greatly alter its meaning and tone. Stories are of course most usually told in the past tense, but as we have seen, many contemporary writers favour the present tense which can give a strong sense of contemporaneity, intimacy, and immediacy. In short doses the future tense can create interesting and challenging effects.

Narrator and author

In most omniscient nineteenth-century novels there is little distinction between narrative and authorial voice. The authors (George Eliot and Charles Dickens sitting at their writing desks) *are* the narrators: to all intents and purposes, they address us, the readers, with their own voices. In many novels, however, the narrator is quite distinct from the author – the narrative voice is a 'cloak' which the author has adopted for the purposes of telling the story, and from which he keeps a discernible distance. This is often most clear, as we have seen, in first-person narration – although many a poor author of a first-person novel has been mistakenly taken for her character!

The observer-narrator Nick in *The Great Gatsby* is quite distinct from the author F. Scott Fitzgerald.

In postmodern texts the author intrudes once again, this time to provide comment on the constructed nature of the story. Either we get a strong sense of the author's presence in the way the story is very obviously manipulated (alternative endings, deliberate changes of tense or narrative voice) or, as in John Fowles' *The French Lieutenant's Woman*, the author breaks into the story to comment directly on the issues.

Needless to say, one piece of work can employ more than one of these types of narrative voice.

A It's very stimulating to dip into books to see the range of possibilities, and once you've collated them you can have some fun.

Have one person make eight columns on the board and give them titles which correspond to the various components required to make up a story, with some of the columns filled in, as in the table overleaf.

Now brainstorm to fill in the other columns. Your characters can be as daft as you like – a bug in a bed, if you want. Under the heading *Catalyst* you will need to write the kinds of happenings that will force your characters to relate to each other, and out of which action will come.

Now everyone must choose one item from each column. Clearly, certain combinations aren't possible – you can't choose omniscient narration if you've chosen first person (unless your first-person narrator is God!) – but apart from that your choice is unrestricted. Now write for at least ten minutes using the combination you have chosen.

I have done this exercise in a room without a board, and although it was more trouble to organise it threw up even more exciting results. We wrote the items on small pieces of paper (we had to do enough copies of everything in the latter columns for everyone to get one) and put them into eight bags and passed them round the room like bran tubs. This time there was no choice involved, and although people got some seemingly impossible combinations, ingenuity was stretched, and the stories that emerged were quite amazing in their wit and innovation. Afterwards, of course, they can be read out aloud.

Character 1/	Character 2/	Place/	Time/	Catalyst/	Tense/	Person/	Authorial Stance/Mode
					Past	*First*	*First-person narration*
							Letter
							Diary
					Present	*Intimate third*	*Observer-narration*
					Future	*Omniscient third*	*Detached omniscience*
						Second	*Intrusive author*

B   A second exercise should follow up this one, to be done in time for the next workshop session. Retaining their characters and basic situation, each person should now make different choices of narrative voice and authorial stance, and of tense if they wish, and rewrite their story. Each member should make a note of their creative discoveries during this process: the comparative limitations and freedoms of the different narrative voices used; and a group discussion of the issues can follow.

3   Right Way Round, Back to Front or Inside Out: Structuring a Story

By structure we mean the way in which the elements of a piece of writing are arranged: the order in which events, incidents, points of information and even images or specific phrases occur, and the pace or frequency with which they are revealed.

An important aspect of structure in fiction is *plot*, that is, the organisation and arrangement specifically of events and action. To a great extent plot structure comes instinctively; we structure stories all day long in our daily lives, telling each other about that bad-tempered bus conductor who chucked the old lady off the bus because she'd forgotten her pass, the rotten lecturer whose boring lectures we complained about and who then gave us unfair marks in revenge, and the way that we plot them – the order in which we relate the events – depends on what we feel about them and how we want to make our listeners feel about them and the characters involved.

In my experience it's a bad idea, for new writers especially, to get too hung up about the rules of plotting before beginning – it's too inhibiting – and it's best to think about the matter when you have a piece of your own to consider.

Workshop 1
A   Begin therefore by telling stories. Either write a story about a crisis that took place in your life or the life of someone you know, or work in pairs and tell the stories orally. In the latter case, think about it for a minute or two first, so that you can recall how it all happened, right from the beginning. The

listening partner should jot down (neatly!) the events in the order in which they are told, and at the end of the story give the notes to the teller, as a record of how he or she instinctively plotted the story.

B   At this point the whole group can consider the matter of plotting in a more academic light.

The classic plot shape

As has been outlined in Chapter 5, our conventional Western plot follows the linear conflict-crisis-resolution pattern, with its roots in the ideal plot defined by Aristotle in the *Poetics* as having a beginning, a middle and an end.

The classic plot-shape, of both short stories and novels, can be drawn as shown in the diagram below. A classic story begins with a situation in which there is potential for *conflict*, but in which nothing has so far happened to set that conflict off. (In Flaubert's *Madame Bovary* we have a restless wife with no opportunity to express her restlessness.) Then something happens (the *catalyst*: equivalent to Aristotle's *beginning*) (the advent of Madame Bovary's first lover) to disrupt the status quo. This catalytic event may open the story with a bang, or it may be preceded by a passage of scene-setting in which the status quo is established. Once the catalyst has taken effect, there is usually a build-up of *conflict* and tension, a series of scenes or moments in which matters complicate, and culminating in a *crisis* (the equivalent of Aristotle's *middle*) (Madame Bovary's despair culminating in her suicide); followed, often very quickly afterwards, by a *resolution* (Aristotle's *end*).

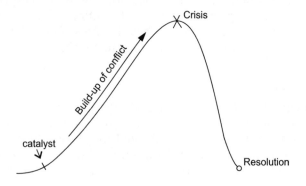

The novelist E. M. Forster, in his classic work *Aspects of the Novel*, made the important and useful distinction between story and plot and stressed the *causality* of plot. The story, he says, consists of merely the events as they happened in chronological order; the plot is the portrayal of those events in such a way as to show their causality, how one *gives rise* to another (rather than simply happening prior to it). *The king died and then the queen died* is a story, he says, but *The king died and then the queen died of grief* is a plot.

C   Having considered the classic plot, each group member should now take some time to study his or her own story, to see how closely or otherwise it fits the same shape. If it did not, would it benefit from being made to do so, would there be a greater sense of significance and suspense? Could you alter the order of events to this end, add or take out anything?

D   Finally one of the stories should be workshopped by the whole group. In one of my groups Deirdre volunteered her story to be worked on. Deirdre was heavily pregnant at the time and she had written about the occasion, not long before, when her last lecture of the day was cancelled and she set off eagerly in her car for home and the unexpected extra time with her husband. Half-way home, she was forced off the motorway by a lorry and narrowly escaped being killed. We were all moved by this story, but mainly because we knew her, and she was sitting there before us, evidence of her vulnerability and that of her baby, hugely pregnant and still bruised and in pain. In fact, there was room for improvement in the structure of her story to make it moving to someone who did not know her. We sketched the events on the board in the order in which Deirdre had related them:

Class cancelled.
Deirdre gets in her car feeling happy to be going home; moves onto motorway thinking how pleased she is to be pregnant, even though her pregnancy clashed unintentionally with starting college.
Lorry suddenly overtakes her, cuts in too closely.
Deirdre swerves, her car hurtles out of control towards the edge of the road.

Deirdre comes to a jolt at the side of the motorway, shaken, trembling.
Kind man stops his car and looks after her, rings her husband on his mobile phone.
Deirdre's husband comes to get her, and shaken, Deirdre contemplates her lucky escape.

The group felt that there was some important element to this story which Deirdre had failed to realise in the execution. We asked her questions. What was the story really about? Was it about the vulnerability of pregnant women? Or (as it seemed at present to be on the surface, although we felt sure it was not meant to be) about the cruel hand of chance – just when you're at your happiest, fortune will have a good go at knocking you down? No, Deirdre said, it was neither of these. I asked her to look at the list of what she *had* written for clues as to what the story was really about. The clue was in the second item, the part about getting pregnant at the same time as starting college. What Deirdre really wanted to write about, and wanted this story to portray, was her conflicting feelings about motherhood (her excitement about her coming baby, her need at such a time to be in her husband's protective company) and her self-fulfilment at college.

   What Deirdre had left out was her *conflict*, a main ingredient of the classic short story. We discussed how the plot might be adjusted to realise this theme. We felt that the beginning needed an addition or change to establish early on the conflict in the mind of the Deirdre of the story – rather than her being simply happy about everything at this point. It was felt that the way the story existed at present, it depended too much on coincidental event, rather than E. M. Forster's causal connections. Wouldn't it be better, and a more organic story, if Deirdre's conflict made her over-anxious to get home and therefore drive too fast on the motorway; this and her guilt and worry about college could make her lose her concentration, resulting in the accident and her near loss of both her goals? What about cutting out the last two items (the rescue and the husband's arrival) and ending on her shaken realisation, at the side of the road, of how much she has nearly lost, and maybe an implication of some resolution of her attitude?

Deirdre was delighted. She said that that was how it *really* was, it was just that her choice of events and the way in which she had juxtaposed them had failed to realise it.

From this it can be seen that it really doesn't matter if a story doesn't come out right the first time: you can always work on it afterwards to knock it into the shape you want.

The non-classic plot

In the above process, because we got nearer to the story that Deirdre did want to tell, there was very much a feeling of excavation, of uncovering the buried ideal form of the story that had always existed underneath all along. It doesn't have to be like that. As E. M. Forster pointed out, a plot can reverse the time-sequence of a story: *The queen died, and no one knew why, until it was discovered that it was through grief at the death of the king*. We could have reversed Deirdre's story completely, started with the crash and worked backwards to uncover the reasons it happened. Detective stories always work in this way, beginning at the end, as it were, and working backwards, usually to the moment of crime, though they still very much conform to the shape of conflict, crisis, resolution. We could have jumped in and out of Deirdre's story, bringing in flashbacks to her early marriage, her moment of discovery that she was pregnant; we could have interspersed it with her college reports or contrasting scenes from the lives of her friends. We could have used the elements of her real-life story to make an entirely fictional plot, changing the motives of the 'Deirdre' character and her final resolution: perhaps she wasn't really happy about college at all and decides at the end to give it up? Perhaps after all she didn't want the baby? As we have seen in previous chapters this is how most fiction works – a sometimes impenetrable mix of the factual truth and the imagined. Many writers speak of discovering a greater truth in this way, often about themselves. (I should issue a word of warning here: it must be clear to the reader that Deirdre's story has potential for upsetting revelations for the real-life Deirdre herself, and such public reworkings of autobiographical material should always be done sensitively and with a willing author. As discussed in earlier chapters, it's easier for new writers to begin on the material ready-provided by their own experience, though this exercise of public rewriting could be carried out more freely with entirely – or purportedly – fictional pieces.)

When my first novel, *The Birth Machine*, was first published, the publisher asked me to change the order of the opening chapters. As I had originally written the book (and as it appears in the current edition), the novel opened at an international scientific conference with all its razzmatazz and 'objective' scientific world-view, and then spiralled in through the first four chapters to the lonely viewpoint of a woman on a hospital bed undergoing the procedures being feted at the conference. The publisher, a feminist press, required me to move the fourth chapter, and the woman's viewpoint, to the beginning, since they wanted to enable their readers, whom they expected to be women, to identify with the protagonist straight away. While for me this shift of emphasis and change of structure crucially changed the meaning of the book – making it primarily about women's experience of childbirth rather than wider issues of objectivity, subjectivity, science and logic – its reception proved the publishers to know their readers. For me there now exist two versions of this novel, intended for different circumstances and audiences, but with equal validity: I could not for the life of me say which was the 'right' one.

A story is something like a knitted sock: we can turn it inside out, we can unravel it and knit it up again in a different pattern altogether, adding stripes of colour or sequins if we want to, and the way in which we arrange the events of a story can very much affect the story's meaning.

Workshop 2

A   Take a story from a newspaper, one with human interest. Cut a circle out of card and write down all the events of the story – both those which are actually narrated in the article, and those which can be deduced – around the edges of the circle. Punch a short pencil through its centre so that you can spin it like a top. Sit in a circle around a table and spin the 'top' in the centre.

B   Begin writing the story with the event which lands nearest to you. Alternatively, you could write the events on a piece of paper and put them in a lucky-dip bag (though you would have to make sure there are enough pieces of paper to go round).

Read out and compare the results. Discuss the differences in stress and significance, and consequently the differences in meaning, which the different structures have created.

4   Postmodern Possibilities

In the introduction to this chapter I outlined some of these. This workshop covers just a few possibilities – you will find more suggestions in the Writing On section.

A main preoccupation of postmodernist writers is with exposing the constructed nature of stories, and the way they depend for their meaning on the social context in which they were composed.

Workshop 1
Umberto Eco's *The Name of the Rose* is the story of a manuscript found in the present day and written in the fourteenth century. Filtered thus through modern eyes, the fourteenth-century story takes on richly ironic significance. Working in a group is an excellent way of doing this kind of thing.

A   First, one person writes on the board a list of historical eras suggested by the group, and also a list of geographical locations. They can be as wild and wonderful as you like.
B   Then each person chooses one era and one geographical location and writes a short story – only a paragraph or so – set in both. Stop after five minutes, whether you have finished or not.
C   Next, swap stories and read the story you have been given.
D   Now choose a new historical and geographical setting, and imagine that this story, this manuscript has been found in it.
E   Write the story of how it got there including, if you like, the story of the imaginary person who wrote it. If the story was unfinished, there will be the reason for that to consider and write about, and speculation as to what it would have been. To be finished for next workshop.

F   Make journal notes and as a group discuss your findings.

Workshop 2
A   Take a well-known tale, say a fairy story, and as a group do a postmodernist reworking. Use the board and rub out and add where necessary.

Alternative endings.   Consider alternative endings, and discuss their social and political implications.

Open and closed endings.   Consider at what point the story could be concluded to give it an 'open' rather than a 'closed' ending – an ending which leaves open the possibilities, for what might eventually happen in the story, or for the reader's interpretation of what does. You might consider taking the story *beyond* its traditional ending – what happened when Cinderella and the Prince woke up the morning after their wedding? Discuss the implications – for the satisfaction quotient/stimulation-challenge quotient of the story.

Circularity.   Individually, choose a point from somewhere near the end of the story, and rewrite the story in such a way that you begin with it, come back to it twice in the middle, and finally end with it, all the rest being flashbacks or flashes forward in between.

B   Take a look at *Black Water* by Joyce Carol Oates (for circularity) and *The French Lieutenant's Woman* by John Fowles (for alternative endings and authorial intrusion). At home, rewrite a different well-known story using at least one of the techniques discussed above *and* making authorial intrusion. To be ready for next meeting.

Workshop 3   *Genre: convention versus postmodernist disruption*
The best way to learn to write conventional genres – detective fiction, sci-fi, chillers, historical, family-saga, romance (if you must!), allegory, fairy tale, is to read them avidly. A large part of the process of learning to write is instinctive mimicry, much

as babies pick up language, which is why I recommend that you read *all the time*.

Once you have mastered a genre, you will probably want to put your own individual stamp on it. Many postmodernist writers go a whole lot further and play games with genre forms. *The Name of the Rose*, though set in the fourteenth century, is cast in the mode of a modern detective novel, a kind of spoof which provides thought-provoking comment on how we come to acquire and possess knowledge. As noted already, writers like Angela Carter and Margaret Atwood have used conventional genres in new ways. Margaret Atwood's *Bodily Harm* makes considerable use of the macho thriller mode – its images, setting, storyline – but disrupts it with flashbacks and the kind of preoccupations usual to literary, and in particular feminist literary novels: a striking reversal, and a challenging juxtaposition.

A   As a group, try recasting a well-known tale in another genre. Use the board. What rearrangements of events might be necessary? What needs to be changed? What added or deleted?

Finally, was the change of genre possible? Or did the story itself, in order to switch genres, need to change beyond recognition? Discuss the implications: How far is form or genre the essence of the meaning of a story?

B   At home, try using a genre in a postmodernist way: disrupt the form, turn it on its head, make authorial intrusion if you like. It may not work – you could even make a mess – but you don't need to ensure the presence of an adult! Record your discoveries in your journal.

C   Next meeting, swap these stories with a partner. Read your partner's story. Make notes and discuss with each other your reactions. How far did the disruption work, excite the reader? How far did it simply break the spell and alienate?

Workshop 4
A   Read beforehand and discuss Grace Paley's short story 'A Conversation with my Father'. This is a story in which the narrator discusses with her dying father his complaint that she does not write stories which conform to traditional notions of

character and structure. Consider how far this story itself does or does not conform to those traditions.

5   Longer Fiction

Clearly, most of a novel must be written outside the workshop, at home, but there are various ways in which a workshop can provide a framework and guidance and support for the writing of it.

Firstly, as indicated in the early part of this section, there are exercises which can train you to keep going and trust your instincts. If you are writing a novel as the workshops progress, the workshop can provide deadlines which are another great incentive to keep going.

Secondly, a workshop can help you plan. (More about this later.)

Thirdly, a workshop can provide valuable feedback – very important when you're on a long haul.

Workshop 1

A great way to get going is to write some group novels. A Sunday newspaper carried out a very public form of this recently: each week, a different well-known novelist was invited to contribute an episode, following on from the chapter written the previous week by another.

A   This is best done as homework, though it need not be. Everyone contributes a beginning and hands it on the next person on the rota, who writes the next episode, and so on. Make the novels short – stop after a few weeks so that the results can be enjoyed by all. Everyone should know the schedule beforehand, so that they know when they should be working towards the end. It should be treated as fun, and you shouldn't worry about any inconsistencies. The main value of the activity is that it doesn't feel like work or distract your creative energies from other writing because other people are providing your stimulus, yet you can be delighted and motivated by the speed with which pages can be covered, and the creative buzz of it all.

Planning

Planning a novel can be a very individual matter. Some nove-lists do far more preparation than others, and the preparation can take different forms. Jack Kerouac's *On the Road* was what he called a 'spontaneous' novel, typed in a thunderous non-stop rush in less than a month on sheets of paper taped up into twelve-foot lengths, but for years beforehand he had been filling notebooks with notes for a 'road novel', notes which previously hadn't led him anywhere. The basic point is that ultimately you will find for yourself how much planning *you* need to do. It may be different for each novel you write. Your relationship to the material will be different on each occasion. Some novels are simply a question of organising a story you already know very well. Others are a matter of exploration, and you will be writing to find out where the story leads. Or you may *think* you know what you are going to write, and find that in the writing you are led in directions you had never expected – this has certainly happened to me. In any case, a workshop can help you try out planning and handling plans once you have them.

In my experience (that is, for my own writing) the best thing is to have a *flexible* plan, and many other writers have told me that they find the same. A plan (more or less detailed on different occasions) gives you security before the long haul, gets rid of that feeling of stepping out into the void. But you should never let it become rigid, or start dictating to you against your better instincts as the story unfolds. Be prepared to change course, as in the part of this section on STRUCTURE, to alter the order of events, or even to scrap the plan half-way along the journey and make another. I always think of my plans as safety nets thrown out across the void: you can follow any route across the net, you can backtrack if you want to, you can add or pull off stars (the events, images – even whole characters) or change the places where you stick them; if you get brave you can throw the safety net away altogether. Of course it's great if the plan you started with turns out to have been exactly right all along! My endings I usually (though not always) allow to stay blank: often the excitement of writing is in going forward to find out what's throbbing silently and invisibly in that dark space.

Planning out a novel in terms of *chapters* – one chapter to one episode or set of episodes – is a time-honoured practice, though I don't do it: I find that the moments in my novels which dictate the ends and beginnings of chapters – crises, epiphanies and moments of movement forward – often happen on a psychological or emotional level rather than that of event, and I discover them only as I go along.

Workshop 2

A   As a group, make a plan for a novel. Work on a table or a floor (as long as the group isn't too big), or better still, rig up a corkboard. (You will need to be able to move the parts of your plan around.)

For this exercise, use the classic story shape (see the diagram above). Take a large sheet of paper and draw this shape on the paper. Have several small sheets of paper ready, and some coloured felt-tip pens (or coloured paper, of at least two different colours). As in the exercise in part 3 of this section, brainstorm a character, but this time do it quickly and make a quick decision. Now think of a journey to send your character on (quick brainstorm) (every novel is a kind of journey, geographical, emotional or psychological). Agree (for now) on a starting-point and a destination, and a goal for your character in reaching the destination, a goal which can be achieved by only one. Write this down on a piece of paper of one colour and place it at the right-hand end of the story curve. Now plot the journey; think up obstacles, setbacks and highlights along the way, and finally a crisis: for example, does his goal seem to be unreachable? or change, so that he finds he was on the wrong course after all? Write all these down on separate pieces of paper of the same colour and place them appropriately on the curve. You may find there is disagreement about the order, and your plan will be necessarily flexible already. Try them in different places. You have a plan for a simple novel.

B   Now complicate it. Brainstorm a second character who is out for the same goal. With pieces of paper of a different colour plot the course of this character in the race to the destination. At what point does she enter the action? At what point, if ever, do the characters meet? Move your other character's pieces accordingly. What alterations does this make to the crisis? Does it become a different kind of crisis altogether? **C** Record your reflections in your journal, and be ready to start making plans of your own.

Hilary Mantel is a novelist who is known to work along these lines, making differently coloured cards for different characters and episodes, and moving them around on her corkboard as necessary. If I am writing a novel with several parallel strands I'll plan them in vertical columns marked with different colours, with the linked events sitting side by side. I began with this scheme for my hi-tech childbirth novel, *The Birth Machine*, but a short way in abandoned it in favour of a plan made up of concentric circles linked at various points by arrows or spokes, since the novel was a series of severally layered flashbacks. Several writers I know, particularly those whose inspiration comes from images, pin up pictures and motifs on corkboards near their desks, and move them around as necessary.

Try out as many methods as you need to. Ultimately you will find your own.

Workshop 3   Serialisation

To present your novel in serial form for group discussion is not only to rekindle an old tradition – the novels of Dickens and Elizabeth Gaskell first appeared as serialisations in periodicals – but to put into practice the postmodernist ideal of reader-writer interaction. It can be both stimulating and comforting to get week-by-week feedback to keep you on course. Photocopy chapters and distribute them to other members a week prior to discussion. All members should read and make notes in the interim and be well prepared for discussion (this way several people's latest chapters can be discussed in one session). (This kind of thing only works properly if it is well organised and all members are committed to the process.)

Time management

There's no getting away from the fact that you need *time* to write a novel – whether it's a routine period set aside each day, or a couple of months of full-time intensive activity. And of course time must be paid for somehow. 'A woman must have money and a room of her own if she is to write fiction,' said Virginia Woolf in her 1929 essay *A Room of One's Own*. Woolf was chiefly concerned with the financial inequalities between (middle-class) men and women, and the differences this makes to their creative production, but of course the same principles apply to inequalities of class. It's perhaps no surprise that for a long time working-class voices and perspectives were largely absent from novels, which require time, leisure and space to be written.

If you are studying on a course specifically for writing novels, you will get the time anyway and that's great; but the course won't last for ever and at some point or other you will probably need to learn to manage limited time.

Firstly, grab what time you can and, if your time is limited, guard it jealously: be strict with yourself and make it clear to others that you are committed to your writing period – it's all too easy, in a culture which values rationality over creativity, to feel you don't *really* have the right to go off and write. (Mark out your perimeters as cheerfully as you can – by the very same token, it does not do to alienate people to your writing activities!) This is one of the most difficult sticking-points for those with children, and achieving writing time can involve some very practical manoeuvres which might seem on the surface quite divorced from creativity – over childcare, timeshare and other problems.

Scheduling

It might seem obvious, but it's worth stating that on a longer work it's best to *schedule*. Do some rough mathematics and work out how long you've got overall, and therefore how much you should aim for each day. It's surprising and satisfying to find how much a deadline can push you on. On the other hand, you should be realistic and not over-ambitious in your daily aims, or you'll only go and get frustrated. It's hard to make rules about this: everyone writes at different rates, and all of us write at different rates at different times. You could decide to try for a certain number of words in each session (that's what I do), or you could plot out your schedule along the pattern of your plot-plan, aiming to cover certain episodes or chapters within certain time-spans. In any event, like your plot-plan, your schedule should be *flexible*: you should not worry if you fall behind; simply reschedule accordingly – something I have ended up doing each time. You will probably find, like me, that the last part of a novel comes more quickly, and you make up for lost time at the end.

Serialisation for group work is of course an excellent way of helping you to schedule.

Most novelists like or need to keep going once they've started, which means making sure that they have some time every day to spend on their novels. I stick to this principle as far as possible, but generally have weekends off – unless I'm completely fired up – without any noticeable ill effects. Some writers have told me that even if they don't have time on a particular day actually to write, they will make sure they have at least a few moments to 'be with their novel': thinking about it, looking at what they've written – just generally keeping the lines open and buzzing. If it can be organised, many people find it best to have the same period of time set aside each day: a familiar set of circumstances – such as the same light, the same pattern of sounds around you – can be a good shortcut back into the inner world of your novel when you need to get started quickly. If you have the luxury of choice, find out which time of day is the one when you work best, when the ideas and connections come quickly. Fay Weldon is one of many who have reported that the best time for them is early in the morning, when they are still in touch with their dream-worlds, and their minds uncluttered by mundane daily issues.

If you can't sit in bed in the morning writing, however, there are other ways of coping. What if you sit down to write for your appointed two hours, and you just *can't* get into it, can't get out of your head all the earlier hassles or excitements of the day? Try laying your hands on the desk, palms up; lean back, take deep breaths, close your eyes and roll your eyeballs back up into your head. Some people always start with five min-utes' yoga or meditation. These are the activities which induce alpha waves in the brain, associated with creativity. There are all sorts of stratagems on record for linking back in and undoubtedly you will find your own. There's leaving off each day before you've quite finished, so that there's always something to start with next day. There's reading over what you wrote the day before. Some professional writers I know start by rewriting the last paragraph or so from the day before – one, who writes her first draft by hand, actually writes *over* the words again, physically linking herself to the previous day's output. If you really do seem to be blocked, a trick that's worked for many – and which can be used in group exercises where you're forced to keep writing – is simply to write or type the first word that comes into your head and then to keep writing it over and over. More often than not, other words will pop up, ideas will start connecting, and before you know it, the creative juices have started to flow again.

Finally, *don't worry* if nothing comes in the end – all writers have fallow patches. It could simply be that you don't know your story well enough to go on writing it yet – haven't 'dreamed' it fully enough yet. Write something else, or do something different. Go for a walk, have a bath (brilliant for alpha waves) and you might end up, like Archimedes, shouting Eureka!

Writing On

Igniting the Spark

- Play word-association games to get the connections buzzing.

- Develop your receptivity and let your senses lead you: smells can trigger memories which lead to stories; music can do the same. See Chapter 3 for ideas.

- Brainstorm first sentences – as mad as you like. Choose one, go ahead and write the rest.

Flexing the Imagination and Innovating

- Stare into the fire, or into the centre of a glass marble, or even at a flat brick wall, and see what pictures start to form. Write down the scene, and the story that takes place there.

- In Jane Rogers' novel, *Her Living Image*, a young girl steps in front of a moving van. There follow two alternating stories, the one if she'd been run down, and the other if she hadn't. Think of similar moments when the course of things could be very different. Write the parallel stories. Or choose an event that really happened – in your own life, or from the newspaper – and write the alternative possibility.

- Jorge Luis Borges compiled the *Book of Imaginary Beings*. Write an imaginary being of your own.

- Compile your own (short) *Book of Imaginary*... (Fill in the missing word.)

- Write an imaginary world, one in which the laws of physics, for instance, may have changed.

- Think up unusual viewpoints: animals (Read Scott Bradfield's 'Dazzle'), a Martian's view of British suburban life, of the insights of someone suddenly plunged into an unusual situation. Read Franz Kafka's short story 'Metamorphosis'.

- Use as stimulus unusual pictures; alternatively, find a picture of a really mundane scene and find an unusual way of writing about it: an unusual character/viewpoint, some of the postmodernist ideas we've discussed.

- Imagine the parallel universe accessed by, say, a magic elixir, a special phone card, digital stick-on patches.

- Try time-warps; imagine coming back from the future and confronting your present self, or the present-day world.

Point of View and Narrative Voice

As above, and also:

- Choose a well-known story and write it from an entirely different point of view (one of the other characters, or change the authorial stance).

- Write dual and multiple narratives: the same story from more than one character's point of view.

- Try telling the same story in several different narrative voices (any you haven't tried from part 2 of the Workshop section).

- Look at Alice Walker's *The Color Purple*. Write a story in the form of letters.

- Try writing a story in diary form (look at Sue Townsend's *Adrian Mole*).

- Unreliable first person. This is one of the most difficult and subtle things to achieve in fiction, but you should certainly have a go. First, write a short paragraph from the point of view of a character who has been wronged by another and is in the moral right. Now write the first-person justification of the other party, keeping in mind as you write that he/she was in the wrong. Have a partner read this second piece and tell you what impression he/she gets of the character.

Genre

- Tell each other real-life stories, then try casting them in different genres (fairy tale, sci-fi, etc.).

- Read some allegories and fables (Aesop's Fables, Orwell's *Animal Farm*). Take a real-life political story from the news and turn it into an allegory or fable.

Symbols

- Look at *Moby Dick* by Herman Melville and *Lord of the Flies* by William Golding. Consider how the whale in one and the island in the other symbolise some major aspect of the human condition. Write your own story, with a different setting – hospital, school, airline, sewer – where the setting operates as such a symbol.

More Postmodern Possibilities

- Take a well-known traditional story and let the characters interrupt and comment on the story.

- *Faction.* Truman Capote's *In Cold Blood* and Joyce Carol Oates' *Black Water* are examples of faction. They take incidents which are factually and historically true and publicly recognisable, and while preserving and acknowledging their real-life status, imagine the emotional story between the hard facts. This is not so much the seamless alchemic fusion between fact and fiction we have considered previously, but a different form, in which the seams between the two are intended to be clearly visible. Research a well-known event from the news and give it this treatment.

Limbering up for Longer Fiction

- Keep a notebook.

- Take a human interest story from the news. Plot the life-stories that followed for all of the participants.

- Keep your eyes and ears open: pick out people at bus stops, in cafés, waiting rooms. Write the story of how they got there, write the story of where they are going. Invent and plot their life stories. Listen to how they talk, watch their gestures. Be a starer like me, but try to be more surreptitious than I often am!

Booklist

Aesop, *The Fables of Aesop*, trs. S. A. Hansford (Penguin, Harmondsworth, 1964).

Allende, I., *The House of the Spirits* (Black Swan, London, 1986).

Atwood, M., *Surfacing* (Virago, London, 1979).

Atwood, M., *Bodily Harm* (Virago, London, 1983).

Atwood, M., *The Handmaid's Tale* (Virago, London, 1987).

Atwood, M., *Cat's Eye* (Virago, London, 1990).

Aristotle, 'On the Art of Poetry', in *Aristotle Horace Longinus: Classical Literary Criticism*, trs. T. S. Dorsch (Penguin, Harmondsworth, 1965).

Baines, E., *The Birth Machine* (Starling Editions, Manchester, 1996).

Borges, J. L., *The Book of Imaginary Beings*, trs. N. Thomas di Giovanni (Penguin, Harmondsworth, 1974).

Bradfield, S., 'Dazzle', in *Greetings from Earth* (Picador, London, 1993).

Brontë, C., *Jane Eyre* (Wordsworth Classics, Ware, 1992).

Brontë, E., *Wuthering Heights* (Penguin, Harmondsworth, 1994).

Burroughs, W., *Naked Lunch* (Harper Collins, London, 1993).

Capote, T., *In Cold Blood* (Abacus, London, 1984).

Carter, A., *The Bloody Chamber* (Penguin, Harmondsworth, 1981).

Eco, U., *The Name of the Rose*, trs. W. Weaver (Minerva, London, 1992).

Erdrich, L., *The Beet Queen* (Flamingo, HarperCollins, London, 1994).

Faulkner, W., *The Sound and the Fury* (Picador, London, 1989).

Fitzgerald, F. Scott, *The Great Gatsby* (Wordsworth Classics, Ware, 1993).

Flaubert, G., *Madame Bovary*, trs. G. Hopkins (OUP, Oxford, 1981).

Forster, E. M., *Aspects of the Novel* (Penguin, Harmondsworth, 1990).

Fowles, J., *The French Lieutenant's Woman* (Picador, London, 1992).

Gibson, W., *Neuromancer* (HarperCollins, London, 1993).

Gibson, W., *Virtual Light* (Penguin, Harmondsworth, 1994).

Golding, W., *Lord of the Flies* (Faber & Faber, London, 1962).

Gray, A., *Unlikely Stories, Mostly* (Penguin, Harmondsworth, 1984).

Gray, A., *Poor Things* (Penguin, Harmondsworth, 1993).

Greene, G., *The Power and the Glory* (Penguin, Harmondsworth, 1971).

Johnson, B. S., *Christy Malry's Own Double-Entry* (New Directions, New York, 1985).

Johnson, B. S., *House Mother Normal* (New Directions, New York, 1986).

Joyce, J., *Ulysses* (Penguin, Harmondsworth, 1969).

Kafka, F. A., 'A Crossbreed', in *The Great Wall of China and Other Stories*, trs. M. Pasley (Penguin, Harmondsworth, 1991).

Kafka, F., *Metamorphosis and Other Stories*, trs. Willa & Edwin Muir (Minerva, London, 1992).

Kelman, J., *How Late It Was, How Late* (Minerva, London, 1995).

Kerouac, J., *On the Road* (Penguin, Harmondsworth, 1991).

Maitland, S., *Women Fly When Men Aren't Watching* (Virago, London, 1993).

du Maurier, D., *Rebecca* (Arrow, London, 1992).

Melville, H., *Moby Dick* (Penguin, Harmondsworth, 1994).

Michael, L., *Their Angel Reach* (Secker & Warburg, London, 1994).

Morrison, T., *Beloved* (Picador, London, 1988).

Oates, J. C., *Black Water* (Picador, London, 1992).

Orwell, G., *Animal Farm* (Penguin, Harmondsworth, 1989).

Orwell, G., *Nineteen Eighty-Four* (Penguin, Harmondsworth, 1987).

Paley, G. A., 'A Conversation With My Father', in *Enormous Changes at the Last Minute* (Virago Modern Classics, London, 1979).

Pickard, N., 'Things Being Natural', in *Metropolitan Issue* 3, Manchester, 1994.

Raine, C., *History: The Home Movie* (Penguin, Harmondsworth, 1994).

Richardson, S., *Pamela* (Penguin, Harmondsworth, 1985).

Roberts, M., *Daughters of the House* (Virago, London, 1992).

Rogers, J., *Her Living Image* (Faber & Faber, London, 1984).

Rogers, J., *Mr Wroe's Virgins* (Faber & Faber, London, 1991).

Rushdie, S., *Midnight's Children* (Picador, London, 1982).

Seth, V., *The Golden Gate* (Faber & Faber, London, 1986).

Spiegelman, A., *Maus* (Penguin, Harmondsworth, 1987).

Sterne, L., *Tristram Shandy* (OUP, Oxford, 1983).

Swift, G., *Waterland* (Picador, London, 1992).

Tennant, E., *The Adventures of Robina* (Faber & Faber, London, 1986).

Tennant, E., *Faustine* (Faber & Faber, London, 1986).

Townsend, S., *Adrian Mole from Minor to Major* (Mandarin, London, 1991).

Walker, A., *The Color Purple* (Women's Press, London, 1982).

Weldon, F., *Puffball* (Sceptre, London, 1994).

Woolf, V., *To the Lighthouse* (Vintage, London, 1992).

Woolf, V., *A Room of One's Own* (Penguin, Harmondsworth, 1945).

7 | Writing Verse

John Lennard

Wherever possible, the poems referred to in this chapter are included in The Norton Anthology of Poetry, *4th Edition (New York & London: Norton, 1996), and the page references are given within the text, as '(N999)'.*

Listen! When anyone speaks, some syllables are more stressed and higher pitched than others. Only a robot would say 'how-is-it-go-ing, then?-all-right?'; a person would say 'HOW's it GOing then? All RIGHT?', with their voice rising and falling. The patterns of stress and pitch vary from language to language, from person to person, and according to what is being said, the urgency and emotion: and, as you can see if I put the stresses in capitals and divide the syllables into pairs, sometimes | the PAT – | tern's VE – | ry REG – | uLAR; | AND SOME-| times it | CHANges | irREG-| ular-| ly: but there is *always* a pattern. Nor is this pattern of sounds wholly lost in writing: it is often suppressed, especially in reading non-fictional prose; but poetry (like drama), even when printed and read silently, remains close to the spoken and the heard, so the play of stress and pitch is unavoidably active in both writing and reading poetry. Writing without it is impossible, and the choice is simply whether you attend to it, writing to a design, or allow it to happen haphazardly.

In the same way, all poems begin and end, and must be organised on the page – into lines, and often groups of lines: which means that all poems have a form. The lines, and the groups, may be regular in one or another way, as in limericks and sonnets; or they may be irregular, creating a new form unique to that poem: but in all cases there is a form, so again the choice is not whether to have a form, but whether you attend to the form.

Poetry has varied enormously over time (as you can see by paging through the *Norton Anthology*), and because people have often been taught poetry narrowly at school there are common misconceptions about 'what poetry is'. Before the twentieth century most poetry in English was written in regular *metres* (or patterns of stress), so that each line has a similar rhythm; and in prescribed forms, so all the lines are either of the same length, or vary in a regular way. Poems of this kind often have a regular pattern of end-rhymes (called the *rhyme scheme*): but this does not mean that 'all poems rhyme', nor that 'if it rhymes it's a poem'; and in the twentieth century (especially since T. S. Eliot's *The Waste Land* [1922]: N1236) *free verse* (where the metrical pattern varies from line to line) and *open form* (where the line lengths and rhyme scheme are irregular) have become increasingly popular. There is still metre, and form: but they are freed from preset rules and limits. You may want to write more traditional poetry (and many poets, like Tony Harrison, have continued to use regular metres and forms), or you may want to experiment with free verse, but in either case you will need to understand metre and form, to make them regular or to control their irregularities.

Metre and form are very general terms, and each can be subdivided in many ways (some of which are explored in the Workshop Writing and Writing On sections). They also interact and overlap with other elements of the poet's craft: the layout of the poem on the page, the division into lines and the use of line breaks, the use (or absence) of punctuation, the use (or absence) of rhyme and other sound-effects, the choice of words, and the syntactical relations between words. Each element has particular effects, and each is a different tool for a poet to use – so that using an element inappropriately may make a poem turn out quite differently from the way you wanted it to be. The comparison with tools is a useful one: sculptors might know that they wish to sculpt a sad-looking male figure in bronze resin, or a happy woman in wood, but to do so they must know what they are doing technically, and what tools to use – not just a chisel, but what kind of chisel; not just a mallet, but a mallet of a particular weight and size; not just wood, but a wood chosen for its special grain and colour. A sculptor ignorant of these things is unlikely to create the sculpture he or she imagined, and a poet ignorant of the poetic craft is similarly limited.

Knowledge of the elements of craft is also helpful in one of the most difficult parts of writing poetry – learning to improve poems after the moments of initial inspiration and composition. Once you have something written or typed on paper, but find that it isn't quite what you wanted, or that something unexpected has happened, the elements of craft provide a way of analysing and understanding what went wrong. Suppose, for example, that you were writing about your parents, and your relationship with them, and your poem began:

> My daddy couldn't stand it when I cried
> He punished me by shouting and with smacks

Both these lines might be 'true', and say what you want them to say, but nevertheless are not quite right, perhaps because they trip off the tongue rather jauntily, whereas you wanted the poem to be slower and sadder. Why is that? and how can you slow them down? One reason for the speed of the lines is their metre, which you can see if I put the stressed syllables in capital letters:

> My DADdy couldn't STAND it when I CRIED
> He PUNished me by SHOUTing and with SMACKS

Although you could vary these stresses in some ways, the pattern as I have shown it clarifies one basic problem, that there are many unstressed beats between the stresses, and that the pattern of each line is similar: using 'u' for an unstressed beat, and 'x' for a stressed one, both lines go 'ux uuux uuux'. Both the runs of unstressed beats and the pattern repetition speed the lines up, and make them read aloud like a chant, as in a limerick:

> There WAS an old MAN with a BEARD,
> who SAID, 'It is JUST as I FEARED...'

Here the pattern of each line is 'ux uux uux', and the speed is made greater by the rhyme. So one thing that you could do to revise your lines is to break up the runs of unstressed syllables, like this:

My father could not stand me when I cried,
And punished me with both his voice and hand

My FAther COULD not STAND me when I CRIED,
And PUNished me with BOTH his VOICE and HAND

By changing 'daddy' to 'father', 'couldn't' to 'could not', and 'it' to 'me' (in the first line), and 'by shouting and with smacks' to 'with both his voice and hand', the pattern of stresses has been changed, and is no longer identical in both lines. As a result, the pace of the lines has been slowed, and the jauntiness lessened: these lines are not likely to sound like a chant to any reader. Of course other changes are involved, which also have consequences, and you might, for example, want to keep 'smacks' (rather than 'hand') for the sake of a rhyme, or the simple sound of the word; in this example, though, my point is that if you cannot think about the metre, it would be harder to identify and correct the jauntiness of the first draft.

This may seem at first a cold and technical way of trying to improve your poetry, and incompatible with 'inspiration': but unless you can get it right first time, every time, you need some way to revise work, and craft-based technical analysis is a tried and tested option. An allied method of self-improvement used by many poets to learn the craft is imita-tion, modelling a new poem of their own directly on an existing poem by an established poet: the imitation may be done gravely or parodically, but in either case the exercise will help you to understand why and how the poem you are imitating works as it does. That knowledge can then be brought to bear on your own work in revising it, and in preparing a ground *for* inspirations, so that you stand a better chance of getting poems more nearly right first time, and have a better sense of what is and is not likely to work.

Such preparation, and the processes of revision, are vital: very few poets publish first drafts, and many successful poets exclude their early work (however revised) from collected editions. The great Romantic myth of the genius-poet who needs only to look at something to produce perfect and spontaneous poetry about it remains a powerful ideal: but it is a very elitist conception of the poet, and for aspirant poets is forbidding and misleading. My advice would be to ignore it (or to remember very clearly that it is a myth and an ideal), and concentrate instead on that craft which even the greatest Romantic poets used constantly, and which anyone can learn.

Some aspects of craft suggest quite abstract rules, effects which are more-or-less properties of particular metres or forms. It is broadly true, for instance, as my example of revision suggests, that (in English) metres in which pairs of unstressed beats are repeated read rapidly, and lend themselves to the comic – as happens in limericks, *ti-ti-TUM-ti-ti-TUM-ti-ti-TUM*, where the *ti-tis* are to the line as a skip is to walking. Conversely, the metre of most of Shakespeare's great speeches is *ti-TUM-ti-TUM-ti-TUM-ti-TUM-ti-TUM* (called 'blank verse', or 'iambic pentameter'), where the alternating stressed and unstressed beats prevent the line from skipping, inhibit unintended comedy, and help to sustain serious attention to the content of the speech. Of course, many individual lines vary the strict pattern of 'iambic pentameter', a line of five iambs (5 × *ti-TUM*), but some conform exactly, and in every line the pattern is there as a model to vary from. As in twelve-bar blues the variation and distortion may be great but the simple and immensely strong basic structure can be heard through everything.

As has happened to blues, though, the intrinsic qualities of a particular metre (or form) can become, over time, an extended baggage which the metre (or form) drags with it. Is it really impossible to write non-comically in a metre that skips? can you write a cheerful blues? These are serious questions, and the other vital aspect of learning about poetic craft is to identify, and learn to use, the baggages that particular metres, forms, or other craft-elements drag with them. If the Chancellor of the Exchequer gave the Budget speech in limericks, you would be surprised; but a limerick is probably the only kind of poem you would *not* be surprised to find in a pub toilet, for as a form it has particular associations. Equally, sonnets have a

long history of use as poems of courtship, in which male
wooers freeze and burn in love, but are disdained by chaste
and icy women; so when W. B. Yeats chose to write his poem
'Leda and the Swan' (N1095), about the brutal rape of Leda by
Zeus in the form of a swan, he created a tension between his
new content and the form's established history. That choice,
and Yeats' manipulation of the tension created by it, were as
much a part of his writing of the poem as any decision about
particular words or rhymes. Yeats, an Irishman, was writing in
Ireland in 1923, during the Irish civil war; and the sonnet
became an established English form in the 1580s and '90s,
largely at the court of Elizabeth I, who was then pursuing a
very aggressive policy in Ireland – so the tension and violence
which Yeats brought to the sonnet form draw some of their
power from the sonnet's English history: and this is not
chance. In similar ways, poets as different as Tony Harrison
(from Leeds, N1764) and Derek Walcott (from St Lucia, N1709)
both feel compelled to interact with older canonical poetry,
as a source of power and tradition, but also feel antagonistic
to a canon formed by a social elite in the south-east of
England, and imposed on them by nationalism and imperialism; and neither is able emotionally or politically to write in
ignorance of a history which includes poetic histories and
baggages.

Such large issues may not be what you wish to write about,
but they are only an example writ large: for social and political
pressures surround everyone, and every poem bears, however
lightly, their weight. You might want to write about Jack the
Ripper, fox-hunting, Mrs Thatcher, feminism, or your own
children: and in no cases would you wish to write the poem
as a sonnet without knowing what you were doing, and what
you might be thought to be implying – especially if you hoped
to see the poem in print.

It will be evident that I believe poetry to be written for and
with both your eyes and your ears. Never hesitate to read your
own work aloud, as you write and as you revise. Readers read
with many senses, and poems that leave the ear dissatisfied
are as disappointing as those which fail to please the eye (and
the mind). The rightness of a poem is as often aural as formal
or conceptual; and in the most practical terms, success as a

poet means invitations to read aloud, for publicity and money, so it is worth being able to do it well.

Similarly, knowledge of the poetic craft is an aid for both writing and reading poetry. Far more than in manuals or histories, the lessons of poetic craft are found in the poems which give the craft its substance, history, and perceived value. In many of the workshop exercises which follow you will be asked to read as well as to write, or offered examples from the *Norton Anthology* as illustrations of effects or techniques; and without the reading the writing will be a damn sight harder. It always is.

Workshop Writing

1   Ways into Verse

People write poetry for different reasons and in different ways. It may be a job, the most enjoyable thing you do, a course requirement, or just another way of writing. Poems may rhyme or be blank (as in *blank verse*), which means 'unrhymed'. A poem may be an argument, a plea, a song, a joke, a curse, or an image. It may be addressed to yourself, your lover, your family, city, culture, nation, or world: so it may be private or loudly public. But if it's a poem, then whatever else it may also be, it is in words and it isn't prose.

For me, the handiest distinction between poetry and prose is that poetry uses one unit of words that prose does not: the line. Alternatively, poetry uses one form of punctuation which prose doesn't: the line break. There's more about this in Workshop 5, but in the first place what it *doesn't* mean is that poems are chopped-up prose; and what it does mean is that if you are writing poetry you are writing lines *as well as* making sense. However straightforward or complicated the sense, however long or short the lines, there must be some reasons why the lines are as they are, and the line breaks where they are. The reason may be to make it clear that the lines are rhythmically similar, and have a pattern of end-rhyme; or to give visual stress to end-words which don't rhyme; or because each line is one image (or word, clause, sentence...): but there will be a reason, and if it's an interesting reason that readers can readily understand, so much the better.

To begin, then, you need to experiment with writing lines. At first try anything you like to get words on paper; but when you read over your work be judgemental: which lines do you like? Which do you think work well? Why did you begin and end that line as you did? You might then try these exercises:

lines with one clear image;
lines with one clause;
lines with a set number of syllables (10 is a handy length).

When you feel ready, you should go on to try sequences of lines each governed by the same principle. The most interesting question that arises is whether each line is to be syntactically self-contained, or whether the sense will run-on from line to line:

- Write ten consecutive self-contained lines, and then ten in which the sense runs on (so that full stops etc. are in the middle of lines). Which set of lines reads aloud better?

- What happens if you spread one image over two or three lines? Is it more or less interesting to read? to listen to? Are some images better in one line, and others in several lines?

In conclusion – later workshops require more exact ways of shaping and combining lines, but before you begin to do that you need lines to work with! The integrity or coherence (imagistic, syllabic, aural, or visual) of lines is a basic feature of all poetry, with which you will be confronting your readers. You *can* do almost anything, but you *always* need to know *what* you are doing – and *why*!

2   Metrical Lines

Metre (the pattern of stressed and unstressed beats in a line) is conventionally analysed as the repetition of a basic unit, called a *foot*, and the description of a metrical line therefore specifies the type of foot, and the number of such feet per line: thus *iambic pentameter* means a line of five iambs, *trochaic trimeter* a line of three trochees, and so on.

The great bulk of English poetry uses one of four basic feet:

duple feet

| the iamb | *ti-TUM* | or | ux | iambic |
| the trochee | *TUM-ti* | or | xu | trochaic |

triple feet

| the anapæst | *ti-ti-TUM* | or | uux | anapæstic |
| the dactyl | *TUM-ti-ti* | or | xuu | dactylic |

These feet are most commonly used with between three and seven per line:

trimeter	three feet per line	trimetric
tetrameter	four	tetrametric
pentameter	five	pentametric
hexameter	six	hexametric
heptameter	seven	heptametric

These nine terms, in their twenty combinations, can be used to describe most poetry in English. This does not mean that every line will be exactly, thumpingly regular – for that would be very dull. What it does mean is that in most lines most of the words will fit the specified pattern, and in some all will: and where that is true, the irregularities (such as a trochee in an otherwise iambic line) will be heard as an interesting variation. Take, for example, Shakespeare's famous line from *Hamlet*.

> To be or not to be: that is the question

Like much of Shakespeare's poetry, this is an iambic pentameter, but it has one extra syllable, and the fourth foot is usually pronounced as a trochee:

> To BE | or NOT | to BE: | THAT is | the QUES- | tion
> u   x | u   x | u   x | x u | u   x | u

Speak the line aloud: the rising rhythm of the first three iambs, the pause (at the colon) and the following trochee (THAT is), and the return to rising rhythm (in the last foot and the extra unstressed beat) are clearly audible, and make the line metrically interesting, because less predictable. (Compare it with 'To be or not to be, is that the point?') Look up Hamlet's speech (3.1.55 ff.) and scan some more lines: as well as iambs (ux) and trochees (xu), you may find a *spondee* (xx; *TUM-TUM*), or a *pyrrhic* (uu; *ti-ti*). How regular are the lines? and does Hamlet ever stop being clearly and audibly iambic? In the exercises that follow, I have written as regularly as possible; but always remember that good metrical verse can contain at least as much variation as Shakespeare's.

This workshop investigates the basic use of regular metres by making two distinctions. The first is between *duple* feet (iambs and trochees, ux and xu), which have two beats, and *triple* feet (anapæsts and dactyls, uux and xuu), which have three. Some effects of duple versus triple rhythms have been discussed above, triple rhythm tending to comedy – but this needs qualifying by the second distinction, between *rising* and *falling* rhythm. Rising rhythm is produced by iambs (ux) and anapæsts (uux), where the stressed beat comes last and tends to raise vocal pitch and volume in reading aloud; it is close to common speech. Falling rhythm is produced by trochees (xu) and dactyls (xuu), where the stressed beat comes first, and pitch and volume then tend to fall away; it is rarely anything like common speech.

Try first to write some lines in duple rising rhythm: iambic tetrameter (ux ux ux ux) and pentameter (ux ux ux ux ux) are the commonest metres. Long strings of iambs | ocCUR | in COM - | mon ENG – | lish SPEECH |, and only need isolating ('occur in common English speech') to become a line (here an iambic tetrameter) which can take its place in a metrical poem:

> I'm FASciNAted BY the WAY
> that FOReign WORDS no-ONE can SAY
> ocCUR in COMmon ENGlish SPEECH
> exTENDing OUR linGUIStic REACH.

Use rhyme only if you want to (some people find rhyme easier), but write four connected lines in iambic tetrameter;

then recast the same thoughts, as far as possible in the same words, as four lines of iambic pentameter:

> I'm fascinated by the way in which
> so many foreign words no-one can say
> with ease occur in common English speech
> extending our linguistic reach abroad.

Then, reverting to the tetrametric version as a base, recast it again in iambic trimeter:

> Amazing: foreign words
> no-one can say are used
> quite commonly, and make
> our language bigger still.

- What has happened with each recasting to the pace and density of your poem? Read each version aloud: how must your voice accommodate the constant rhythm and different line lengths?

Again reverting to the first version as a base, recast it as an anapæstic tetrameter (uux uux uux uux):

> What a WONderful (NOT to say STRANGE) thing it IS
> that we USE foreign WORDS that we CANnot
> proNOUNCE all the time in our daily exchanges of speech
> thus extending our language's stupendous reach.

- Read the iambic and anapæstic versions aloud, and get others to read them aloud as well: is there more variation in the readings of the iambic or the anapæstic? Is the version in triple rhythm more comic?

Now recast the first version again, in trochaic tetrameter (xu xu xu xu):

> FASciNAting! FOReign PEOple
> OFten UTter USEful PHRAses
> we can use while mispronouncing
> to substantial verbal profit.

It's much harder for most people to write trochaically.

- Read aloud your original version (in iambic tetrameter) and the new trochaic version: what qualities are unique to one version? and what qualities do they have in common?

- If there are members of the workshop with distinctive national or regional accents, ask them to read both versions aloud: how do their accents cooperate or interfere with the different rhythms?

The easiest way to write trochaically is by stringing together words which are themselves trochees: 'FOReign PEople / OFTen UTTer USEful PHRAses'. It works, after a fashion, but the staccato rhythm becomes monotonous, because the feet and the words coincide. My lines 3–4 are more interesting 'WE can USE while MISproNOUNcing / TO sub-STANtial VERbal PROfit'. It isn't very good, but the poly-syllables 'mispronouncing' and 'substantial' consolidate and enliven the rhythm, inflecting and modulating the thump-ting-thump-ting to which trochees tend. What begins to result is a potentially subtle and expressive rhythm not to be heard from iambs.

The best-known trochaic poem is Longfellow's *Song of Hiawatha* (1855), written in unrhymed trochaic tetrameter (which is as well if one's hero is called Hiawatha, and his wife 'Minnehaha, "Laughing Water"'). The poem is fun (read any 100 lines aloud), but relies heavily on a chanting delivery, repeating phrases and lines; and Longfellow does not begin to do all that can be done with trochaic rhythm. For a more varied display try Robert Browning (1812–89): two of his great trochaic poems are included in the *Norton Anthology* – 'Soliloquy of the Spanish Cloister' (N913) and 'A Toccata of Galuppi's' (N926) – but a collected Browning is well worth sampling. Rudyard Kipling (1865–1936) was also unusually skilled with trochees, and reads aloud excellently. To see/hear something of great skill, try to scan 'Recessional' (N1077), deciding what is rising and what is falling. (Remember that trochaic words, such as 'MAzy' [xu] and 'ERRor' [xu] can be fitted in to iambic lines, as in Milton's 'With mazy error under pendant shades': With MA– | zy ERR– | or UN– | der PEN – | dant SHADES: ux | ux | ux | ux: four words out of six are trochaic, with a falling rhythm, but the line is a regular iambic pentameter, with rising rhythm.) Then, considering Kipling's more iambic lines or stanzas to be more affirmative (the voice surges along), and his more trochaic parts to be more doubtful (the voice halting slightly), consider the poem's history: Kipling, since Tennyson's death (in 1892) probably the most popular poet in the Anglophone world, sent it as a letter (he was not paid) to *The Times*, on the occasion of Queen Victoria's Diamond Jubilee in 1897 (the largest feel good-about-imperialism party ever held).

Many speakers (as opposed to the poets) of trochaic poems have in common a degree of madness or obsession, like Browning's Spanish monk, whose every stratagem against Brother Lawrence reveals his own self-corroding hatred. It is the very abnormality in common speech of long runs of trochees which makes the monk's speech so liable to sound strange, its patterns of stress, non-words, and twisted syntax jarring to the reader's ear; and it is interesting to choose a speaker with an obsession or instability, and write trochaically for that voice – as a free-standing poem, or as part of a larger work in which one or more voices are predominantly trochaic, but others iambic.

Triple falling rhythm, created by dactyls (xuu xuu etc.), is so rare in English that its effects, while unpredictable, tend to sound very contrived. Experiment with it, to see and hear for yourself, but be warned that most people find it unwieldy, and success at any length elusive.

In conclusion – in the session(s) of this workshop you've been learning to describe poetic rhythms and metres, and modulating them by manipulating the basic foot and the line length. Before about 1900 most poems in English were written fairly strictly, in accordance (within conventional limits of variation) with a prescribed metre and/or form; and before the Jazz Age both professional and public opinion located much of a poet's skill in the dexterity with which they observed prescription. In this century free combinations of metres and the exploration of variant forms have been powerful and popular – which means a new way of using metre formally, but commonly uses the same basic elements as before. By considering the proportions of duple and triple, rising and falling rhythms in your own work – however it got itself written in the first place – you will gain access to one of your poem's main technical control-boards.

3   Limericks

Besides the quatrains of songs, the limerick is probably the best known and most widely composed poetic form. Almost always comic, often obscene and/or witty, and trippingly memorable, it was popularised by Edward Lear (1812–88; see N942 for examples); and in the twentieth century has gone from strength to strength.

In its strictest prescription the limerick is a pentain (5 lines), with lines 1, 2, and 5 rhyming in anapæstic trimeter, and lines 3–4 a rhyming couplet in anapæstic dimeter:

ti-ti-TUM ti-ti-TUM ti-ti-TUM	*OR*	uux uux uux	A
ti-ti-TUM ti-ti-TUM ti-ti-TUM		uux uux uux	A
ti-ti-TUM ti-ti-TUM		uux uux	B
ti-ti-TUM ti-ti-TUM		uux uux	B
ti-ti-TUM ti-ti-TUM ti-ti-TUM		uux uux uux	A

The letters in the last column (AABBA) show the *rhyme scheme*, the three A-lines rhyming with one another, and the two B-lines with each other. (This is the standard method of annotating rhyme, so that AABBCC would indicate three couplets, ABAB a cross-rhymed quatrain, and so on.) This is the ideal form, but in practice the lines are often *catalectic*, missing one or more beats – most commonly the first unstressed beat of each line. The form is then:

ti-TUM ti-ti-TUM ti-ti-TUM	*OR*	ux uux uux	A
ti-TUM ti-ti-TUM ti-ti-TUM		ux uux uux	A
ti-TUM ti-ti-TUM		ux uux	B
ti-TUM ti-ti-TUM		ux uux	B
ti-TUM ti-ti-TUM ti-ti-TUM		ux uux uux	A

This variant was used by Lear, as the type beginning 'There was a[n] [adjective] [person] from [place]' ('There WAS | an old MAN | from PeRU', for example). Use catalectic lines if you wish: but consistency helps, and if one A-line is catalectic, the other two should also be so – though the B-lines might reasonably be of two complete anapæsts each.

Most limericks make each A-line a complete clause, and the pair of B-lines a complete clause, so that the poem proceeds 'uux uux uux STOP uux uux uux STOP uux uux | uux uux STOP uux uux uux! END': but this is mere habit, and among the most interesting limericks are those which set the clause (a grammatical unit) against the line (a poetical unit) with idiosyncratic variety. (It's the same as with the trochaic words and feet in Workshop 2: exact regularity gets boring fast.) There is no restriction on rhyme, but rather an encouragement to find clever, silly, or funny rhymes for a difficult rhyme-word (and see N1328–29):

> A percussionist playing the timpani
> was twice warned that he'd better not skimp any
> more notes in the score;
> and then shown the door
> for omitting two-thirds of the symphony.

It isn't perfect, but illustrates one popular form of comic rhyme, where in the first line the last stress (uux uux uuX) is filled by the stressed first syllable of a polysyllabic word (here 'uux uux uuTIM-pa-ni', or 'uux uux uux-u-u): the line becomes too long (or *hypermetric*) and the other A-lines must follow suit. You can also have fun with eye-rhymes, words which look as if they rhyme but don't (bough, cough, dough, enough); and W. S. Gilbert (1836–1911; N1041), of Gilbert and Sullivan, who disliked limericks, wrote this little masterpiece:

> There was a young man from St Bees,
> who was stung on the neck by a wasp:
> when asked, 'Does it hurt?'
> he replied, 'Not at all –
> but I'm glad that it wasn't a hornet.'

- Try to state as concisely as possible what Gilbert has done, and how it is funny. Is it still a limerick?

A similar lesson in form is offered by this famous example:

> There was a young man from Japan
> whose poetry would never scan;
>   when asked why 'twas so
>   he replied, 'Well, you know
> I always like to get as many words into the last line as I
>   possibly can.'

Such fundamental distortions of form are often one-offs, but provocatively illustrate the benefits of moulding form, observing-while-challenging the prescription; and there are many degrees of distortion to explore. Try any or all of the following, in any order:

- a limerick that is a single, grammatical sentence;
- a limerick that is five sentences (lines 3 & 4 are tough);
- a reverse limerick in which lines 1, 2 & 5 are dimeters, and lines 3–4 trimeters (i.e. uux uux / uux uux / uux uux uux uux uux uux / uux uux);
- a limerick that rhymes ABCBA and ones that rhyme ABABA/ABABB;
- a limerick taking as its first A-rhyme your own name, or the name of your hometown;
- a limerick about a famous person, rhyming on their name;
- a limerick in which *alliteration* (where as many words as possible begin with or contain the same consonant) or *assonance* (where a vowel is repeated) is important;
- a limerick that is obscene but politically correct;
- a limerick that is scrupulously polite but politically incorrect;
- a limerick that a child of 3 or 4 would laugh at.

4 Clerihews

A distant cousin of the limerick is the clerihew, named after its inventor Edmund Clerihew Bentley (1875–1956), who suggested it in *Biography for Beginners* (1905): it is a quatrain of two couplets (AABB); the couplets should be of unequal length, and it is common for all four lines to be of different lengths; but the first line is always someone's name. Bentley himself wrote many, my own favourite being about Nell Gwynne, one of Charles II's mistresses:

Nell
fell
when Charles II [read: Charles the Second]
beckoned.

All you need to begin is a name: your own, that of anyone you like (or dislike), or any famous person; the odder it is, the better. Like limericks, clerihews challenge your skill in finding (or creating) rhymes; and in making the rhymes as telling as possible. Politicians are sitting ducks ('Ronald Reagan / wanted a cosmic ray-gun / but SDI / didn't fly'; 'John Major-Ball / became plain John Major, that's all: / the 'class-less society' / on a nominal moiety'), but clerihews lend themselves to satire generally, and it is often possible to make a clerihew sufficiently sharp to become uncomfortable:

Michael Jackson
was born a black son,
but after repeated plastic surgery he's now quite
white.

- Agree among the whole group a list of ten or so famous names, mixing people from many walks of life; then each participant should write a clerihew for each name.

- Of the clerihews beginning with the same name, which are most and least successful/memorable, and why?

- Of all the clerihews, which is funniest, and why? Which is saddest?

In conclusion – limericks and clerihews are among the easiest forms to use, swift-footed, readily written, and small but tough enough to handle roughly. Although both offer rich varieties within their compass, both are relatively limited, and offer a compact multigym in which to exercise the muscles of rhyme, metre, and tone. This can profitably be done on paper, and in groups: but once the forms have been grasped, these little

poems can also be exercised in your head, when bored, travelling, or engaged in tasks which fill the hands but fail to occupy
the mind.

5   Syntax, Lineation and Punctuation

I mentioned in Workshop 3 the play of clauses (units of
grammar) against lines (units of poetry). The articulation and
division of sentences are indicated with punctuation, and one
can regard the line (and the stanza, if any) as additional
forms/units of punctuation particular to poetry. In some
ways the line makes a crucial difference between prose and
poetry, and Christopher Ricks once defined that difference by
saying that 'prose *has* to go to the end of the line, but in poetry
it's an option': one can see what he means by putting line
breaks, a form of punctuation usually particular to poetry,
into a paragraph otherwise laid out as ordinary prose. One
immediate consequence is that a half-rhyme that wouldn't
stand out in prose (usually/poetry) is displayed; both metre
(parTICuLAR to POetRY, ux | ux | ux | ux) and alliteration
(punctuation, particular, poetry) also become audible; and
more generally one's reading focus is twitched, and alerted.

It is this readerly attention (from Latin *tendere*, to stretch)
upon which poetry can play. The clauses and lines, and the
punctuation (including layout) that marks, displays, and controls their relations, are primary determinants of how sense
and expression build into structure: their fluidity and pressure
are at the poem's heart, and the relations between grammar
and form are more important than either can be alone.

To begin pondering those relations, each member of the
workshop group should bring in one of their own poems
typed out as a continuous prose paragraph, with the line
breaks and all other punctuation (commas, full stops, capital
letters, etc.) left out. Swap paragraphs: and try to work out,
from the prose paragraph in front of you, how the original
poem was lineated and punctuated. Then compare the original
and the new versions.

- How did you decide where to put line breaks? and other
  marks/units of punctuation?

- How are the line breaks and other marks/units of punctuation related in each version? Are lines *end-stopped* (with a mark of punctuation after the last word)? or *enjambed* (where the sense carries over the line break)?

- Have poems which originally had short lines tended to be relineated with longer lines? or vice versa?

A similar exercise can be undertaken with retyped, unpunctuated prose versions of canonical poems; and where, as in Eliot's *The Waste Land*, punctuation includes the type font, spacing, and position on the page, versions in prose layout can be very extraordinary to read. What would one make, for example, of lines 273–83?

> the barges wash drifting logs down greenwich reach past the isle of dogs weialala leia wallala leialala elizabeth and leicester beating oars the stern was formed a gilded shell red and gold

Even with the rhyme as a guide, not, in all probability, what Eliot made of it:

> The barges wash
> Drifting logs
> Down Greenwich reach
> Past the Isle of Dogs.
>   Weialala leia
>   Wallala leialala
>
> Elizabeth and Leicester
> Beating oars
> The stern was formed
> A gilded shell
> Red and gold

Eliot makes it very clear that the question is as much 'what is acting as punctuation? and how?' as it is 'where does the punctuation go?'; and clear that these questions have immediate consequences for syntax, the sense a reader will be able to make of the lines. Such problems are also visible in the monologue by Molly Bloom which ends Joyce's *Ulysses*, where there are about 40 pages without marks of punctuation, and in Beckett's novels. Extracts from these texts can valuably be discussed: other readers will see possibilities that you have missed, and vice versa.

A different but also extreme degree of lineation is visible in Robert Herrick's (1591–1674) poem 'Upon His Departure Hence', written in iambic monometer:

Thus I
Pass by
And die,
As one,
Unknown,
And gone:
I'm made
A shade,
And laid
I'th' grave,
There have
My cave.
Where tell
I dwell,
Farewell.

In one sense the poem could not be simpler, but its animating tension is shown at once if the rhyme and punctuation are notated first with the rhyme as dominant (AAA, B,B,B: CC,C D,DD. EE,E.) and then with the punctuation dominant (AAA, B, B, B: CC, CD, DD. EE, E.): translated back into layout, these would produce:

Thus I pass by and die
As one, unknown, and gone:
I'm made a shade, and laid
I'th' grave, there have my cave.
Where tell I dwell, *Farewell.*

Thus I pass by and die,
As one,
Unknown,
And gone:
I'm made a shade,
And laid i'th' grave,
There have my cave.
Where tell I dwell,
Farewell.

The hinge of the poems stands out clearly: the junction of the C-rhymes (made/shade/laid) and the D-rhymes (grave/have/cave), and the commas which organise the sequence as 'made+shade, laid+grave, have+cave'. And a further twist becomes audible: that whereas the A-, B- and E-rhymes (I/one/tell) are quite distinct, the C- and D-rhymes (made/grave) share a vowel, and half-rhyme with one another: so the distinction of the triplets is blurred aurally just as it is blurred syntactically.

- In reading Herrick's original aloud should you pause after each line? after the marks of punctuation? or only at the end of each triplet?

- Devise your own layout for the poem: what features do you hope to display for the reader?

- Write a short poem in dimetric couplets (for example, 'ux ux (A) / ux ux (A) / ux ux (B) / ux ux (B)', and so on) – a poem that is (as it were) 2×2 rather than Herrick's 1×3. How does it respond to variant lineation?

This timberyard measure of regular poetry, expressing the line length and units of rhyme as dimensions (so that blank verse is '5×1', trimetric couplets '3×2', tetrametric quatrains '4×4', and so on) is a useful shorthand way of thinking about the shape of poems; and as for particular DIY jobs you need particular cuts of timber, so too with poetry: different basic shapes confer different strengths and weaknesses.

To experiment with punctuation one needs to know what the available resources are. One principal form of punctuation, the use of space – between words, lines, stanzas, paragraphs, poems, sequences . . . – is almost infinitely malleable. Many off-the-peg arrangements are available, the conventional layouts for, say, continuous prose, cookbooks, addresses, letters, telephone directories, newspapers (headlines, columns, captions, and display boxes); and poetry has conventions too – set to the left margin or centred, the use of indentation to display rhyme or line length – but (especially in this century) has also been prone to spatial experimentation. Without being too serious, try, either individually or collaboratively, to:

- write a poem in columns;

- write a poem as a recipe; or take a recipe from one of the more lyrical cookbooks, and organise it visually as a poem;

- write a poem in which the standard layouts for (i) an address; (ii) an entry in the telephone directory; and (iii) an official form or form-letter are visually quoted.

The domestication of word-processing technology has made the rapid and sophisticated redesign of the *mise-en-page* (the putting-on-the-page) much easier, and if you have access to a word-processor you will find it very worthwhile learning what it can do and how you can make it do it. Even in straightforward word-processing programmes (I am using Microsoft Word 5.1 on an AppleMac Classic II with System 7), letters or words can be raised or lowered, displayed in

italic or **bold** fonts, increased or decreased in size, be set in many dIfferENT **fonts and** DESIGNS: outline, and shadow, for example, or ~~strikethrough~~. As well as standard lower- and UPPER-CASE letters, an intermediate form, small capitals, may also be available; and these possibilities can, *of course, be combined*. Lines may be set in single-space, double-space, or space-and-a-half; they may be justified to either margin, centred, or otherwise tabulated; and the positioning of the text in relation to the margins of the paper, plus the content (if any) and design of the header and footer zones and side-margins, are wholly malleable, for the poet to determine.

- If sufficient word-processors are available, their use during workshops is well worth exploring, to encourage everyone to practise hands-on control of the layout and presentation of their own work.

- If only one or two word-processors are available, the best option may be to enter a well-known poem and system-atically mutate its *mise-en-page*, printing out successive copies which can serve as prompts for arguments and dis-cussion.

- If no word-processors are available, pens, scissors, paste, and photocopiers are handy.

For some poets, if they compose on screen, decisions about their use of these resources may be integral to the process of composition; for others, especially those who scribble down rough drafts and work them slowly, decisions about the *mise-en-page* may be the last things to be done in preparing a fair copy. Some people will welcome the chance to attend to these 'details'; to others it will seem irrelevant to the central concerns of their poetry: but unless you *never* write things down and your work consists wholly of performance, you will have to prepare texts – for yourself, for workshops, for readers; and for publishers' readers – and a professional competence in handling layout will stand you in good stead. For many, it will prove a tremendous poetic resource.

The other form of punctuation is the set of marks, and these you simply have to know, as you know the alphabet. The most important are the four stops, the comma [,], the semicolon [;], the colon [:], and the full stop [.]. Most people use commas and full stops in everyday writing, but the conventional uses of semicolons and colons are now rarely taught in schools, and many people are uncertain how to use them. One way is to think of them as indicating pauses, so that if, in reading aloud, a comma is a one-beat pause and a full stop a four-beat pause, then a semicolon and a colon are two-and three-beat pauses respectively. Another measure is syntactical force: a comma separates clauses where the sense is continuous; a semicolon separates clauses (or groups of clauses) where the sense is related but not continuous, such as items on a list; a colon separates (groups of) clauses whose sense is self-contained and brings them into relationship within a sentence; and full stops separate complete sentences from one another. The best way of learning these uses is by paying attention to their use in everything you read, rather than by trying to learn 'rules' for their use from a grammar-book, and in your own poetry which marks you use, and where, is very much up to you (but remember and try to help your readers!). You could write long sentences, which go on, and on, with only commas between clauses, like this, or you can write many short sentences. One after another. Each short. Each sharp. Like that. Or you can write, as most poets do, in ways somewhere between the two; and whatever you do, your decisions will be different in one poem than in another, and will be affected by other decisions: where the line breaks are, whether the poem is narrative, lyric, or in dialogue, and so on.

There are many other marks also, including the tonal markers [!?], for signalling exclamations and questions; round brackets (or lunulae) [( )], which allow you to place one clause in the middle of another; the breakers and joiners [-/] [dash, hyphen, and slash], which separate words or clauses from one another, or join words together (as in 'red-gold', 'tree-lined', 'and/or'); and inverted commas ['''''], for signalling speech. Each mark (and there are more!) has specific conventional uses which may be observed or exploited, and to ignore the possibilities of punctuation can be as serious a handicap as to abandon the vowels, painting the keys for A, E, I, O, and U black on your keyboard. Sounds crazy, nu? But for all the use most writers make of the marks of punctuation available as standard on QWERTY keyboards those keys might as well be painted black.

Some books with detailed information about the marks, their histories, and how to use them, are given in the Recommended Reading at the end of this book; but the main thing to remember is that, especially in poetry, *there are no hard-and-fast rules*: there are only *conventions*, which may be observed, but may also be disregarded or deliberately broken. Grammarians, style handbooks, and old-fashioned teachers will try to tell you that there are rules, that you should always do this or that: but it cannot be binding advice, only suggestion. One can do anything – provided that (a) one knows what one is doing, and (b) that a reader can follow what one is doing: the conventions are there for a good reason – they make reading possible – and if you break too many of them at once the results will probably be unintelligible. Joyce may have spent 17 years writing *Finnegans Wake*, but not many people are willing to spend 17 years reading it; Eliot's *The Waste Land* and *The Hollow Men*, however, substantially reinvented the conventions of punctuation, with spectacular consequences for much modern poetry.

As you read, learn to read the punctuation too, observantly and thoughtfully; remember in particular that, as T. S. Eliot said, punctuation 'includes the *absence* of punctuation marks, when they are omitted where the reader would expect them'.

Workshop exercises which can help, and which bear periodic repetition, include:

- Looking carefully at poems which make particular use of a specified mark. For colons and semicolons try Keats's 'Ode to a Nightingale' (N845); for lunulae Theodore Roethke's 'I Knew a Woman' (N1392); for hyphens Geoffrey Hill's *Mercian Hymns* (N1722); and for commas Seamus Heaney's 'The Strand at Lough Beg'.

- Reading aloud, from your own work and that of others, experimenting with the length of pause you feel the poet's punctuation requires.

- Having one member of the group dictate a canonical poem, signalling punctuation and lineation only with pause, tone, and cadence (the rise and fall of voice): how 'correctly' could anyone hear the punctuation and layout?

These exercises (accompanying research and reading) will help your sense of punctuation: it won't happen overnight, but perseverance and practice pay off.

In conclusion – a poet's use of syntax (the order of words), lineation (their division into lines), and punctuation (their articulation and layout-display) all interrelate constantly, fluidly, and powerfully. Either as an integral part of composition, or as a necessary task of presentation, these elements must be competently and profitably handled. Poets may on occasion set themselves a more-or-less specified task, which will impose technical restraints, but neither syntax, lineation, punctuation, nor their relations can be reduced to or operated by fixed rules; and their productive use depends on and demands groundwork – and then practice.

6   Diction and Rhyme

Diction has a range of meanings, but is defined here as 'the choice of words, with the causes and consequences of that choice'. The unexpected word, and *le mot juste* (the perfect word), have an obvious potential in any writing; but odd considerations come into play when the writing is poetry – metre, rhyme, register, and lexicon, to name only the obvious heads.

The constraints which metre may impose are visible in various parts of Workshop 2: if you are writing iambically, the word 'DISapPOINted', say, though naturally trochaic, can be accommodated by three iambs (u DIS—| apPOIN—| ted x); but the word 'voCABulary' is much trickier, for it has only one natural stress, and its presence within an iambic line must either distort the metre or oblige a distorted pronunciation of the word. This doesn't mean that you can't do it; only that to do it satisfactorily will require effort. A similar difficulty will attend the use of many polysyllables within duple metres, but the presence of such polysyllables can be the making of a rhythm. In 'The Garden' (N442), Andrew Marvell (1621–78) wrote of lying about in a garden in summer as 'Annihilating all that's made / To a green thought in a green shade': and the power of the lines has much to do with the pentasyllable 'Annihilating' and its eleven following monosyllables.

- Draw up, as a group, a list of words and phrases which sound hard to accommodate iambically ('flowering alstromeria', 'moon-landing', 'M25', and 'chief secretary', for example, all from today's papers) and try it. It's worth beginning on a small scale, to find out what sort of line your word or phrase needs to occur in for one of your poems to be able to digest it; and where in the line? beginning, middle, or end? When you have a line, what sort of poem might accommodate it? Once you have an idea of form, you may find it easier to go to the beginning and work towards the set word/phrase, working up a head of metrical steam before attempting the hard bit.

- Draw up a list of commonly used but foreign words and phrases (*fin de siècle, coup d'état, schadenfreude, et in arcadia ego*): what rhythms do they bring with them? and how might those be used in English poetry?

- Choose, as a group, a single word, and then, individually, use it repeatedly or with particular emphasis in a sequence of lines. Small polysemic words, such as 'cast' and 'hand', can produce good results. Be ready to explain what you were trying to do, and how.

- Compile a sequence of words, randomly, from a dictionary or printed text, and use them in order, then in reverse order, in a sequence of lines.

Straightforward dictionary-reading, as a means of increasing your vocabulary, is not to be sneered at – *les mots justes* are not always in everyday use – but in dictionaries and in poems words do not always behave identically.

A substantial vocabulary is also a help in finding rhymes, and while the basic problem posed by the need to combine rhyme and sense needs no comment, it is worth thinking clearly about what and where rhyme is. In English, rhyme occurs when two words or phrases have the same (i) final stressed vowel and (ii) following sounds: thus cat/mat, abroad/ignored, and adventure/debenture are all full-rhymes, meeting both criteria. There are, by implication, the following variants:

half-rhyme 1: *vowel rhyme*, where the vowel is the same, but not the following sounds: bite/fire, courage/bunker;

half-rhyme 2: *pararhyme*, where it is the vowels that differ: bite/fate, honour/winter;

eye-rhyme, where words look as if they rhyme, but don't: bough/dough, picturesque/queue;

autorhyme, where a word is rhymed with itself: Amen/ Amen (see *Macbeth* II.ii.29–30).

Where full-rhyme tends to confirm the sense, half- and eye-rhyme often make for dissonance and questioning; and auto-rhyme, while in one sense not a rhyme at all and in another the most perfect rhyme, often has profoundly disturbing effects on the reading voice. Rhyme may also vary in position: end-rhyme is commonest, but *initial* and *medial* rhymes (between words at the beginnings, or in the middles, of lines) should not be forgotten.

- Experiment with quatrains in couplet-rhyme (AABB), in cross-rhyme (ABAB), and in arch-rhyme (ABBA): what are the effects of each pattern?

- Experiment, using the same rhyme words in each version, with sestets rhyming AABBCC, ABABCC, ABCABC, ABC-BAC and ABCCBA: how is the A-rhyme affected by the distance apart of its component lines?

- Beginning with the same line every time, and trying to make the content of the successive versions as similar as possible, write a short sequence of couplets using first full-rhyme, and then, in succession, vowel, para-, eye- and autorhyme (each on their own), and finally a version in which successive couplets use the various forms of rhyme: how well, for example, do vowel and para-rhyme sit alongside one another? para- and autorhyme?

- Choose a given rhyme (the stalwarts death/breath and love/move are good ones) and employ it initially, medially, and terminally: how do its effects interact with its position?

Variation and pressure within rhyme are highly desirable, but if the rhyming is too loose it will disperse into alliteration and assonance, useful cousins of rhyme but not the thing itself.

Register and *lexicon* are related, but distinct: the register is the appropriateness of the words you choose, their decorum either in relation to your subject or to your reader. Just as you might choose to say 'copulate' in one situation, 'sleep together' in another, and 'fuck' in a third, so you must choose which is most appropriate to your poem. The rich swear words of English are one obvious site of difficulty, terms of racial abuse another; but poetically related problems are posed by scientific terms (you might write 'DNA', but probably wouldn't write 'deoxyribonucleic acid'), philosophical terms, slang, euphemisms ('toilet'? or 'bogs'? or 'little girls' room'? 'the khazi'? 'the heads'? – a wealth of choice!), and so on – all are groups of words which might cause offence, be misunderstood or plain incomprehensible to some readers, or look or sound awkward, pretentious, or 'unpoetic' on the page. A lexicon, however, is simply a group of words generated by or associated with a particular person, profession, or situation: a professional jargon, for example. Any particular poem may seek to use or to avoid any particular lexicon.

- The problems of offence posed by 'obscene' and racially abusive terms are best explored and considered in calm and disciplined group discussion. Philip Larkin's notorious 'This be the verse', Tony Harrison's magisterial *v.* (in the excellent Bloodaxe edition that includes newpaper comments and the Channel 4 log-book of complaints and praise when the poem was broadcast), and Derek Walcott's 'The Schooner *Flight*' (N1714) are all worth discussing carefully before any practical exercises involving attempts to use such words in poetry are undertaken.

Group experimentation with writing for speakers of a different gender than oneself is also best preceded by exploratory discussion of the group-members' assorted beliefs and sensitivities on the subject.

- As with the obscene and the polite limerick in Workshop 3 choose a register (perhaps by specifying the relation of your speaker to their listener/reader) and write within it. As a complication, try to write for a speaker who knows there is a register they should use (for example, they need to be formally polite) but who has difficulty in maintaining it (because they are angry or distressed, perhaps).

- Try to write as if by, and for, children of particular ages, genders, and cultures. And then adults.

- Compile as a group parallel lexicons in different registers, for example the vocabularies which might be used by a doctor and a patient in discussing the same subject (say, 'hit his head + swelling + dazed + painkillers' against 'cranial trauma + œdema + concussed + analgesics'): write poems using one or other lexicon exclusively, and a poem which combines them.

- Compile lists of words linked by their form (for example, feline, canine, porcine, serpentine etc.), or their secondary meanings (for example, hand/deck/house/pack/deal/

calling/business: cards) and write poems exploring and exploiting these groups. The aim is to make the secondary meanings trigger one another into enriching the primary meanings (a principal means of binding poems together).

- Change lexicons in mid-poem while keeping the register as undisturbed as possible; and change registers in mid-poem while remaining within a given lexicon.

The 20 volumes (or one CD-ROM) of the *Oxford English Dictionary* do omit things, and contain mistakes: but the *OED* is a massive achievement and resource. One virtue is that it gives older senses of words, and illustrates most senses, obsolete or current, with quotations; it also gives etymologies (the derivations of words). Use it and learn from it.

In conclusion – whatever else poems may be, they are sequences of words, and choosing 'the best words in the best order' (Coleridge) is crucial. Certain words pose problems, and may be ideological dynamite: their properties must be recognised and explored; as must those of rhyme which can make quite innocuous words undergo sympathetic detonation. Control of register and lexicon is a powerful influence on artistic success and the reactions of readers. Finally, remember that lexical shock has its uses, but other severe limitations.

7 Sonnets

The skills you have been developing can be harnessed together in writing a sonnet. The criteria are:

> fourteen lines;
> iambic pentameter (at least for the first one!);
> any rhyme scheme, from AAAAAAAAAAAAAA to ABCDEFGHIJKLMN.

The last criterion is deliberately open (there are *c.* 191 million ways of rhyming fourteen lines), but if you'd rather start with a specific task, three stricter sonnet forms are common in English; do remember, though, that they are only popular possibilities. They are:

the Petrarchan: ABBA ABBA + a sestet (CDECDE or a
variant);
the Shakespearean: ABAB CDCD EFEF GG;
the Spenserean: ABAB BCBC CDCD EE.

Examples of Shakespeare's and Spenser's sonnets are in the
Norton Anthology (N165, 234); and Wordsworth's 'Composed
Upon Westminster Bridge' (N727) is a Petrarchan sonnet
(with a CDCDCD sestet). The *Norton*'s layout is conventional,
and interesting variations can be produced by introducing or
eliminating spaces between groups of lines: 4/4/4/2 (three
quatrains and a couplet) or 8/6 (an octave and a sestet) are
the traditional configurations for sonnets, but anything is possible (12/2;7/7;2/3/9 etc.).

Besides the intrinsic demands of the form – the observation
of metre; the creation of a rhyme scheme; the control of syntax;
its relation to lineation; the deployment of punctuation;
and the weaving of sense and diction – the interest lies in the
opportunity to handle the baggage sonnets drag with them.
Since Petrarch (1304–74) sonnets have been strongly marked as
poems of ideal love and/or frustrated courtship: renaissance
sonneteers burnt, froze, and scribbled in anguished chastity;
romantic sonneteers yearned admiringly towards the vistas
and ideas they loved; and among the most intriguing modern
sonneteers are post-imperial and commonwealth poets who
have mapped the tangled loves and hates of Britain's imperial
embrace onto the traditional colourings and situations of
the sonnet. In the *Norton Anthology* the best examples are a
small selection of Geoffrey Hill's sonnets (N1724–25), but
to appreciate Hill's work properly one needs to read
whole sequences: begin with 'Funeral Music' and 'An
Apology for the Revival of Christian Architecture in England'.
The sonnets of Wole Soyinka (especially 'Apollodorus on
the Niger') are also superb; as are Michael O'Siadhail's
'Perspectives', and some of Robert Lowell's unrhymed sonnets
from *Life Studies*. Tony Harrison has brilliantly revived the
16-line Meredithian sonnet in his continuing autobiographical sequence 'The School of Eloquence' (N1764–66).
Significant older sonneteers in the canon include e.e.cum-
mings (N1283–84), George Meredith (N1007–09), Dante

Gabriel Rossetti (N1005–06), Gerard Manley Hopkins (N1062–67), Elizabeth Barrett Browning (N856), William Wordsworth (N726–27), John Milton (N378–79, 406), and John Donne (N287–89).

Try to find, among the subjects to which you and your poetry are naturally attracted, one which will respond to the imposition of sonnet form. When you have found the subject, try different types of rhyme and rhyme-schemes; densities and ranges of punctuation, registers, and lexicons; degrees of metrical observance and laxity; degrees of clippedness or longeur in syntax. All play their part.

Much of this work will of necessity be solitary, but:

- group feedback and criticism of completed sonnets;
- group brainstorming to help with metrical, lexical, or find-the-rhyme binds that individual sonnet(eer)s have got themselves into;
- comparative/competitive attempts to accommodate some specified rhyme scheme, rhyme, word, or topic; and
- having other people attempt to sight-read your work aloud

are all useful resources. Above all, don't be intimidated: that figure of 191 million possible rhyme schemes means that, though thousands of sonnets have been written in English, many very good, there are millions of possibles untouched by poetic hand.

In conclusion – the sonnet has been in continuous use in English since the sixteenth century, and has proven a form which almost all canonical poets have used. It's big enough to stand on its own 70 feet, but small enough to be do-able, roughly and readily, in limited time; and re-do-able as often as you like. Wordsworth referred to the sonnet's 'scanty plot of ground'; and Donne to building 'in sonnets pretty roomes': either way, sonnets are sturdy and versatile poems offering rich opportunities to learn writing to form.

Writing On

- Try to write a serious limerick. One can make the subject matter serious easily enough, as in this about Sir Walter Raleigh, who first imported coffee and tobacco into England, and famously laid his cloak over a puddle the Queen was about to step in:

> Sir Walter was handy with cloaks,
> and caffeine, and packets of smokes:
>   a mighty romancer
>   of insomniac cancer,
> I thank him – and hope that he chokes.

It has gravity as well as levity, but that tripping triple rhythm and rhyme hold a stubborn strain of comedy which is hard to remove. To try to do so teaches you a great deal about the grain of the metre and form. The equivalent test for sonnets would be to write one embodying indifference.

- The use of inverted commas to signal direct speech is fairly recent (the first book to use the exact modern conventions was Charlotte Brontë's *The Professor* of 1857). Before that such signalling was less easily available to writers: among other systems, italics, line- and stanza-breaks, and parenthesisation of attributions of speech – as: Well (he said) I don't agree – were used. Write, using inverted commas, a poem containing as much speech and dialogue as possible, and then remove the inverted commas: how can you make your speech(es) and dialogue clear to a reader without them? You may find it helpful to look at lines 139–72 of *The Waste Land* (beginning 'When Lil's husband . . .') in Eliot's drafts (published by Faber) and then in the published version; Tony Harrison's 'On Not Being Milton' and 'Them and [Uz]' (N1764, 66) are also suggestive.

- Some poets have experimented with shape or pattern poems, where the words and lines are arranged into an outline of the subject: examples include George Herbert's

'Easter Wings' (N330), Lewis Carroll's 'Fury Said to a Mouse', and John Hollander's 'Swan and Shadow' (N1664). Spaces can also be used within the shape to add details. Try it, at first with a simple object (a cup, a window, the crescent moon), then with a stylised image of a more complex object (a flower with petals, a sitting cat, a stick figure), and finally with something genuinely complex (a cross-section of a house, a face, Celtic knotwork). Be warned that, unless you know your word-processing programme well, this may prove easier on typewriter than computer.

- Other ways of playing with layout are suggested by e.e. cummings's 'r-p-o-p-h-e-s-s-a-g-r', where the letters of 'grasshopper' hop about the page; and D. J. Enright's 'The Typewriter Revolution', which depends on a typewritten appearance. An unpublished poem by Chris Rappleye about finding one's way out of mazes with balls of string (as in the Minotaur story) was written as a single long line – about 30 feet long, typed on paper cut into ribbons and stuck end-to-end. Experiment in any way you can think of with the physical substance and visual appearance of your work: you never know when the game will throw up something to use in earnest.

- 'Imagists', such as H. D. (N1202), sought not a shape but an image, a simple and clear, but resonant, picture or appre-hension, and tried to capture it in short, uncluttered lines. Try it. At other times you might want to be very baroque or cluttered – but as many new writers tend to overwrite, the discipline and minimalism of Imagist work can be useful.

- A particular problem is posed by titles. Look through any big anthology and consider the variety of titles: those which simply quote the opening words, those which flatly describe the content, and those which pose puzzles about poem or/ and poet. A title is an opportunity, the first thing many readers will read, and it seems a shame to omit a title; but you don't want to put readers off with some wilful obscurity that amuses you but confuses everybody else. Go through your portfolio supplying (alternative) titles; and try giving the same poem with different titles to different members of the group. How do the titles shape or prompt their responses?

- Repetition, of words, phrases, lines, and stanzas (as a refrain, for example) offers the disturbance of autorhyme, but also rhythm, circularity, and closure. Experiment with repeated words within the line, and repeated lines within the stanza/poem, as well as with a poem that has a chorus (as many ballads do). Another form which includes highly structured repetition is the *villanelle*: 19 lines (usually iambic pentameter), in 5 tercets and a quatrain, or '(5 × 3) + 4'; the rhyme scheme is $A^1BA^2//ABA^2//ABA^1//ABA^2//ABA^1//A^2$ (where $//$ = a stanza-break, and A1 and A2 always denote the same line). In other words, line 1 is repeated as lines 6, 12, and 18, and line 3 as lines 9, 15, and 19. Examples include William Empson's 'Missing Dates' (N1360), Theodore Roethke's 'The Waking' (N1391), and Dylan Thomas's 'Do Not Go Gentle into That Good Night' (N1465). Much depends on getting the two lines repeated as refrains right, for if one or both is somehow wrong, the mistake is compounded with each repetition: but if you can find a line that will bear repetition, the achievement of a villanelle can be deeply satisfying.

- Don't get hung up on rhyme: it's far better to have loose rhymes than to twist sense to achieve a perfect clang. On the other hand, rhyme makes odd conjunctions sound out: orchard/tortured, boat/goat, station/nation, culture/vulture. Going with these unlikely rhymes and looping the sense round them can work well, especially for poems intended to be read aloud. Regional and national accents interact interestingly with rhyme, mainly on a north-south axis in England (Tony Harrison uses this wonderfully) but also between cultural groups, classes, and the situations in which people are speaking. Experiment with rhyme in as many ways as you like – and if you start to see spots (or phonemes) in front of your eyes, set rhyme aside for a bit and think about another aspect of the poem. Rhyme can be intended – but it can also look after itself.

- Some words have histories that make them rewarding in unexpected contexts; others have etymologies that make them difficult and embarrassing to use. A current example is 'Holocaust', used in English since 1956–8 to refer to the Nazi genocide of European Jewry and other groups; and meaning 'A whole burnt offering; a sacrifice wholly consumed in fire' (*Shorter OED*). Clear enough, perhaps, who was sacrificed and who did the sacrificing; but sacrificed to whom? in propitiation for what? Are we happy to label that appalling history with a word whose radical meanings are religious? Israelis and many Jews of the diaspora prefer the Hebrew word *Sho'ah* (the title of Claude Lanzmann's epic documentary), meaning 'destruction'. If there is a word which bothers or interests you, investigate it thoroughly (and perhaps collaboratively), looking it up in many different dictionaries, chasing its related meanings and cousinly words, and the phrases in which it occurs. Write a poem activating as many meanings and associations of the word, on as many levels, as possible.

- One of the most intriguing canonical sonnets is Keats's 'On the Sonnet' (N842), which rhymes ABC ABD CAB CDE DE. By configuring it as four tercets (4 × 3) rather than three quatrains (3 × 4), Keats stood the form on one of its heads. Write a sonnet in triplets (sets of three lines all rhyming: AAA BBB CCC DDD EE) or tercets (sets of three lines with at least one not rhyming, as in the Keats).

Booklist

The Norton Anthology of Poetry, 4th Student Edition (Norton, New York & London, 1996).

Evans, G. et al. (eds), *The Riverside Shakespeare* (Houghton Mifflin, Boston, 1974).

Browning, R., *The Poems*, ed. J. Pettigrew, 2 vols (Penguin, Harmondsworth, 1981).

Brownjohn, S., *To Rhyme or Not to Rhyme: Teaching Children to Write Poetry* (Hodder & Stoughton, London, 1994).

Bugeja, M. J., *The Art and Craft of Poetry* (Writer's Digest Books, Cincinnati, 1994).

Chisholm, A., *A Practical Poetry Course* (Allison & Busby, London, 1994).

Eliot, T. S., *The Waste Land: A Facsimile and Transcript*, ed. V. Fletcher Eliot (Faber & Faber, London, 1971).

Fussell, Paul, *Poetic Meter and Poetic Form* (rev. edn, McGraw-Hill, New York & London, 1979).

Harrison, T., *Selected Poems* (Penguin, Harmondsworth, 1987).

Harrison, T., *v.*, 2nd edn, with press articles (Bloodaxe, Newcastle-upon-Tyne, 1989).

Hill, G., *Collected Poems* (Penguin, Harmondsworth, 1985).

Hobsbaum, Philip, *Metre, Rhythm and Verse Form* (Routledge, London & New York, 1996).

Hollander, John, *Rhyme's Reason: A Guide to English Verse* (new edn, Yale University Press, New Haven & London, 1989).

Hyland, P., *Getting into Poetry* (Bloodaxe, Newcastle-upon-Tyne, 1992).

Larkin, P., *Collected Poems*, ed. A. Thwaite (Faber & Faber, London, 1988).

Lennard, J., *But I Digress: The Exploitation of Parentheses in English Printed Verse* (Clarendon Press, Oxford, 1991).

Lennard, John, *The Poetry Handbook* (Oxford University Press, Oxford, 1996).

Lowell, R., *Poems. A Selection*, ed. J. Raban (Faber & Faber, London, 1974).

O'Siadhail, M., *Hail! Madam Jazz: New and Selected Poems* (Bloodaxe, Newcastle-upon-Tyne, 1992).

Parkes, M. B., *Pause and Effect: An Introduction to the History of Punctuation in the West* (Scolar Press, Aldershot, 1992).

Parrot, E. O. (ed.), *How to be Well-Versed in Poetry* (Penguin, Harmondsworth, 1991).

Sansom, P., *Writing Poems* (Bloodaxe, Newcastle-upon-Tyne, 1994).

Soyinka, W., *Mandela's Earth and other poems* (Methuen, London, 1990).

Walcott, D., *Collected Poems 1948–84* (Faber & Faber, London, 1986).

8 Narrative Fictions for Film and Television

MERIEL LLAND AND ROBIN NELSON

Introduction

The word 'cinema' has its roots in the Greek word for motion, 'kinema', and this etymology points the screenwriter to an important lesson: that narrative film and television *show* their stories through *motion* or movement.

Writing for film and television is not simply about thinking visually (as one might in composing a photograph or painting) but thinking through connected action. Whilst the degree of emphasis placed on the 'action' or movement varies from script to script, one of the key pleasures offered by film and TV drama is the opportunity to see events in action. Remember the spectacle of the fully realised dinosaurs of *Jurassic Park* (1993) or the launch (and loss) of the liner in *Titanic* (1998)? Recall the shift in dynamic at the opening of *Middlemarch* (BBC, 1993), as the sleepy middle England rural town is disturbed by the arrival of reforming Dr Lydgate who simply observes 'the future' in the building of the railway as the post-horses drive him towards an adventure.

In a less elaborate sense, the spectacle of motion offered by film and television can be glimpsed within the more frequent chase sequence, dance sequence, shoot-out or make-over scene. When Uma Thurman and John Travolta take to the floor in *Pulp Fiction* (1994) the audience is being invited to enjoy far more than a spark of attraction between two characters; when Dustin Hoffman is transformed into his female alter ego in *Tootsie* (1982), the pleasure of his make-over (transformation) is that we are shown – through movement and action – the tension of his predicament. The screenwriter is the choreographer, orchestrator and architect of this and more subtle events. As a writer for both TV and film, you will create the blueprint for action; a framework through which visual action, spoken and musical elements are crafted together to show a story.

This story is shown in time: the average duration of a film for TV or cinema is 90–100 minutes. The duration of other TV drama forms varies, but in any instance there are quite precise parameters. This means that, as a writer, you have a temporal framework in which to build your story. Within the 90 minutes of an average film, you must establish your possible world, the conflict which mobilises the action of the story world and a resolution to that conflict. To learn how to achieve this structure, begin by looking closely at those who have successfully employed the conventions of film narrative. With all writing, you can learn from the best, but this method is particularly useful to film and TV writing. This means 'reading' screenplays, TV movies and films with the same attention you would give to a playscript or the content and structure of a novel or poem. Watch, read and write continuously; these activities feed from each other in helping you to develop your craft. To illustrate this idea of critical/creative reading, we offer in this chapter worked examples of reading of two film texts: *Shallow Grave* (1994) for cinema, and aspects of *Middlemarch* (1994) a six-part serial for television. For workshop purposes readers may substitute other examples from mainstream TV and film.

Finally, remember that the screenplays you will produce remain always starting-points because television production and film-making are ultimately collaborative processes. The writer's blueprint is often literally reshaped by the script editor and/or director, and it is realised by the actors, cinematographers, film/video editors and a host of other production personnel. It may also be influenced by market research and projected audience response, for film- and TV-making nowadays are expensive businesses requiring substantial investment on the promise of ratings or box-office, merchandising and rental returns. In the limited space of this chapter, we concentrate on the processes of writing the script and make no attempt to deal with the business side of writing a 'treatment' to 'pitch' at a potential producer. For these aspects we recommend Trottier's *The Screenwriter's Bible* (1995). A short glossary is appended to explain as required some technical terms used. For a biting view of the motion picture industry in action take a look at Robert Altman's *The Player* (1992). But don't let Michael Tolkin's script and Robert Altman's direction – with their emphasis upon the greed and power of Hollywood – deter you from your screenwriting, even though it might helpfully shatter the illusions of the most romantic.

Workshop 1   Watch, Watch, Watch!

Go to the video store. How do they categorise their stock? Read the information given on the reverse of the video cassette case and note down how the video is defined: 'Horror/Adventure', 'Comedy/Romance', 'Serial Killer/Police/Action'.

You will already know far more about writing for screen than you might imagine; narrative films rely upon what the audience already knows for much of their effect and we are often unaware of just how many of the conventions of cinema and television are familiar to us. When we go to see a movie, or watch a TV drama, we expect the story to be brought to resolution. If we view a Comedy, we expect to laugh; if we watch an Action picture, we expect to be excited by the adventures of the hero/heroine; if we choose a Horror movie or a Thriller, we expect to be unnerved by the experience. These expectations are shaped by the characteristics of the GENRE.

Genre is the word used to describe the kind of text and experience on offer. For example, it may be a Western, a Road Movie, a Police Series, a Buddy Picture, a Hospital Drama, a Sci-fi Adventure, an Historical Epic. In the theoretical study of film and television, the considerable significance of genre – of established narrative forms and the linguistic tropes (figures of speech) which characterise them – has been brought out (see Neale, 1980; Cook, 1985). For our purposes, it is enough to recognise that, although we like to think of ourselves as creative writers producing original material, we all in fact draw upon our store of models from previous writings. Suppose, for example, we aimed to write a new hospital drama for television. It would be almost impossible to do this today without an awareness of *Casualty, ER, Holby City* and other familiar Hospital Dramas. This 'borrowing' is not a weakness but a strength when used effectively. Firstly, it is important to speak to people in a language form which they understand because it is familiar: in the Detective or Mystery genres there is a pleasure in not knowing whodunnit but generically knowing that we will know whodunnit. Secondly, in industry terms, the products of screenwriting are frequently sold on their similarity to films or TV dramas which have previously been popular. Remember, it was not possible to keep the title of Alan Bennett's *The Madness of George III* for the American market because everybody would be asking what had happened to *The Madness of George I* and *II*.

Of course, there is a danger of the 'formulaic', a kind of 'film-by-numbers' which is tedious because overfamiliar. The trick is to understand genre, to draw on generic features, but to spring small surprises to thwart expectations and lend the script an aspect of freshness. Genres establish the content and the 'atmosphere' of the film but they may be used flexibly or they can overlap and merge. Frequently today, films combine genres: the Romantic Comedy, the Comic Horror, the Romantic Epic, the murder-mystery/Buddy movie (see 'Writing On' below) They do this in an attempt to draw on the popular features of more than one genre at once and hence bring in two established audiences whilst producing something a bit different – as mercilessly exposed in *The Player*. Audiences appear actually to take pleasure in variations on a theme, in products which confirm and exercise their generic knowledge, making them feel at home, but which discomfort them a little with a new twist on the formula. Precisely because we know that you know quite a lot about genre – even though you may not be aware of it – we leave you to bring out the features of selected genres through the following exercises.

Workshop 2   Draw on Your Imaginary Library

Think of your favourite films. To what genres do they belong? Begin to itemise their characteristic features.

Workshop 3   Cross-check the Key Features

Return to the video store and hire one or two examples of videos within the same genres. View these films and make notes on their characteristics. Compare these ideas with your initial notes on genre.

Workshop 4   Genre Spoofing

You may well have seen Dawn French and Jennifer Saunders in one of their genre spoofs, for example of British TV period drama or of *Titanic*. Much of the fun comes from bringing out, and accentuating, generic features. Write a spoof of key scenes from a James Bond film. Alternatively, try scenes from an episode of your favourite soap, just slightly heightening generic features. Some soaps almost parody themselves at times, so the keynotes are easy to spot. Make the music-over in *Neighbours*, for example, just that bit more sugary or slightly overdo the mounting tension of the 'cliffhanger' scene to end the episode.

Workshop 5   Generic Collaborations

Read the screenplay for one of your selected film examples. Compare the screenplay with the film. Has the shooting of the script strengthened the generic 'feel' of the film? If so (and it probably will have done), how?

To learn to write narrative fiction for the screen you need to be reading screenplays as well as watching films and TV dramas. These activities will help to give you a sense of the media, the genres in which you are writing, and what is possible within them. Watch and read analytically: ask yourself why a particular scene is placed next to another, why a character is introduced in a particular way and how a scene or sequence comes to interest you. Screen stories pose questions which maintain audience interest; sometimes the questions are overt (who killed the body found in the opening scene and why?). But more often they pose questions implicitly, or offer 'questions in disguise'. The audience will try to make sense of the images with which they are presented. To do this, they ask themselves questions inferred from the action: what is the relationship of Character A to Character B, of Location A to Location B? As a writer you make use of our desire to 'make sense' of things.

- Look at the opening of *Titanic*. What are the divers looking for? What is the significance of the portrait? Who made it? Why was it made?

- Look at the opening of *Trainspotting* (1996). Why are the boys running; from what or whom? To whom does the voice-over belong?

- Look again at the opening 5 minutes of the genre movies you selected. What questions do they pose?

Workshop 5   Economy

Film and TV dramas are expensive; each shot costs and therefore each shot must count. The guiding principle of screenwriting is economy. The world you are about to craft has to be of the same density as that of the novelist, yet in film and television you will recreate that world using very few words and a limited number of images and sounds. To achieve this density, screenwriters cut and revise their scripts for maximum effect.

- Take a film you know well and select an extract at random from the tape. View for 3 minutes and ask yourself what you have learned from the clip. What information does the clip provide concerning the main story or plot? What do we learn about the characters? What is exciting or interesting about the action? Does the clip *foreshadow* a future event in the film or provide *backstory* on the motivation of any of the characters? Does it pose a question? Note how much information you have gleaned from the short extract.

Characteristics of the Cinema and Television Media

Modes of Writing

Writing for film and television shares a number of features with other kinds of fiction writing. Mainstream cinema and TV forms are typically narrative – they tell stories with characters in action. There are, of course, exceptions to this generalisation. Some postmodern films (*Pulp Fiction*, for example) play with time and space to disrupt the linear narrative sequence of the text. Likewise, some postmodern TV (*Ally McBeal*, for instance) is multiply-coded, fragmented and ironic. But cinema and television remain predominantly narrative media. The appeal of digital Special Effects and the extended use of music for its own appeal must at least be set against – if not located in – a narrative. In the 'Writing On' section, we offer some exercises in postmodern modes but, for the most part, this chapter deals in popular narrative forms. It does so partly because these remain dominant in commercial writing practice but also because, if the aim is to subvert or play ironically with conventions, you need to understand those conventions in the first place.

Besides characters, action and linear narrative apart, however, there are significant differences between story-telling in prose form and film/TV narratives. The writer's keynote, 'show not tell' has particular resonance, as noted, for predominantly visual media. It used to be said that writing for the stage comprised 75 per cent words and 25 per cent visuals whilst writing for cinema was 75 per cent visuals and 25 per cent words. Television occupied centre position in the continuum at approximately 50:50 words/visuals. Today, however, TV drama increasingly aspires to the cinematic, particularly in 'one-off' slots. The single play, initially the staple of TV drama, is now increasingly rare. Screen One, Screen 2, Film on Four have gradually replaced Armchair Theatre, The Wednesday Play, Play for Today. Where once TV drama (in Britain at least) had close associations with radio and theatre and was dialogue heavy, single-play forms are now effectively films for television. In this chapter's work on structure, the 'one-off' TV vehicle will accordingly be treated as film separately from television's distinctive narrative modes.

Communicative Means

Visual 'story-showing' is vital in film and television. To mark a sharp contrast with novels, films/TV dramas have pictures, but rarely do they have an overt narrator (*Trainspotting* and its televisual derivative, *The Young Person's Guide to Becoming a Rock Star*, C4, 1998) are exceptions that prove the rule. Film and television use dialogue, visual imagery, soundtrack. Writers must convey all they want to convey, including point of view (which character you want people to like or identify with) by these means. Seeing it (as we do with TV news footage) may offer greater credibility than saying it. As TV drama increasingly approximates to cinema, visual style becomes more important in that medium too. With more information being visually conveyed, dialogue, in both film and television, is increasingly sparse. The exercises in the section on visual story-telling invite you to make the dialogue do several things at once.

Technological Forms of Cinema and Television

The technologies and viewing conditions of cinema and television remain significantly different from each other, as indicated in the table below. We have suggested that, technologically, television aspires to cinema. The current developments of digital imaging (improving image resolution), digital surround sound (improving sound quality), and widescreen TV sets (to afford cinematic 'aspect ratio': the depth of the screen image relative to its width) could make a difference to the future of television (bringing it ever closer to cinema). Time will tell, but prices will have to come down and viewing conditions change. The table below charts the differences between the two media:

CINEMA	TELEVISION
Big screen image	Small screen
High-quality image chemically produced on exposure to light and projected by light	Electronically produced low resolution pixel image but digital format much improved
Aspect ratio (depth to width) varies from 3:4 to 3.5:5 and wider in widescreen formats	Aspect ratio 4:3: traditionally 3:4 but widescreen 'cinematic' formats emergent
Digital surround sound	Poor sound quality but digital surround sound
Experienced as complete narrative	Segmented: dramas viewed in a ceaseless stream of programming 'flow' (Williams, 1984)
Audience in darkness, giving undivided attention to screen	Viewers in lit, domestic spaces with many distractions
Concentrated involvement in dreamworlds	Glance not gaze

There are implications here for the screenwriter. Cinema viewing conditions are disposed towards the undivided attention of the viewer over a sustained concentration span of one to one-and-a-half hours. The story overall needs to be gripping but, since people have paid to come in, they tend to stay and become drawn into the illusion of a possible world – unless it's truly awful. The experience of watching television, in contrast, is characteristically fragmented. Programmes are typically shorter than cinema films and interrupted both by advertisements and by domestic distractions. Thus, the means of grabbing and holding viewers' attention varies between media, with implications for structure (see below). In television, minute-by-minute analysis of viewing figures (ratings) is now undertaken by all TV companies (or their agents) to develop individual programmes and to inform schedulers' placement of slots. The consequent need for 'hits', 'hooks' and 'cliffhangers' for each narrative segment differs from the building of tensions over time in a feature film.

Structure

> When I first started writing I think I thought that structure
> was for critics. Audiences and writers didn't bother with
> it. ...When I began to explore 'structure' in my own
> way...I found it not only helped but [was] positively
> stimulating.   (Ian Heggie, 1990, p. 120)

We place emphasis upon structure because it is particularly
vital to screenwriting. Quite simply, if you can't deliver scripts
for television to suit scheduled slots or screenplays which
match the budget, then your work will not be realised. Some
writers think of structure as a constraining force inhibiting their
creative freedom. At worst, slavish adherence to established
structures can indeed lead to formulaic writing. But it need not
do so. Understanding the structural features of the medium you
aim to write for is essential. It is an aspect of the craft of writing.

Two structural models are offered here: the plot-resolution
model for film and the single TV play (or its successor, the film
for television), and the 'flexi-narrative' (Nelson, 1997) model of
popular TV dramas. We give a thorough coverage to the first
although it inevitably figures in other chapters in this book since
it is the dominant mode of narrative form in our culture. Note
that there are particular inflections and time implications of the
model as developed in film and television. Moreover, much
innovative practice FUNCTIONs in reference to this model,
if only by departing from it. Indeed the 'flexi-narrative' mode
is a compound version of plot-resolution structures. If you feel
you have fully grasped the plot-resolution model before the end
of the next section cut to the following one. Workshop exercises
to guide your practice are offered after each model.

The Plot-Resolution Model and Step-Plan Outline
cinema film, single play/film for television

While individual films exploit structure in different ways,
there are typically three elements to a story: a beginning,
a middle and an end. Nearly all mainstream narrative
screenwriting follows this pattern which we will call the

PLOT-RESOLUTION MODEL. To illustrate the point we shall trace the features of the plot-resolution model through the film *Shallow Grave*.

The beginning will establish the characters, story situation, location and tone of the film. It will probably achieve this in the first 10–15 minutes of running time but perhaps in less. We can call this 'Act One'.

The turning point from the establishing scenes into the main body of the action (the middle) will emerge through a big event or major conflict. The conflict, or big event, marks the end of the beginning, or establishing scenes, and it will imply a question. From this point you enter the action of the story as the consequences of the big event/conflict are visualised. For example, in *Shallow Grave*, the beginning includes a series of interviews for a new flatmate, his selection, and the subsequent discovery of the new flatmate dead in his room with a suitcase full of money. This situation acts as a catalyst to the main question of the film: should the protagonists keep the money or report the death and discovery of the cash to the police? The main question is resolved by the decision to keep the money, which impels the big event (the dismemberment), main action and further questions: how is the body of the dead flatmate to be disposed of, can the three protagonists hide their actions, and what impact will the cash have on their friendship? This we can call 'Act Two'.

In addition to these questions, the beginning of *Shallow Grave* also contains apparently unconnected scenes of violence and torture perpetrated by an unknown duo of thugs. Thus, the viewer is encouraged to speculate about the relationship between this duo and the main action. As the middle section of the film develops, it becomes clear that the protagonists are facing the threat of discovery not only by the police, but also by this glimpsed criminal fraternity. This sets the trio within a kind of pincer movement in which they are placed under mounting pressure from without (from both the cops and the robbers) and growing tension from within as the presence of the money causes their internal relationships to break down.

This rising pressure, and its intermittent and temporary release, generates a mounting tension as the film reaches climax. Covertly, the trio have each become committed to securing the cash for themselves and this culminates in an overt and violent showdown in which each attempts to outwit the other; this overt sequence we will call the end. The conflict of the story is at a close, the resolution is fast (approximately 10 minutes of screen time) and the *dénouement*, or return to harmony-with-difference, brief. This is 'Act Three'.

Scripting the plot-resolution model

- The script can be divided into three sections: the beginning, middle and end. The beginning will run for approximately 10–15 minutes (10–15 pages) and will culminate in a big event and major question as turning point. The middle (approximately 60–70 pages) will explore the consequences of this big event or question and will frequently involve the protagonists becoming more committed to their goals (in *Shallow Grave*, it is not until David has dismembered the corpse that he is fully committed to protecting the money; in *Gone with the Wind* [1939], it is only after Scarlet declares 'I'll never go hungry again' that she is fully bound to the story). This section of the film will also introduce and exploit subplots (see Workshop 4 below) to work with the developing narrative. The subplot both feeds and is fed by the main action; its presence can extend the story world, provide additional questions to intrigue the audience and counterpoint to the on-going action. This 'main' action will rise to a turning point at which the story reaches climax or crisis point – the worst that might happen has happened and the end (of the film) is nigh.

- In this climax (approximately 10–20 pages) the questions of the story begin to be resolved and this marks the close of the film. Resolution is generally swift because, once the questions and conflicts generated by the story have been concluded, audience interest is lost. Therefore, writers delay the final moment of resolution as long as possible. The film *Seven* (1995) exploits this technique expertly as we watch Brad Pitt decide whether or not to pull the trigger on the man who murdered his wife. This act will bring to completion the sequence of *Seven* sins illustrated in the murders of the messianic serial-killer and the audience remains locked into the question of 'will he/won't he', then, 'should he/shouldn't he' as Morgan Freeman's voice-over ends and the credits begin.

- The screenplay is 90–100 pages long and each page of script will equal one minute of screen time (see below for script layout in the established industry standard which ensures the equation of page to screen time). You need to remember this time-frame when crafting your script.

In sketch form, the plot-resolution model looks something like this:

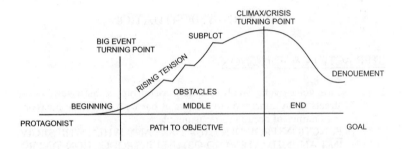

Workshop 1   The 35 Step Outline of the Plot-Resolution Model

Having looked at the map, try to follow it. It may be best to work initially with a familiar story.

Take 'Little Red Riding-Hood', 'Cinderella', 'The Three Pigs' or another well known fairy-tale as your 'story outline'. Write a brief synopsis of the story in note form. Ask yourself who is your protagonist (central character)? What is the main goal of your protagonist and what obstacles prevent that goal from realisation? What do you think the theme of the story might be? You can interpret your fairy-tale in any way you choose; you might want to emphasise one element over another in response to your understanding of the theme or to focus on one of the less familiar characters and show the story from their perspective.

Workshop 2   Marking the Steps

Having broken the synopsis down into three parts, the beginning, middle and end, set yourself the task of showing the story through 35 main events or steps; allow yourself 4–6 steps for the beginning, 25 steps for the middle and 4–6 steps for the end. Concentrate on making each of these steps visual. Don't worry about the format, notes are adequate at this stage. The example used below to assist you is for Act One of *Shallow Grave*. The upper-case comments refer to the FUNCTION of the step and underpin the action; such pointers should stimulate your thinking but are not part of the step-outline itself.

ACT ONE – THE SITUATION

STEP ACTION & FUNCTION

1   Face, voice-over [David discussing friendship] & fast visuals of the streets of an unnamed city. Arrive at flat with candidate for room, read names of occupants on name plate.
FUNCTION: PROVIDES THE WHERE AND WHEN WHILST GIVING AN INTIMATE [AND OBTUSE] INTRODUCTION TO PROTAGONISTS.

2   Interviews for new flatmate.
FUNCTION: ESTABLISHES RELATIONSHIP BETWEEN ALEX, JULIET AND DAVID.

3   Squash court discussion of their [lack of] success in finding roommate.
FUNCTION: CLARIFIES INITIAL PROBLEM – UNSUITABLE APPLICANTS FOR ROOM. DISCLOSES THE COMPETITIVE RELATIONSHIPS BETWEEN THE TRIO.

4   The arrival of Hugo. NB his self-assured manner and confidence in conversation with Juliet. Dinner with Hugo. He is asked if he ever killed a man and action switches to cashpoint scene.
FUNCTION: PROBLEM APPARENTLY SOLVED BY ARRIVAL OF HUGO WHO ACTUALLY CATALYSES THE MAIN – AS YET UNKNOWN – PROBLEM. TRIO IMRESSED BY HUGO'S CASH.

5   Cashpoint scene: mugging. Point of view of the cashpoint machine.
FUNCTION: OCCURS WITHOUT CONTEXT BUT JUXTAPOSITION SUGGESTS ACTION CONNECTED TO HUGO'S MYSTERIOUS PAST. INTRODUCES SUBPLOT.

6   Hugo moves in, is unseen for a time and then discovered dead in his locked room with a suitcase full of money.

      FUNCTION: ESTABLISHES THE MAIN DILEMMA FOR THE PROTAGONISTS – DO THEY KEEP THE MONEY AND THUS HAVE TO CONCEAL/REINVENT HUGO'S DEATH – OR NOT? MOTIVATION: GREED.

The maximum length of a screenplay is 100–110 pages, the average length being 90–100 pages. In this model, one step will translate into 3 pages of script.

The check list below might help to frame your thinking. The figures in the left-hand column refer to the amount of time dedicated to each section; the notes to the right summarise the objectives of the section.

screentime	pages	STEPS	OBJECTIVE
15 m	1–17	4–6	ACT ONE Establish situation. WHO? WHAT? WHERE? WHEN? Motivation/intention of protagonist. MAIN GOAL ESTABLISHED.
70 m	18–85	25–30	ACT TWO Complications. Obstacles. Subplot. Sequence of conflicts. WHY?
20 m	86–100	4–6	ACT THREE CRISIS POINT. CLIMAX. Will protagonist achieve goal? Resolution. [VERBAL AND ACTION] THE END

Now review your step outline and experiment with the rearrangement of events. Showing a story well is about maintaining rhythms of tension and release. Are the scenes you have outlined occurring in the best order? Do they vary pace, maintain conflict, pose questions? How might you reorder them to better effect? In practice, this is an on-going process of maximisation to which the screenwriter will return throughout.

Workshop 3   Scenes and Sequences

Having now completed your step plan, it's time to explore the dramatisation of the scenes you have established.

- Study the first 10 minutes of five movies and think through the devices used to attract the audience's attention. Make notes.

- Take Act One (the beginning) as your focus and attempt to write the opening sequence. How are we going to meet your protagonist? What are you going to reveal about her/his environment? How are you going to show her predicament? How are you going to hook your audience? Use the opening of the script to establish the particular world of your movie. (Think here of the feather which deserves an Oscar for its linking performance in *Forest Gump* [1994] or the mechanical monkey crashing its silent cymbals in *Rebel Without a Cause* [1955]. An equally good example might be the hyperreal sequence which opens *Blue Velvet* [1986].) Allow yourself an hour for this task, then reread your sequence. Read it out loud and consider your work in relation to the following questions:

    How does the opening intrigue the audience? (Think here of plot and character.)
    What kind of mood does it establish?
    What questions are posed by the sequence?
    What do we know of our central character? Is s/he interesting and engaging?
    Does the script establish motivation for your characters?

Make notes of your responses and revise your sequence.

- Repeat the exercise with other pivotal steps from your fairy-tale outline. The pivotal steps refer to those events upon which the story turns: the big event, the emergence of a major obstacle, the crisis in action which forms the climax of the script. As you re-read your scenes, ask the following questions of your work:

> Is my protagonist truly challenged by his/her situation?
> Is there conflict?
> Am I intrigued by what might come next?
> Do I care about my characters?

Workshop 4   Pace and Subplot – Increasing Complexity

> Screen time is a most mysterious thing: the same scene must be written differently depending upon where it comes in the narrative, beginning or middle or end. Because the more information an audience has, the less additional information it requires. And the ladling out of when and where something is necessary is one of the requisite components to skilful story-telling.   (Goldman, 1985, p. 120)

You will now have an opening, big event and crisis point for your movie outline. The task remains to build into and out of these pivotal moments; to craft the structure and pace of your script. As you do so, remember to vary scene length and tone. Try to contrast light scenes with dark; dialogue scenes with action scenes and to ensure that a CAUSAL relationship exists between scenes. This is also the point at which to begin to develop the subplot.

Look again at the step-outline for the opening of *Shallow Grave*. Think about how the script intercuts the scenes concerning the thugs (the cashpoint episode during the dinner with Hugo) with the main action. Initially we have no explanation of the connection between the narrative threads, rather, the cashpoint scene *foreshadows* a future connection and, as time passes, the audience recognises that this violence will emerge as interwoven with the main story. Also, remember the introduction of Cameron who is interviewed as a prospective occupant of the flat? We re-encounter Cameron in the post-dismemberment scene at the Hospital Ball where he takes his revenge on the scoffing Alex. Both of these storylines are examples of subplot.

The subplot helps to maintain interest in the main storyline and provides the opportunity for moments of tension or release throughout the course of the film. The subplot needs to be closely connected to the main events of the film and the success of the subplot can be determined by the extent to which it is woven into the main action. The presence of the subplot works rather like the flexi-narrative of television drama (see below) in terms of audience interest: it provides a wider range of engaging action and high points, it poses questions about plot developments to come and thus it allows the writer to broaden the scope (and appeal) of the screenplay. The strongest subplots develop simultaneously both their own storyline and the main action.

Exercises in subplotting

- Return to your fairy-tale scenes. Do you have a subplot in operation? Try to rewrite your opening sequence to include the introduction of a subplot. Taking Cinderella as an example, we might cut between scenes introducing us to the plight of Cinders at home with her step-family and the plans of the Prince's mother to match-make a suitable partner for her son. Perhaps the Prince is too concerned with affairs of state to consider taking a wife? Or perhaps we begin with Cinders as a baby and her own mother and father discussing her future. Was there some token of love exchanged between the parents which they pass on to their child, something Cinders could later offer to the Prince or something the step-sisters try to steal, or which Cinders sells in order to secure her survival? These are crude examples but they would establish other threads within the main story.

In *Pretty Woman* (1990), a remake of the Cinderella story, the relationship between Julia Roberts and her flatmate provides a subplot which not only serves to make clear for us how the Roberts character differs from other prostitutes but also how her friend too has dreams which can be realised. The treatment Roberts receives when out shopping in LA is a further subplot which provides both social commentary and an opportunity for a little mid-movie revenge and comic high point, while Richard Gere's business activities allow the audience to witness the ruthless nature of his world and to engage with the future of the company he is aiming to take over. The threatened company is personalised in the form of the old-school values of its President and his concern for his workforce. This subplot contributes to the romantic climax of the script in a substantial way whilst widening the presentation of its concerns.

- Re-view *Shallow Grave* or a film you know well and for which you have the screenplay; ask yourself the following questions:

    What kind of pattern of tension and release do you detect within the film?

    When and how are subplots introduced?

- How does the film suggest the internal conflicts of its characters?

- Compare the film with the screenplay and pay particular attention to scenes omitted from or rearranged within the film: why has the screenplay been edited in this way? In *Shallow Grave*, a whole storyline concerning Hugo's involvement with drugs has been cut from the film – why?

'Flexi-narrative': Popular Narrative Forms and Structures
dominant TV drama forms: **series, serials, soaps**

Broadcast television has developed its own distinctive narrative form, the soap opera, but has adapted other established forms to suit its purpose of maximising audience appeal and, therefore, numbers. Series, involving the same characters and environments, have episodes in which the key narratives are complete in themselves. Serials are ongoing narratives, developing the story, characters and perhaps the situation over a period of typically 6/7 or 13 weeks. Soaps, notionally, are endless fictions involving a group of regular characters and a common situation. In practice some narrative strands are brought to a conclusion, whilst others are left open to leave the 'cliffhanger' for the next episode. Over time, the central set of characters may change completely, but other popular characters will have been introduced in their places to draw audiences.

Increasingly typical of contemporary television is the 'flexi-narrative' (Nelson, 1997) hybrid of the series/serial form which is attractive to schedulers in its combination of 'hooks' to bring in the audience. It is the structure of this multi-narrative form that we must now address. Consider the following sketch plan:

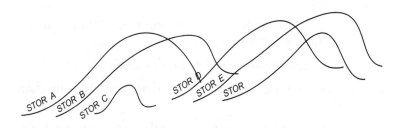

It is evident that the shape of a multi-narrative drama is made up of several Plot-Resolution models overlaid. They do not, of course, all start at the same time. It would be literally impossible to lay out the necessary exposition of five or more narrative strands simultaneously. The introduction of narratives, then, is staggered. In the above outline (based on an actual episode of *Casualty*), two or three stories are introduced and inter-cut at the outset, whilst some storylines do not start till a third to a half way through the episode. The first complete storyline (A above) in the episode – as compared with the on-going story arcs involving the series' regulars (X, Y, Z) – reaches its climax as the exposition of the new stories (D & E) is laid out. It has its *dénouement* as the new stories are beginning their ascent of complications. Storyline C is interesting. It is a narrative fragment complete in itself in one narrative bite.

Its <u>FUNCTION</u> in the *Casualty* episode is almost certainly comic relief, setting in relief, that is, the more grim stories of accidents, loneliness and family break-up.

Key features of flexi-narrative

- The pace of TV drama has increased markedly with the pace of modern communications and with people's sharpened ability to read television. On average, the 30–90 second narrative bite (similar to the speed of advertisements) is the base unit.

- Intense competition for audiences in a multi-channel TV environment has increased the need to grab and hold viewers' attention by cutting from highpoint to highpoint of the drama. The flexi-narrative form keeps the emotional temperature at a high level. It leaves out all unnecessary lead-ins/lead-outs to and from a scene and leaves the audience to imaginatively fill in the gaps.

- TV drama is written in a highly commercial context. Writers have to write accurately to suit established slots, typically 27/30 or 55/60 minutes, and in popular forms, such as flexi-narrative.

- To work to a formula does not preclude creativity and good writing. The best series' episodes are multiple-plot dramas, each narrative strand of which throws the others into relief, making the whole greater than the sum of its parts.

Workshop 1   Flexi-narrative Structure

Watch an episode of a favourite 'flexi-narrative' drama (*Casualty; London's Burning; Soldier, Soldier*, etc.). Separate out each storyline. Draw a rough diagram of the episode based on the model above. Analyse in detail the first five minutes, noting how narrative strands are inter-cut. Time each narrative segment, that is the duration of a part of one storyline before the cut to the next. (To do this for the whole episode is laborious – a lot of stop-starting and tape rewinding with a stopwatch. The first five minutes should give you sufficient insight.)

Workshop 2   Micro-stories

Write 30 one-liner storylines for a popular flexi-narrative. If it were for *Casualty*, you'd need one-liner accidents. For example:

- road builder cuts high-power electric cable with pneumatic drill – electrocuted;
- fraught mum forgets chip pan when phone rings – multiple burns;
- 'boy racer' smashes stolen car – trapped;
- frail, haemophiliac, old man gashes hand opening a can of soup – bleeding to death;
- double-decker schoolbus hits low bridge – many children injured.

Try to avoid clichés. Keep a notebook to jot down new story ideas as you hear them on the bus or in the pub, or when you read them in the newspaper.

Workshop 3   Maximum Appeal

Select five storylines to weave into an episode, bearing in mind the need to appeal to all sectors of the potential popular audience (ages, genders, cultures). Consider also possible inter-relationships or parallels between the stories such that the episode might add up to more than the sum of its parts.

Workshop 4   Multiple Plotting

Take your storylines and develop each one as a plot-resolution narrative. You need not go as far as a full step-plan, but you must be clear about the arc of each story. Choose the lead story for the episode. Draw up a chart of starting-points of each storyline.

Workshop 5   The 'Zap Factor'

Write the first four minutes of an episode of a 'flexi-narrative' series/serial familiar to you (e.g. *Casualty, Soldier, Soldier,*

London's Burning). Introduce three of your chosen narrative strands. Bear in mind that TV viewers have a lot of channel choice. If your story doesn't grab them, they'll zap to another channel with the remote. Think, too, of the need for clear but economical exposition in story-telling.

Workshop 6   Sustaining the Temperature

Proceed to develop your script, remembering that the average duration of a narrative bite in flexi-narrative is 60 seconds. A long narrative segment – perhaps for exposition when you introduce a new storyline – is unlikely to exceed three minutes. A number of 'hits' are required to sustain high emotional temperature. The key here is to cut from highpoint to highpoint of the drama of each of your storylines. Of course, some less intense moments, or comic relief, are necessary to vary the intensity.

Workshop 7   Practical Resource Check

Having completed your draft, review it in practical production terms. Although some TV drama has relatively big budgets, resources are finite. Have you introduced any unnecessary characters or locations which you can cut before the script editor gets to them? Are the scenes you have written workable in the mode of production available? If it is a multi-camera studio location with 'live editing' have you kept the scene tight and dialogue-based? If the mobility of a film camera is available, have you made the most of visual story-telling, keeping the dialogue to a minimum?

Visual Story-telling

Workshop 1   Look Again

Look again at the decision-making sequence in *Shallow Grave*. What do you notice? How much dialogue is involved? What does the soundtrack contribute to the sequence? Or again, look at the DIY store scene in which the trio get 'tooled up' for the dismemberment of Hugo. Is the tension-building of this scene a product of dialogue or visuals? Could one element retain its effect without the other? Hire the video of *Middlemarch* and look carefully at the opening sequence (see Workshop 5 below).

Workshop 2   Sound versus Visuals

Hire a film with which you are unfamiliar. Listen to the opening of the film with the TV set turned away from you. Make notes on your understanding of the film and any things you don't fully comprehend – think especially about atmosphere suggested by the music and the brevity of the dialogue. Now watch the sequence visually and aurally. Compare the two experiences.

Workshop 3   Biopics

Imagine you are to introduce yourself in a biopic (film biography) of your life. Select three objects and one event to introduce yourself to the audience WITHOUT dialogue. Write this sequence.

Workshop 4   Story-board

Draw up a story-board for an advertisement. Take a sheet of A3 paper and divide it into 24 frames of equal size. Leave space beneath each 'screen' to write directions. Tell your story in just 24 visual frames, noting in the 'directions' space the kind of shot (e.g. Close-Up, Medium Shot, Long Shot), the movement from shot to shot (e.g. CUT, DISSOLVE, X-FADE). Note also the duration of each shot (e.g. 3 seconds); the whole story should take 90 seconds. Dialogue should be kept to an absolute minimum and music, or effects soundtrack, should be employed.

Repeat the exercise to make a mainly visual version of the fairy-tale used above.

Workshop 5   Think Genre

In the opening sequence of Andrew Davies' adaptation of George Eliot's *Middlemarch*, we see 'a man riding into town'. This trope is familiar to us all in Westerns: a man rides into town to cause mayhem or to clean up corruption. But *Middlemarch* is a 'serious' novel about social reform in 1830s England, not an American Western. Nevertheless, generic thinking by the production team allowed them to turn into a visual cinematic sequence what takes thousands of words in the novel. Dr Lydgate is a young doctor seeking to reform medical care. He is coming to *Middlemarch* to set up in practice and he dreams of opening a new hospital. The opening sequence shows him approaching in a horse-drawn coach. The musical soundtrack, Vaughan Williams' 'Variations on a theme by Thomas Tallis' connotes 'Englishness'. The beat changes as the sleepy rural village is disturbed by the coach bearing Lydgate. It passes a team of workers cutting and laying the railway. Two words are uttered by Lydgate, 'the future'. In this dynamic sequence, drawing on the Western genre but adapting it to a new context, the story is located visually in its geographical and historical setting, a central character is introduced and his disposition illustrated, and a key theme of change through social reform established. Think visual, think genre. There are just two words of dialogue!

Take a novel with which you are familiar and write an equivalently economic opening sequence.

Dialogue Tips

Cinematic and televisual dialogue needs to be lean, economical and clear. It usually emulates 'natural' speech but is actually highly edited. The first step in learning to create convincing dialogue is to listen and observe. Listen to people on the bus, in MacDonalds, walking the corridors, in the bar, the supermarket ... and note not only WHAT they say, but HOW they say it. Forms of naturalism remain the dominant conventions of film and television, creating the illusion of a possible world in which we are invited to believe.

Naturalistic speech

That is speech which sounds as if it could come from the characters in the situation presented, remains the benchmark of most film and TV drama. BUT unedited everyday speech may be:

- unintelligible, because it is too disjointed, overlapping or interrupted;
- boring because it is rambling or long-winded;
- ineffective, because it doesn't move the action on.

Because visuals dominate in film and television, dialogue in good scripts is very economical, doing more than one job. Dialogue may convince us that it echoes everyday speech, then, but it is invariably shaped or stylised.

Convincing dialogue:

- Avoids proper sentences: typically we don't speak with correct grammar.

- Is disjointed, overlapping: in conversation we support, counter, affirm, make noises.

- Deploys jargon, shorthand: context permits people to use shorthand, even specific jargon. A balance must be struck, however, between a ring of authenticity and exclusion of the audience.

- Avoids 'ping pong' exchanges: such dialogue offers a feed-line (perhaps a rhetorical question) anticipating a specific answer. The 'receiver' then serves a similar cue to the 'server'. And so, boringly, the dialogue bats back and forth.

- Avoids 'caption-speak' – stating what it would be better for the audience to deduce, or the problem of characters telling each other what they already know to convey information.

- Is distinguished according to class, age, gender, regional/ ethnic origin; different registers being deployed in different situations and at different times.

- Should arise from the character in the situation.

Aim to be economical in your dialogue:

- Join the scene late and leave it early.

- Dialogue <u>FUNCTION</u>s:
    to give information
    to reveal emotion
    to advance plot
    to characterise speaker and character addressed

... and it attempts to do so in an unobtrusive manner. Strong dialogue overlaps these functions and lines develop plot and character simultaneously, thus maintaining audience interest. Make each line do more than one job (at the edit stage, cut those not doing so).

- In some genres (e.g. action/adventure) every scene must move the action on – ambiguity/implication makes an audience work hard; full explanation doesn't.

- Strive for a subtle relationship between SHOWING and TELLING: for example the characters' displaced feelings (i.e. their hidden/unconscious agenda) might come out through small action (e.g. sips from mug 'have you put sugar in my coffee again?' reveals marital tension).

Characterisation and Dialogue

No rules but a number of ideas...

- Characters may originate in many ways – you may observe an action-detail (the manner in which somebody uses a napkin, strains their tea, holds their knife, etc.) which will encourage you to explore them in your script. The more individualised a character, the more interest s/he will hold for the audience so stay with the particular and avoid stereotypes.

- What does your character care about? What are her/his concerns? How do you show them? Remember that the goals and targets of a character are illustrative of those concerns.

- Characterise your cast for diversity and contrast – this will increase conflict and widen audience appeal.

- If the aim is a certain naturalism, then your characters need to think and speak within their own frame of reference. A City stockbroker will not speak, think or behave in the same way as a Norfolk farmer.

- Know your characters' speech (vocabulary, accent, pace, rhythm, intonation), and mannerisms (physical characteristics, characteristic movements, gestures), but be careful not to overdo such 'business' as it can become tiresome.

- Remember that interest in characters is one of the principal ways of maintaining interest in your film, therefore take the time to know your creations. Research their worlds, social activities and occupations. You will learn much about your characters as your script develops but having the basic attributes outlined can help clarify your thinking and your writing.

Workshop 1 'Are You Listening Carefully?'

Tape a conversation and replay it. Transcribe it. Practise trying to emphasise and punctuate it in different ways. Note the circumstances of the speakers, focus on the degree of familiarity and intimacy that vocabulary and syntax can reveal. Then begin to edit down that dialogue and use it to generate a short scene or sequence.

In the cinema, and on television, we usually hear dialogue only once. We can't easily re-read. For sure, with video-tape at home we can rewind and replay, but typically we don't. So, keep dialogue short; one or two lines (not sentences) is a good guide. There will be exceptions but keep them to a minimum.

Workshop 2   Dialogue on Actual Lips

Dialogue reflects the speaker, her/his social context and background as well as their reactions to the present context. You need to know how your character speaks and one of the most frequent problems for the writer is creating voices and maintaining 'difference' in those voices. Imagine a supermarket checkout in which a customer does not have the cash to cover her/his bill. Create a brief exchange between the cashier and the customer in which:

(i) the cashier is a farmer's son of 17 years and the customer is a retired professor of mathematics;
(ii) the cashier is a female lone parent of 25 years and the customer is a well-dressed woman in her 40s;
(iii) the cashier is a middle-aged woman with children at university and the customer is a child of 10 years.

Difficult isn't it? To create dialogue in which you can believe you need to know much more about your characters than the information given here. You have to have a sense both of who the people are and what has brought them into the situation; you need their *backstory* and their motivation. From an exchange such as this you could create a whole story-world.

Workshop 3   Dialogue in Action

Good dialogue hooks into the action of the film. An obvious example of this would be the spoken question to which the answer may come in the form of action. In *Shallow Grave*, the initial 'cash dispenser scene' is scripted to be inserted AFTER Alex makes a comment concerning the authenticity of Hugo's money. However, the film has been edited to insert this scene as if in response to David's question to Hugo, 'Have you ever killed a man?' (Hodge, 1996, p. 145). This reordering of the initial script serves to invite the audience to be increasingly sceptical of Hugo's reliability.

Dialogue can also be deployed to provide helpful transition from scene to scene. In a further example from *Shallow Grave*,

Juliet's first meeting with Hugo concludes with his line, 'I'm in search of the self'. The next scene opens on what we take to be the next morning with Alex's line, 'Has he tried down behind the fridge? I mean that's where I normally find things' (Hodge, 1996, pp. 138–9). Here, wit and brief dialogue have made the temporal cut swift and thus made apparent the shifts in mood and tone of each situation.

If you look again at the checkout scenes you created, can you spot ways to hook the words and action together more effectively?

Workshop 4   Reworking Drafts

Film and television provide the opportunity to use action, performance, music, ambient sound, SFX, and so on to tell your story and direct attention. Dialogue is ONE of these tools but try to use as much of the medium as possible. Remember, the screenplay is NOT a filmed stageplay. Can you cut any dialogue and replace with other sound? Can the scenes or sequences you have created be reordered to better effect? Do your characters sustain audience interest? Is the plot sufficiently challenging? Is it credible? Don't be afraid to change things.

Task (a) Read your script aloud. Make a tape of the reading and review it. As you listen, note any awkward phrases or problematic transitions, and rework.

Task (b) Collect together a group of friends and/or family to read out your work. Tape the read-through and ask for comments at the close. Listen to the tape and rework.

Script Layout

Screenplay Format

Screenplays and teleplays consist of three parts: (i) Headings (also known as 'slug lines'); (ii) Description; and (iii) Dialogue.

Formats do differ. The important point is to be consistent within whichever convention you choose to use. What follows is a general guide to screenplay format. Since so much television drama is now made cinematically (i.e., shot on a single camera with post-production editing rather than edited 'live' in a multi-camera studio), most contemporary screenplays are laid out as films. A brief note on layout for television scripts follows after screenplay format.

MATERIALS
Print on white paper. Cover of coloured light card. Exclude biography, cast list/suggestions.

TITLE PAGE
Including your name and address.

FONT AND JUSTIFICATION
Use a font or typeface which is 10-pitch, such as Courier. Set this to 12-point and keep the right margin unjustified.

MARGINS
Left margin – 1.5 inches. Set at 15 from left paper edge.
Right margin – 0.5 inches. Set at 80 (8 inches) from the left paper edge. The margin is, typically, left ragged (rather than justified).

TABS
You indent to distinguish between direction, dialogue, actor's instruction and character's name. Set your tabs in the following way:

- Left margin at 15 spaces (1.5 inches) from the left edge of page.

- Dialogue at 25 spaces (2.5 inches), or 10 spaces from the left margin.

- Character's name at 37 (3.7 inches), or 22 spaces from the left margin.

- Actor's instruction at 31 (3.1 inches), or 16 spaces from the left margin.

SPACING

- Single space within an action/description and a character's name above the dialogue.

- Double space between action/description and a character's name above the dialogue.

- Single space between a character's name and her/his own dialogue.

- Double space between one character's dialogue and the name above the next character's dialogue.

- Double space between a scene heading – INT. COFFEE BAR. DAY. and the action/description passage that follows.

- If using CUT TO and FADE IN, double space between these directions and scene heading.

HEADINGS

A Master Scene heading contains three elements:
   (i) The location of the camera – is it outside or inside?
  (ii) The place.
 (iii) The time of day/night.

DIRECTIONS to the production team detail location of shot and time, i.e. INTERIOR [INT.], EXTERIOR [EXT.], STREET, BAR, CLASSROOM, DAY, NIGHT, EARLY MORNING, DUSK. These elements are given in capitals and justified to the left, e.g. EXT. CAR PARK – DAY
If a scene moves rapidly between an interior and exterior shot, then the direction
INT./EXT. may be used.
LEAVE TWO LINE SPACES AFTER THE HEADING.

DESCRIPTION

Narrative description is written in the present tense. Double space between paragraphs and do not indent. Be economical and give only the information required to progress the story while emphasising important events. Try not to exceed 4 or 5 lines, for example:

INT. VAN – NIGHT

In front of the van, David is climbing into the passenger side. Juliet and Alex are already in, with the latter at the wheel. Alex turns to the other two.

ALEX
Why don't we just draw lots for it?
(adapted from Hodge, 1996, p. 166)

Action sequences which may require a lot of screen time can be stretched out on the page by using short paragraphs.

Character names need to be given in CAPS when they make their first appearance in the script. You may also offer a brief description of the characters where relevant.

Important sound effects are given in CAPS.

DO NOT give camera directions unless essential. Use the narrative description to suggest important close-ups or wide-angle shots.

DO NOT indicate exact music playing or blasting from the radio unless relevant. LEAVE TWO LINE SPACES AFTER DESCRIPTION.

DIALOGUE
Dialogue direction contains three elements:
  (i) The character caption, or 'character cue'. This is given in CAPS.
 (ii) The actor's direction. This appears below the character name. This gives a guide to how the character should deliver a line where such information is not given in the action.
(iii) The character's speech.

VOICE-OVER
VO after character's name, for example:

RENTON
(VO)

> Choose life. Choose a job. Choose a career . . .
> (adapted from Hodge, 1996, p. 3)

OVERLAPPING DIALOGUE

Indicate this in the actor's instructions or lay out in two columns.
LEAVE TWO LINE SPACES AFTER A SPEECH.

LENGTH

90–100 pages. One PAGE tends to equal one MINUTE of screen time and studios aim for 90 minute–2 hour features. The formula permits for a little more script time than screen time. Typewritten on one side of A4 paper only.

Layout for Television

The distinctive form of script layout for television places the characters' names, in capitals, to the left of the dialogue (as in a theatre playscript) rather than above the speaker (as in a filmscript). The description of the action may be written in italics (as in playscript stage directions) rather than in capitals (as in filmscript). A margin is set to the left, where the screenplay is centred on the page. It is not necessary to leave the wide margin used by TV studio scripts to indicate camera numbers and directions in your writer's submission. The following extract from the published script version of Dennis Potter's *Cream in my Coffee* will serve as an illustration:

1. A GRAND SOUTH COAST HOTEL

A huge, white, wedding-cake of a five-star hotel, crenellated and towered, against a blue sky. We move in slowly from the sea, across the shingled beach decorated with luscious brown bodies, looking at the grand Victorian palace as though licking it, lovingly, like a huge ice-cream.

On the move, the voice of Sam Browne (with the Jack Hylton Orchestra) singing the 1930s hit 'You're the Cream in my Coffee'.

SINGER: You're the cream in my coffee
           You're the salt in my stew

> You will always be
> My necessity
> I'd be lost without you.

> You're the starch in my collar
> You're the lace in my shoe
> You will always be
> My necessity
> I'd be lost without you.
> (on the last two lines we go...)

2. INSIDE THE HOTEL: 1979

An old PORTER, in hotel livery, is trundling heavily and seemingly not too willingly along a wide hotel corridor leading endlessly away from the lifts. He is carrying two fat and obviously expensive suitcases.

Behind him, looking around them, come a man and a woman. She is in her early sixties, he is in his late sixties. They are BERNARD and JEAN WILSHER – and as though by now used to it, by a self-consciously deliberate act, they are holding hands.

BERNARD: It's a long way from the lift.
PORTER: No, it ain't. 'S only four and a half miles, sir.
  (JEAN *laughs.* BERNARD, *however, is not so sure that the answer isn't a little impertinent.*)
JEAN: (*Nervous little laugh*) Still, we came for the exercise.

(Potter, 1984, pp. 139–40)

Soundtrack

Music is not normally indicated by the writer unless it is essential to the development of plot or to achieve a necessarily distinctive style or tone. But popular music is increasingly used today for its own intrinsic appeal rather than as subordinate to the narrative, particularly in programmes aimed at 15–30 year olds (MTV is a key influence here). Remember, you should avoid trying to be director or producer, but indicate music where it is integral to your conception, or the pleasures, of the piece.

Workshop 1   Image and Sound

Take a scene from your own screenplay writing. Choose two different pieces of music to underscore the scene, each to set a different atmosphere or tone.

Workshop 2   Sound and Image

Choose a favourite piece of music. Write two scenes, one conjunctive with the music (i.e. in which the music soundtrack supports the mood of the scene as you read it), the other disjunctive (i.e. jarring with, or commenting on, the mood of the written scene).

Workshop 3   Diverse Functions

Analyse the range of uses of music in an episode of *Heartbeat* (ITV) and of *Ally McBeal* (C4).

Writing On

Workshop 1   Generating Story Ideas

Successful stories can be summarised as a series of questions. Take the phrase 'what if' and generate a central idea. You can gain practice in this kind of kick-off by suggesting the premise of existing films: for example, What if three yuppies discover their new flatmate dead – in bed – with a bag of money? Do you recognise this premise?

- Listen to the lyrics of ballads, nursery rhymes, folksongs or clapping/skipping songs. Use the often strange imagery to invent a narrative.

- Take a snippet of overheard conversation and invent a story out of this excerpt.

- Make notes on things seen or heard that strike you as provocative; that make you wonder about the history of the speaker, their home-life or background. Assemble these into short scenes and aim to weave a context for their lives.

- Steal. Look through newspapers, old magazines, history books, myths and legends. Try variations and twists of plot.

Workshop 2   Practising Narrative

Invent short summaries of the plots involved in a number of films; allow yourself a single paragraph for each movie.

Create a ONE-page synopsis of your earlier version of a fairy-tale. This should include a paragraph or two summarising the excitement of the plot and perhaps culminating in a question; a reference to the genre of the film; mention of similar films with the emphasis upon how your script differs.

Workshop 3   Mapping Tension

Taking a script you know well, map out a pattern of high-points throughout the screenplay. Look at each of these high-points and mark the beginning of their build-up in the plot (you might find it helpful to use different coloured marker-pens for this task). The high-point will reveal a pattern of increasing tension culminating in resolution and this exercise will help you to see how the plot and subplot interweave to create audience interest. You could also mark out scenes and sequences which vary the pattern of increasing tension in the form of comic relief or a 'spectacle' episode.

Workshop 4   Adaptation

Compare a novel or short story with the film adaptation constructed from it. The adaptation process has much to teach the writer new to the screenplay because you are able to see more clearly those elements of the original story which have been translated into film and thus have screen potential. Look closely at how the film affirms the story and to what extent it makes changes to it. Experiment with sample scene adaptations or alternative adaptations. Jeanette Winterson's *Oranges Are Not The Only Fruit* (1985) offers a good example for study since the novel, playscript, video-tapes and an essay on the process of adaptation by Winterson herself (see Giles and Licorish, 1990, pp. 59–65) are all available.

Workshop 5   Postmodern TV 1: Playing with Time

Another kind of postmodern film and television is *non-linear* in narrative. In the context of the dominant plot-resolution model, shifts in time (flashbacks and jumps through time) are signalled to the audience (through dissolving of the image or fading/cutting to black) so that the audience's sense of progression through linear time is maintained. Echoing, perhaps, the notions of postmodern theorists of the end of history (Fukuyama) or that faith can no longer be sustained in *Grand Narratives*, overarching explanatory accounts (Lyotard), sense-making frames based on linear time may be abandoned.

Return to your version of a fairy-tale and make a list of each key narrative segment (e.g. establishing scene, big event, goal, conflict resolution). Develop subplots, if you have not done so already, and make a similar narrative breakdown. Now cut up your segments and, blind and at random, place them in a new order. Consider the effect of the new narrative non-logic. Does it matter that the narrative does not 'make sense' in linear time? Are other pleasures brought into play?

Workshop 6   Postmodern TV 2: Genre Splicing

Re-read the notes on genre near the beginning of the chapter and watch *The Player*, if you have not already done so. Though mainly for commercial reasons, the producers in that movie are seeking to splice genre X with genre Y to come up with what we might call a postmodern blockbuster, Z. At the theoretical level of film and television studies, there are interesting questions about Z. Is it a 'bricolage', a juxtaposition of snippets of material borrowed from disparate sources without any attempt to harmonise them into a new whole? Alternatively, is it a *syncretic* hybrid, an innovative postmodern form in spite of the fact that traces of the source material are in evidence?

A good example is David Lynch's *Twin Peaks*, the very project of which, 'was to mix a police investigation with a soap opera...Dana Ashbrook, who played Bobby, described *Twin Peaks* as a cross between *Peyton Place*, the well-known 60s soap opera...and *Happy Days*, the 80s sitcom series set in the 50s, but with a touch of vitriol' (Chion, 1995, pp. 103–4).

Have fun, by taking two favourite films or TV series from the past and reworking scenes from them into a new hybrid.

Workshop 7   Postmodern TV 3: 'Pastiche' and 'Intertextuality'

This workshop may be taken as an extension of the previous one or be the stimulus for a new project. In constructing your new hybrid, feel free to 'borrow' sequences and images in a way sufficiently evident that initiates will recognise your 'intertextual' play with previous filmic or televisual tropes. Jameson rather negatively speaks of pastiche occurring where, 'the producers of culture have nowhere to turn but the past: the imitation of dead styles, speech through all the masks and voices stored up in the imaginary museum of a now global culture' (1993, pp. 17–18). Devotees of *Twin Peaks*, and other postmodern TV serials or movies, see more fun in a situation where modern recording technologies bring the histories of images and sounds worldwide simultaneously into the present. For the quotations and allusions in *Twin Peaks*, see Chion (1995, pp. 113–14).

Begin by constructing a 24-frame storyboard of images and sounds which allude to film and television familiar to you. Build up a script idea from there. The process might be likened to music sampling or 'grabbing' sounds, and images, from the stock nowadays so readily available in electronic forms. A collage or bricolage is constructed and reworked.

Workshop 8 Postmodern TV 4: Double-coding or Multi-tracking

Watch an episode of *Ally McBeal*. This form of TV extends the idea of 'doing more than one thing at once' in the sections on dialogue and hybridity above. The dialogue itself may be double-coded, written with an irony inviting it to be read in more than one way. The ironic, double-coded style of present-ation rests on assumptions about a tele-literate audience. It simultaneously offers different kinds of pleasures to a range of different viewers. The whole script may be multi-tracked. In *Ally McBeal*, on one track, the episode deals with a serious social issue (the law case in question). On another track, the narrative is 'soapy', concerning whether Ally will find Mr Right. Ally is thus at once an independent professional lawyer determining her own future and sexual preference, and a vulnerable young woman prey to a host of insecurities pass-ively waiting for her life to be transformed by a prince's kiss. On yet another track, *Ally McBeal* offers the attractions of MTV in its use of music interludes.

Devise a serial drama of this kind. Write an episode which is simultaneously funny and deals with a serious social issue. Include as many popular music opportunities as possi-ble. Sell the idea to an American production company at a high price!

Glossary

ambient sound   The background sound which is audible in the general environment. Because microphone technique for dialogue in film and television typically allows us clearly to hear what is being said, we sometimes forget it is a convention of sound reproduction to suppress ambient sound with a unidirectional microphone.

aspect ratio   Indicates the shape of the picture, the depth of the screen relative to its width. Since the shape of the picture can influence our feelings towards the scene it contains, aspect ratio matters. The standard 4:3 proportions of television differ from some cinemas' 3.5:2.5, though widescreen TV has been introduced as television becomes increasingly cinematic.

backstory Information offered during the course of the film which provides background to and/or motivation for an event or action.

bricolage A compositional principle drawing on materials from a range of disparate sources set side by side without any attempt to harmonise the fragments into a new syncretic 'whole'.

cinema A building in which films are shown.

close-up (shot scale) Face or object fills the frame.

dénouement A term for narrative fictions covering the bringing to resolution and closure (typically of narrative and meaning) of the story. Literally, from the French, 'untying the knot'.

diegetic/non-diegetic Terms used to describe what is within the imaginary world of the screen story, and what lies outside it: e.g. if a character switches on the radio and the soundtrack the audience hears is that coming from the radio, then the music/speech is **diegetic**. If music heard by the audience is not located in the world of the film, then it is **non-diegetic**.

film Throughout the chapter we refer to film as the stream of images and sounds experienced at the showing of a movie (irrespective of the recording medium, celluloid or video-tape, or the means of dissemination: cinema or television).

foreshadow Indicates information, the full significance of which only becomes apparent as the narrative unfolds.

FX (SPFX) Special Effects.

Grand Narratives A term coined by Lyotard (*Grand Récits*) to denote the major 'totalising' interpretative stories cultures tell about themselves. In Western culture, the Marxist accounts of history or scientific rationalism's claim eventually to resolve all problems are two examples. Lyotard holds that Western culture can no longer sustain belief in these overarching, catch-all accounts.

intertextuality Indicates that individual examples of texts relate at least as much to other texts already written as they do to any 'real' world of phenomena. The term is interpreted in a range of different contexts, but serves here to remind creative writers that, no matter how original their work, they inevitably draw to an extent on previous linguistic tropes and forms.

long shot (shot scale)   A shot from a wide camera angle setting the full figure of the character against the environment.

medium shot (shot scale)   Cuts the character off at the waist.

non-linear   Sequential representations of experience according to principles which contradict the conception of progress through linear time (beginning–middle–end). Adopted by writers of fiction partly in reaction against Grand Narratives and partly against the tendency of realism to make sense of experience through a sequence of action/events set in linear time leading to narrative closure. Postmodern strategies often dislocate time (and space).

protagonist   A term for the central character in a narrative fiction who is frequently the driving force of the action.

SFX   Sound Effects.

shot scale   The range of different shots used in film/televison and scaled to the human body (though the subject may be a building or object) relative to the frame. Since the cinema screen and the TV screen are vastly different in size, the scales vary slightly between the two mediums.

syncretic   Seeking to reconcile, or merge, disparate beliefs, practices, philosophies.

Booklist

Cook, P. (ed.), *The Cinema Book* (British Film Institute, London, 1985).

Chion, M., *David Lynch* (British Film Institute, London, 1995).

Giles, P. and Licorish, V., *Debut on Two: A Guide to Writing for Television* (BBC Books, London, 1990).

Goldman, W., *Adventures in the Screen Trade: A Personal View of Hollywood and Screen Writing* (Futura, London, 1985).

Heggie, I., 'Structuring Your Story' in Giles, P. and Licorish, V., *Debut on Two: A Guide to Writing for Television* (BBC Books, London, 1990).

Hodge, J., *Trainspotting & Shallow Grave* (Faber & Faber, London, 1996).

Jameson, F., *Postmodernism, or, The Cultural Logic of Late Capitalism* (Verso, London, 1993).

Neale, S., *Genre* (British Film Institute, London, 1980).

Nelson, R., *TV Drama in Transition* (Macmillan, Basingstoke and New York, 1997).

Potter, D., *Waiting for the Boat* (Faber & Faber, London, 1984).

Reynolds, P. (ed.), *Novel Images: Literature in Performance* (Routledge, London, 1993).

Swain, D.V., *Film Scriptwriting: A Practical Manual* (Focal Press, Boston & London, 1988).

Trottier, D., *The Screenwriter's Bible* (Silman–James Press, New York, 1995).

Welsh, I., *Trainspotting* (Minerva, London, 1996).

Williams, R., *Television, Technology and Cultural Form* (Fontana, London, 1984).

Suggested Reading

Dancyger, K. and Rush, J., *Alternative Scriptwriting: Writing Beyond the Rules* (Focal Press, Boston/London, 1995).

Ellis, J., *Visible Fictions* (Routledge & Kegan Paul, London, 1982).

Hauge, M., *Writing Screenplays That Sell* (Elm Tree Books, London, 1989).

Jenkins, G., *Stanley Kubrick and the Art of Adaptation* (McFarland & Co., North Carolina and London, 1997).

Mehring, M., *The Screenplay: A Blend of Film Form and Content* (Focal Press, North Carolina and London, 1990).

Pike, F. (ed.), *Ah! Mischief: The Writer and Television* (Faber & Faber, London, 1982).

Filmography

Blue Velvet (1986). Dir. David Lynch, script by David Lynch.

Forrest Gump (1994). Dir. Robert Zemeckis, script by Eric Roth from the novel by Winston Groom.

Gone with the Wind (1939). Dir. Victor Fleming (and George Cukor, Sam Wood), script by Sidney Howard (and others) from the novel by Margaret Mitchell.

Jurassic Park (1993). Dir. Steven Spielberg, script by Michael Crichton and David Koepp from the novel by Michael Crichton.

Middlemarch (BBC & WGBH Boston, 1994). Screenplay Andrew Davies; directed Louis Marks.

The Player (1992). Dir. Robert Altman, script adapted by Michael Tolkin from his own novel.

Pretty Woman (1990). Dir. Garry Marshall, script by J.F. Lawton.

Pulp Fiction (1994). Dir. Quentin Tarantino, script by Quentin Tanantino and Roger Avary.

Rebel Without a Cause (1955). Dir. Nicholas Ray, script by Stewart Stern, story by Nicholas Ray.

Shallow Grave (1994). Dir. Danny Boyle, script by John Hodge.

Seven (1995). Dir. David Fincher, script by Andrew Kevin Walker.

Titanic (1997). Dir. James Cameron, script by James Cameron.

Tootsie (1982). Dir. Sydney Pollack, script by Larry Gelbart and Murray Shisgal.

Trainspotting (1996). Dir. Danny Boyle, script adapted by John Hodge from the novel of the same title by Irvine Welsh.

Useful Sites

Cyberspace Film School: www.hollywoodu.com/hfi/.

The Screen Writing Center: www.clearstream.com

Video Plus Direct: HYPERLINK http://www.videoplusdirect.co.uk www.videoplusdirect.co.uk (for all films available on video in the UK).

9 | Drama: Writing for Stage and Radio

MARY LUCKHURST

> In everyday life, 'if' is a fiction, in the theatre 'if' is an experiment. In everyday life, 'if' is an evasion, in the theatre 'if' is the truth. When we are persuaded to believe in this truth, then the theatre and life are one. (Peter Brook)

Drama, according to contemporary theatre histories, has its roots in ritual; in the sacrifices and celebrations held in the name of the ancient gods and in the music, dancing, chanting and singing of a communal act of worship. The doing or 'drama' of these acts can be seen as a profound expression of the respective culture. It has the potential to be both sacred and blasphemous. It may summon up forces that are both light and dark. It may be both idyll and nightmare. It may reassure or chill the blood. Western theatre then, as an organised form of entertainment held in specifically designed buildings, has grown from this – and some would say has been trying to get back to it ever since.

Against this backcloth the writer of drama has often been compared to an alchemist or a sorcerer in their ability to weave spells with words. Words that fly off the page into the mouth of an actor and seemingly take on a life of their own; all the more powerful precisely because they are delivered live and charged with all the intensity of a moment that will never be relived; all the more powerful because they become part of the flesh and body of that actor and demand an emotional response. Words resonate in theatre: they can fly, they can bludgeon, and they can heal. A dangerous place then, theatre,

245

a knife-edge. Certainly. But it's also a place of anarchy and fun. And whilst you, as a member of the audience, have been seduced by the magic and mystery of it all, the playwright, actors, director, set designer and technical crew have pooled their crafting skills and worked on every detail in advance.

This 'danger' in the precariousness of the moment is something unique to theatre. Whilst film and radio drama can work the same powerful effect with words, and film can do yet more with image, they happen once and we watch or listen to the recording. With theatre you were either there or you weren't; you either experienced it or you didn't. This sense of living in the moment brings an intensity to stage performance which cannot be wholly matched by other media.

Whether you want to write for stage or radio it goes without saying that you are writing not for a reader, who has the privilege of controlling time, but for a spectator and/or listener, who is at the mercy of time. This means that you will have to train your eye and ear in linguistic and imaginary realms that are specific to the writing of drama. A sense of your audience is crucial: it is they who measure your success, not publication. Nor can you afford to work in the isolation associated with writing prose or poetry; horrible though it may be to acknowledge, you cannot even afford to regard yourself as the absolute guru of your own work. What you must always bear in mind is that in traditional models of drama the written script is only the first stage in a whole sequence of artistic processes. It goes like this:

1 the writer and the text;
2 interpretation by a director/radio producer;
3 delivery/performance by the actor/s;
4 post-production editing in radio;
5 reception by the audience.

As you can see, drama is above everything else a collaborative process. This can be either a delight or a nightmare depending on the relationships fostered with your collaborators, and new writers often find it extremely difficult to let go of their work and entrust it to another's hands. Don't be lured into thinking that because you can write you can also direct: the two skills entail quite separate talents, and a writer may be too involved with their work to stand back and pass critical judgement on it. A director's strength lies in their vision, in the power to make your words come alive. A talented director will make you see perspectives in the writing and staging that you didn't even realise were there, opening new horizons; a poor director will close down your work and enfeeble it. Remember though that very little can be done to make a bad script work! If you have no or little experience of watching a director at work in the rehearsal room, ask whether you can sit in on a local production; it doesn't matter whether the production is amateur or professional – you'll find that it makes you think about all sorts of technicalities which you might otherwise have overlooked such as the construction of character, the clarity of your writing, the eloquence of the human body and patterns of movement, the significance of stage props and so on. Many established writers have spent hours and hours simply watching directors and actors at work on a text. Every director will have a different slant on a play and a different idea of how that play may be approached and you'll certainly need to think about the style of direction when you write your play. A book like *On Directing* (Giannachi and Luckhurst, 1999) will give you fascinating insights into the way leading directors work in the rehearsal room.

Why sit down and write a stage play? One reason is that drama is the most public of all the arts, and the most direct. A play, the great practitioners have always told us, is life distilled and intensified: it is a story about a particular understanding of life and human kind. At its best it is an explosive concoction and can have a powerful effect on its audience. The finest plays come from a writer's most passionate desire to represent or question something vitally important to them. You take your characters and your audience on an intellectual and emotional journey; and with radio you have the added advantage of reaching an audience of millions.

If you are very familiar with stage and radio drama you will be aware that it is conventionally made up of certain components. Traditionally you would expect to find all or some of the following:

- action
- structure
- plot
- theme
- character
- dialogue
- conflict
- suspense

None of these elements could stand on its own, many of them are interdependent and can work with each other in a myriad of combinations. I will say a little about each of these elements here and in the workshops that follow, but you should be exploring them all the time in your own reading and writing.

According to Aristotle's *Poetics*, a play is 'a representation of man in action' in which the so-called three unities should be consistent in time, manner and action. Unity of time demands that all action in the play happens in 24 hours or less; unity of place insists on a single location; and unity of action requires the play to dramatise only one central story and eliminate action not strictly necessary to the plot. Whilst post-Aristotelian drama has radically challenged these notions, you may still find the philosophy behind the unities a guide in your writing: the compression of these three elements unquestionably focuses and heightens dramatic energy. Clearly film action does not conform to this logic, though you will find films where some or all of the unities have been observed. Breaking the unities still means that you must structure your work tightly, and you must know the chronological order of the action, especially if you rupture it with flashback or parallel narratives. Remember too, that action in drama occurs in the present. By this I mean the point of action that you have chosen to depict, the momentum behind your plot. Look at Arthur Miller's stage play *Death of a Salesman* which takes place in the last two days of the protagonist's life; we do travel back in time, but only through the character's imagination. For this reason beware of writing plays in the past tense: you should probably be writing a novel!

The architecture of plot and structure in drama is a complex matter and gives both new and experienced writers headaches. Radio plays rely entirely on the exchange of words and the creation of a sound and mindscape. Whatever the role of dialogue in your work it must be placed within an organised frame. This frame or structure may be organised in acts and scenes, and its shape will depend on your plotting of action. Your plot is your master plan and organises the development of your story; it drives everything forward, develops characterisation and demonstrates the theme of your work in action. A gripping plot is one which makes use of conflict and suspense as a means of heightening the dramatic potential of your work. You have to keep us guessing. Even Samuel Beckett's famous play, *Waiting for Godot*, which overturns many conventional theatrical expectations and revolves around two people waiting for someone who never arrives, is structured to maximise conflict between character and circumstance, between the characters themselves, and between audience expectation and actual experience. Watching this play we want to believe that Godot will finally arrive – but he doesn't. That tension is all-important – we want to find out who this mysterious person is but we never do.

For years there has been a debate about which matters more: plot or character. I don't know that this is a useful line to follow: neither can exist without the other and both should enrich each other. Certainly, Western drama has seen a general historical development from the portrayal of stock and aristocratic characters to an emphasis upon the psychology of a chosen individual drawn from a wider class, racial or cultural range. There are some basic points you may find helpful. First, characters who are in conflict provide a dramatic dynamic. Second, a protagonist who undergoes change is usually compelling in a way that a static character is not. And third, it is your character's actions that are important, whether verbalised as in radio, or both verbalised and physicalised as in stage and film. What I am outlining here is a cause and effect approach to character inherited from the late nineteenth century, though playwrights such as Bertold Brecht, Harold

Pinter, Caryl Churchill, Marguerite Duras, Samuel Beckett and Sam Shepherd have interrogated the 'fixed' self that the notion of 'character' pre-supposes.

I have left the most important point on the list until last. What is your play about? What is its theme or underpinning idea? Henrik Ibsen's play *The Doll's House*, for example, is clearly exploring the social and political oppression of middle-class women in the late nineteenth century and is asking whether they can find fulfilment in their own right. If you can't answer for your theme then none of the other elements on the list can function. The theme of your drama will relate to your purpose in choosing a dramatic form. What is your purpose? For Brecht theatre was a place which could effect political change: far from being a place where we suspend our disbelief, it is an opportunity to see things at a distance and rationalise our place in the world. For the Brazilian playwright and director, Augusto Boal, performance can be a model for revolution. For Vaclav Havel theatre was a place to counter the communist regime. For Harvey Fierstein theatre is the place to rage against public indifference to AIDS.

To enjoy success in your playwriting you must inform yourself about theatre history and dramatic traditions. In England plays commonly take place in purpose-built buildings which usually have proscenium arch stages, and audiences and actors alike have certain expectations about how the performance will proceed: for example, the actors will normally remain on the stage and not 'break' the so-called fourth wall (the imaginary sheet of glass filling the proscenium arch); the auditorium is normally darkened during performance, and most plays are written and acted in realist modes. Increasingly, individuals are challenging these expectations and mixing together different performance traditions, dance and text, music, mime and text, circus skills and text, film and live performance and so on; but to write a meaningful play or performance text you must have an understanding of the theatrical culture in your country, of what these styles mean and how they can be combined.

In the West plays have also traditionally been classified into specific genres. The systems of categorisation are over-simplistic but as a writer you need to know where you locate yourself between the poles of 'pure' comedy and 'pure' tragedy. For Aristotle tragedy is the rise and fall of a noble aristocrat or a great public figure of male birth (Aristotle considered women unsuitable subjects for tragedy) and ends in death – think of Othello and Hamlet. Tragedy therefore stressed the public, regnal aspects of the protagonist. Comedy, on the other hand, is the reverse, fall and rise, and revolves around the middle and lower social orders – traditional plots involving a man and a woman falling in love, opposition to their love which threatens disaster, a happy resolution to the opposition, and the marriage of the couple concerned – think about Shakespeare's *Much Ado About Nothing*. Needless to say nearly all the great dramatists play with generic expectations in sophisticated ways and many mix tragic and comic elements together in audaciously experimental work – Shakespeare was a master at it, and so was Chekhov, as his play *The Cherry Orchard* reveals. Over the centuries different dramatists have extended the tragic subject to include the middle and lower classes, women, and the ethnic minorities. Far from representing the tragic protagonist as heroic, late twentieth-century dramatists are more likely to portray an anti-hero or anti-heroine alienated by the world in which they find themselves. Is Beckett's *Waiting for Godot* a tragedy or a comedy? There are recognisable elements of both traditions but the whole question of tragic action is problematised. Brecht rejected conventional tragedy because he saw it as individualistic and bourgeois; as a marxist he wanted to depict a larger social canvas and debunk the values of aristocrats and money-grabbers. Boal's 'invisible theatre' took the form of unofficial impromptu performances on the streets of Brazil in order to protest against state controls. If you intend to challenge the conventions of play and theatre-making you must understand how and why you are doing it: most new writers only imagine they do, and most new writers do not even think about genre. If you are writing a comic play make a point of informing yourself of the latest developments and trends, read or go and see the work of Michael Frayn, Joe Orton, Oscar Wilde, Noel Coward, Molière, Ionesco, Alan Bennett, Alan Ayckbourn, Sue Townsend and Terry Johnson. Think about the differences between farce (of Latin derivation, *farcire* – to stuff), black comedy, melodrama, the grotesque, comedy of the Absurdist school, romantic comedy, comedy of manners, satire (Latin *satira* – a medley) and so on. Think about forms of tragedy in the late twentieth century, and read up on the literary history of tragedy as well as the theory – again Aristotle's *Poetics* is a good place to start. What do you know of movements such as Absurdism, Expressionism, Realism, Physical Theatre, Surrealism? The apprenticeship of the playwright is long because you need to know what all the ingredients are before you can cook with them.

Since the 1960s theatre-making has been challenged radically by Postmodernism. Theatre, for some practitioners, is more about the preservation of an elite which privileges the written word above movement, gesture, music and visuals. For the avant-garde a 'play' has come to be associated with structures and formulae which are perceived as inhibiting; the word 'performance' is often used in preference to 'drama' so that it can be opened up to other art forms such as dance, poetry and visual art. The influence of film-making has become very apparent in the fashionable 1990s generation of English playwrights from the Royal Court Theatre – dialogue is often sparse and secondary to visuals, as in the work of Sarah Kane and Mark Ravenhill. An emphasis has been placed on the actor's body as opposed to the actor's character. Site-specific work carried out in areas that are not designated theatre spaces continues to blossom, especially away from London.

Whilst shifts are taking place this is an age that finds room for old and new and revels in diversity. Take your pick. Finally, do your research on the profiles of the theatres you are sending work to. Every theatre has its specific community and puts on plays informed by its audience and its profile. Find out about the theatres which are interested in new work and then find out what sort of new work they look for. Many theatres now have literary managers and dramaturgs who are employed especially to nurture promising writers – these people may be your most important link to theatre and can advise you on companies that specialise in developing new writers. Similarly, make sure you know the guidelines that the BBC issue for radio playwrights; plays have to fit certain slots in the programming schedule and different slots highlight different types of play – which slot are you writing for? Make a note of the producer of any radio play you listen to and enjoy – it's worth sending your play to a named producer. You should also follow conventions regarding the presentation of your work: sloppily fashioned work is not only unprofessional but it also reveals to the reader that you're not serious enough about your writing to inform yourself of protocol and you need to avoid negative first impressions at all costs.

Workshop Writing

1 Stage and Radio: Writing a Monologue

I always use writing monologues as a way into writing for performance: it is an unintimidating start and a form many writers grasp with comparative ease. A monologue is a performance piece delivered by a single actor: it might be anything from two minutes to one hour long. I find that writers can totally focus on character without any of the initial anxiety about plot, structure and visuals. Let your imagination go: try to find the authentic voice of your character and simply let them tell a story in their own words. The following exercise asks a series of questions. Use them as a springboard into your character and their story. Write in the present tense in the first person. There are five stages; spend ten minutes writing for each one.

(a) *Where am I?*
This question implies that your character is in unfamiliar surroundings. Describe the environment through sensory perception. Example: It is dark. When I stretch out my right hand I can feel the coarse cool surface of a brick wall.

(b) *What's that noise?*
Example: It comes and goes and I have to concentrate until there is a pain in my head, but – yes, there it is again; a faint scratching, like a mouse pitter-pattering across bare floorboards.

(c)   *Why didn't I tell X ...?*
Fill in X for your character; it might be a parent, or a lover, or a friend. This is a longing and perhaps a memory for your character so take us back there, paint a vivid image of the remembered person and situation. Example: Why didn't I tell my daughter more about myself? I've always lied to her, always.

(d) *What's this feeling?*
Is your character hungry, exhausted, in pain? Describe.

(e) *What's happening now?*
Describe an external occurrence of some sort. Try to conclude your monologue at a natural point, round it off if you can. Example: 'There is a sudden beam of light and I shade my eyes. The door is wide open, a silhouette in the corridor. They have come to take me away, I know it.'

Taking one stage at a time, read your versions out to each other. How do the characters and the narratives vary? Did one of the group create a particularly effective voice – if so, how? Did you find one section more difficult to write than another – if so why? What sort of atmosphere were you hoping to create? Was your monologue for radio or stage? Explain your choice. Speculate on how you might continue with your own and each other's work.

2   Stage and Radio: Practising Dialogue

All good dialogue is honed down to achieve maximum effect no matter how 'realistic' it may sound: this is just as true of Ibsen as it is of soap operas like *EastEnders*. You want dialogue that pushes the plot on, and reveals something about the characters while sustaining suspense and raising more questions than answers. Remember what is not said (subtext) can be an extremely useful dramatic tool:

(B *is poring over a letter.*)
A: Who's it from?
   (*Silence*)
B: Why?

A: Who's it from?
B: No one you know.
A: So why the secrecy?
B: What?
A: You tried to hide it.
B: It doesn't concern you.
A: Your hands are shaking.
B: Stop this!
A: We share everything, remember?
   (B *sets fire to the letter with a lighter. They watch it burn.*)
B: You share everything. Not me. You.

Clearly B is unwilling to reveal some piece of information to A and this is creating an interesting set of tensions. As yet we don't know what the subtext is: maybe B has received a declaration of love from A's partner; or has B received news of a posting abroad? or is it a letter connecting B with a past they would rather forget? As you write you have to pace the new pieces of information. Don't plunge into exposition. It would be a mistake, for example, to start with:

B: I'm reading a letter about my father's death.

You kill any sense of mystery and tell us what's happening rather than *demonstrating* it through the character's reaction to the news.

A Now continue the dialogue between A and B, forcing a confrontation between them. Neither of them is allowed more than three sentences per speech. Write about five pages, more if you can. Aim to have a climax on the last page: by climax I mean a high point in the confrontation. Don't edit as you go along, or be perfectionist. Write it straight out, keeping your stage directions minimal and describing essential action only.
B Read what you have written carefully and out loud. Does it sound convincing or is it awkward, perhaps too prosodic or verbose? Edit it to sound as clean and straightforward as possible. You'll notice that short, sharp sentences give dialogue an extra intensity and thrust.

C What is your climax? Perhaps one of them walks out on page 5. Perhaps A loses their temper and makes an irrevocably wounding remark. Whatever your climax is, do you build up to it and exploit the dramatic potential of the situation? Add any lines you feel you need and cut those you don't.

D Read your piece out loud again. Try and edit it down further. Does the tension of your dialogue build up? Perhaps your two characters scream at each other for four pages. This is no good. Drama builds up subtly. A single expletive can be powerful on stage. If your piece is full of expletives, cut them and delay the strong language until the end of the scene.

E Now write another page in which there is a mood change. Perhaps one of them starts to cry. Perhaps A reveals that they knew all along what the letter said. This is a plot twist: how effective can you make it?

F If your piece is for stage how would it need modifying for radio or vice versa?

3   Stage: Practising Dialogue

This piece involves three performers: A, B and C. The situation is that all three are lost, and all three react in different ways:

A tends to be insecure and pessimistic about ever finding the way to their destination.

B is garrulous and persuasive and constantly cooking up schemes to save them from despair.

C is clear-thinking and independent and the most practical of the three.

Write a dialogue between the three of them starting with the line:

A: We've lost our way.

You must include one prop: this might be a map or a water bottle; or it might be part of the set, a tree or a broken sign-post.

Include simple stage directions where necessary. Write for an hour. Try to think about some of the following points as you write.

- Are your voices distinct from each other?

- Does one of the characters talk less than the others? How might this affect the piece? Perhaps B grows increasingly nervous and begins to babble, not noticing that the other two aren't listening.

- How do the different actions of the characters strengthen the narrative? Perhaps A sits apart and sulks. Or maybe C keeps a constant watch for signs of life on the horizon.

- Where is the power base in your piece? Who of the three is in control? Maybe C has difficulty hiding his contempt for A. Perhaps B is attracted to A and seeking to impress.

- What sex are A, B, and C? What energies does this set up?

- Have you exploited your one prop for all it's worth? Maybe there's a quiet battle going on for ownership of the map until A tears it up in a fit of pique. Or does B undertake an energetic search for the missing letters of the sign-post? Whatever your prop is it should be integral to the action and the situation.

- Do you reach a resolution? Do your characters move on? Do all of them move on? Perhaps C decides that they stand more chance of survival on their own and leaves the other two. Or is yours a circular piece which ends as it started?

4   Stage and Radio: Where to Begin

The starting point of any drama is crucial. Often new writers have fascinating material at their fingertips but don't know how to find an angle on it. Unavoidably there is exposition in the initial scenes of any stage, film or radio play, but it doesn't have to be laboriously executed. Remember these two points. First, plunge your audience straight into the drama. Second, don't fall into the trap of telling us so much that we can anticipate exactly what is going to happen. Learning to keep a balance between asking questions of your audience and answering them comes with practice. A mystery has us all on the edge of our seats. Effectively, writing drama is like learning how to dangle a carrot in front of your audience at just the right point!

Write six scenes of a stage or radio script involving a kidnap. Your script must have only two speaking characters. Where do you start? Many dramas begin *after* a significant piece of action. For instance, you could begin with a dramatic chase just after the kidnap, or with the victim coming round in a dark room not knowing where they are.

Now write the six scenes of your script again, taking your second character's viewpoint. Try to dramatise the situation. Perhaps your kidnapper is seen breaking into the house, or something goes wrong in the plan.

Compare the two scripts. Which is the most dramatic and why?

5   Stage and Radio: Structure and Plot

Form is vital in playwriting. How you shape and control the dramatic energy in your writing will be the decisive factor in whether or not it works as a piece of drama. There are traditional structures for plays: division into acts and/or scenes. The most common forms are still the three- and five-act plays, but you will also find one-, two- and four-act plays. You will also find twentieth-century plays that are composed of scenes only. These divisions are a means of blocking out your plot which will unavoidably have a beginning, a middle and an end – even if you choose an open ending (unresolved) as opposed to a closed ending (resolved). Look at a traditional dramatic narrative, an example of the 'well-made play'. We have:

- The set-up. A lead into the dramatic scenario and information on the characters involved in it.

- A crisis or climax.

- A resolution, or a pulling together of the plot.

In a sentence, most plots involve a protagonist seeking a particular goal, who either achieves or fails in that objective. Hamlet learns that his father was murdered by the present King; Hamlet confronts the King with his deed via a group of travelling performers; Hamlet kills the King and dies himself. This is the main plot and all the subplots feed into it.

Whether you stick to a conventional narrative or not your play must have a dramatic impulse; by this I mean the fundamental dynamic that is propelling your plot forwards. Romeo and Juliet desperately want to be together but are victims of their warring families. It is their overwhelming desire to be together no matter what the consequences that hurtles the play towards its tragic climax. Every character sheds a different light on Romeo and Juliet's situation, and often their words and actions affect the lovers directly. Remember that in your play nothing should go to waste: every scene, every line, should form a vital part of the whole. Focus is the key.

- Read Frederico García Lorca's *Blood Wedding* or *Yerma*. Discuss the economy of structure and analyse the way in which the tragic endings are reached. How does use of theme and symbol play a role in the overall structure?

- Now write a mini three-act play. Each act lasts five minutes. Dramatise a complete narrative. In the first part set up the characters and the problem, have a climax in the second part and try for a resolution in the third act, whether happy or sad. Take the plot of one of the above plays or invent your own.

6   Stage: Body, Object and Space in Performance

You may find that text is not always the first way into your performance piece. In devised work text is simply one element amongst other components that form the piece. Companies such as Théâtre de Complicité, The Right Size, Improbable Theatre and the David Glass Ensemble are representative of a renaissance of interest in mime, gesture and movement: sometimes there is very little text at all.

What you must not forget in your performance writing is the notion of spectacle. We go to *see* a play or a performance, and not solely to hear it. Often new writers will write televisually and write a two-hour piece between characters who are static. You must think about what your performers/actors are doing. Stillness and silence can also be very powerful performance tools. Performance and theatre are about the live *presence* of bodies before an audience.

- Organise a reading of Samuel Beckett's *Catastrophe* in your group. This is a short text and will take about 15 minutes. Elect one member of your group to be the Protagonist and to stand as directed in front of the others. Cast the other roles. Afterwards, discuss the movement in the piece, and its use of silence. How does this piece work against the conventions of theatre? How did you feel watching, performing, or reading the piece?

- Define a space in your group. You might outline a square or a circle or designate a corner of the room. Try to ensure that it is a simple space and as uncluttered as possible. One at a time, introduce objects into the space and discuss their dramatic/performative potential, for example, a wooden chair, a hat, an open umbrella. Now ask a woman to move into the space. Discuss what happens if she stands, sits, stares out at you, turns her back on you, or curls up into a little ball. Some positions are more powerful than others. Why? Now ask a man to move into the space and adopt exactly the same sequence of positions as the woman. What is the effect of a different sexuality and body shape in the space?

- Write a 10-minute performance piece for a single performer in which there are only 2 minutes of actual speech. Write down your movement instructions very simply. Leave plenty of room for a performer to improvise. Read each others' pieces and discuss them. Choose one and work it through physically and spatially.

If you want to pursue the avenue of devised work you might find Alison Oddey's book *Devising Theatre* (1994) useful. Read the collection of performance texts *Walks on Water* (Deborah

Levy, 1992) and, of course, try to see as much performance work as possible.

7   Radio: Thinking Aurally

With radio you are trying to create pictures through sound. You have to paint your landscape and characters through their words alone. Look at the following scenario.

SOLDIER A IS WRITING HIS DIARY.
SOLDIER A: Monday 4th October 1996. Just after 2 a.m. First diary entry of the day. Can't sleep. I think it's the silence, it's ominous somehow, and any minute I wonder if the shelling'll start up again...

Continue A's monologue, describing where they are and who is with them. Don't barrage your listener with information but do try to conjure a precise location: perhaps a trench, a dugout or below deck on a ship. At the end of your monologue have a link sentence or sound which can lead into a dialogue. For example:

FX: SOUND OF PLANES APPROACHING, A WHINE, THEN AN EXPLOSION VERY NEAR BY. AN AVA-LANCHE OF BRICKS AND MORTAR.
(FX is the notation for 'effects'.)

Or

A: I'll stop writing now. Smithy's beginning to come round and he'll need tending to.

Write about 200 words.
 Leading on from the monologue, write a dialogue involving one or two other soldiers. Remember we can't see what's happening so everything has to be clear in the speech. For example:

A: Smithy? (*coughs from the dust*) Smithy? Smithy, can you hear me?

B: He won't have stood a chance ...
A: I'm right here Smithy.
B: Didn't you hear me, he had no hope.
A: He was sleeping.
B: Can you move at all?
A: (*whimpering*) Sleeping.
B: Only my leg's trapped.

Words of warning: don't endlessly qualify how your characters say their lines. When A whimpers above it is because of a seeping realisation that Smithy has died. Watch the numbers of characters speaking in a single scene. Too many and you'll bewilder us – unless it's a general sound effect for an advancing army or a rescue group. Don't include too many footsteps, doors opening and shutting, and clinking cutlery; you need to think of an entire canvas and avoid linking scenes with banal sounds. Don't have long collages of sound effects: you may know what they are but your listener will have a tough time trying to decipher them. Music is an essential key into mood and often a vital connection device.

Now read what you have written out loud. How might the situation develop? Are they left for dead? Does the enemy invade? These soldiers are in extremis, do they know each other? How might their different characters become manifest? Make notes on plot.

8 Radio: Thinking the Impossible

One of the delights of radio is the sheer extravagance of the world that you can conjure with words and sound effects, which in film would cost millions of pounds. Radio offers you the best chance of pushing your imagination to the limits as a writer: think of Douglas Adams' science fiction phenomenon, *The Hitch-hiker's Guide to the Galaxy*. New writers often overlook the benefits of writing radio scripts and are unaware that many established theatre writers are also radio playwrights; indeed Caryl Churchill began her career by writing radio plays. Unlike film and theatre, radio offers unlimited scope in terms of location and time: your characters can hop between centuries and planets, travel into the future and the past, one moment they can be in New York, the next in Alaska or the Galapagos Islands or on Pluto. Animals can talk, inanimate objects can have lives and distinctive characters, a shoe, a glove, a cloud, a tree, a coffee table can be as fully developed as any human being. There are very few scenarios which are not possible.

- Think of an extreme scenario such as a ship sinking, the dropping of a bomb, a typhoon, an encounter with a dragon, the landing of an alien craft. Now write the scenario: remember that your task as a radio writer is to sketch the scene to the listener and stimulate their own imagination. Remember that for the audience to know that a character exists they have to speak or be referred to. What devices do you use to convey the scene? – over-reliance on sound effects will be undramatic and confusing for your listeners.

- Write a scene between a twenty-first-century time traveller and a figure from the past, perhaps an alchemist, a composer, an astronomer, a slave, a soldier, a hangman, a famous scientist, a maidservant or a pirate. Experiment with the speech patterns of each character and their vocabulary. What are the differences in the way they view the world? What comes of their meeting?

- Adapt a scene from your favourite novel, comic or film for radio. What are the restrictions and freedoms of writing it like this? Borrow a taped radio adaptation of a novel or short story from your library; read the printed form first and then listen to the tape. What do you notice about the way the original work has been adapted? Do you agree with the inclusions and exclusions made by the writer? Now write your own adaptation of the beginning or ending of the novel/short story.

- Write a scene between a human and an animal, an object or an alien.

9   Radio: Techniques of Narration

Some writers have played cleverly with soundscape in their radio plays. Dylan Thomas' *Under Milk Wood* creates an astonishingly rich canvas of poetic voices; Tom Stoppard's *Albert's Bridge* presents men at work on different parts of a vast bridge and a sense of distance is created through the quality of the echoing voices; Orson Welles famously used the effect of a rolling news item to begin his adaptation of *The War of the Worlds* – it was so realistic that thousands of Americans left their homes in a panic, thinking that aliens really had landed on earth; in *Cigarettes and Chocolate* Anthony Minghella uses a long sequence of answer machine messages to emphasise the silence and withdrawal of the central character. Many radio playwrights use the device of the internal monologue in which a character speaks their thoughts.

- Try to think up an original soundscape or way of beginning a radio play.

- Think of an idea for a docudrama – a dramatised documentary style.

- Choose a decade and location for a radio play and think of ways of creating mood and ideas through music.

10 Stage and Radio: A Character's Journey and Dialogue

If you are writing a conventional radio or stage play your protagonist should be capable of surprising us; traditionally a central character who remains static and predictable is understood to be undramatic and makes for a dull storyline. Consider the following simple plot:

- Character A is someone who lives by rote. Theirs is an ordinary, uncomplicated life, but rushed and isolated. A never has time to think about how they are feeling: they just exist and find it difficult to show emotion.

- Something happens in their life which is quite unprecedented and it has a more profound effect on them than anything ever has before. It might be falling in love, an illness, a death, the loss of a job. Suddenly they realise the limitations of their life but are uncertain how to change it.

- Gradually, A learns to express themselves and communicate more fully with others. They learn the pleasure of caring for someone and being cared for in return.

Character B has known A throughout all three stages and may be an acquaintance, a relative, a lover, or a colleague. Write a different dialogue between A and B set in each of the three phases. Try and write a page for each, taking the questions below into account.

How does A change in their interaction with B? In the first phase A may be scarcely communicating at all, relying on routine and cliché, and wrapped up in a superficial way of life. Does A try to reach out to B in the second phase? If so, how? It may be a tentative, awkward moment and B may fail to pick up any sign of change. Perhaps at stage three A suddenly takes B's hand, or bursts into tears, or articulates their feelings in a very moving way. Think about the change in language for A as they become aware of their emotions and try to express them. Think about the stage directions, for example, by stage three A may be a more tactile person.

Compare and contrast your three dialogues. In what ways is B revealed in a different light through A's change? Plot out further conversations between A and B.

11 Stage and Radio: The Double Narrative

If you have a plot where the past is affecting the present or you need to explain certain elements about your characters' past lives, you may want to explore flashback as a device. Flashback takes us straight into the past situation and dramatises the moment. Clearly, if you are flashing back to a distant past you will need to think more about potential casting dilemmas for stage, otherwise production costs will be prohibitive. You also need to be sure that your present and past narratives are interweaving tightly and staying ruthlessly to the point. Look at the tautness in Tom Stoppard's radio play *In the Native State* and you will see what I mean. You will also notice that Stoppard links past and present through an object – a painting that involves all four main characters in the play. Take a look at

Stoppard's stage play *Arcadia* and at Shelagh Stephenson's *An Experiment With An Air Pump.*

- Write a scene set in the past in which a woman is given an object, for example a ring. Now write a scene set in the present in which the woman learns that the object has a grisly history, for example, the ring was taken from a murdered corpse.

- Write a scene in which a son is bequeathed his father's diary which no one in the family even knew existed. Write a scene from the past which shows the circumstances in which the diary was written; for example, was the father a prisoner of war, on-the-run, a drug addict, a spy, a transsexual?

- Write a scene in the present between a couple who have not seen each other for ten years. Now write the scene in the past when they last saw each other: were they fighting for their lives, did one threaten to kill the other, was some dreadful secret revealed? Contrast the relationship from the past with the present day. In what ways have the two changed? Has one changed more than the other?

12   Readings

It is essential for playscripts to be exposed to other people before you submit them for professional consideration. All too often scripts read passably but fail to function because a writer has no visual, aural, or spatial awareness: what seems to work on paper can prove disastrous in practical and technical terms. *Always try out your work,* read it aloud or arrange for others to read it to you. Playwriting is a process requiring an enormous amount of discussion and the testing out of your storylines and ideas on other people.

Once you have a first draft you can arrange a reading of your work. Initially you may cast your friends and hold a small informal reading of your work at home. Whether your work is greeted rapturously or not, your primary concerns are these:

- Has everyone understood the piece in the way you intended?

- Did it have the desired effect? For example, if it's a comedy did your audience laugh?

- In what ways do your readers/audience think you might improve the piece?

Be warned, your first readings will probably be a baptism of fire. It is a strange experience hearing your words in the mouths of other people. The word in performance has a completely different life to the word on the page and unexpected things happen. Everyone will tell you how you *should* have written it! Have courage, keep your mind open, listen and make notes. At a later date you may reject 95 per cent of what was said, but the 5 per cent that you don't could be absolutely key to cracking a problem or revealing something that you simply hadn't seen. If you do seem to have a lot of problems with your reading, arrange a workshop: this might be anything from a brainstorming session to improvisation exercises or an attempt to actually walk through the particular scene of the play.

Once you feel you have a good enough draft you might approach a local theatre company, or your local hospital or community radio team for a reading, or ask if they can put you in touch with actors and directors who have an interest in new writing.

- Hold group sessions where you spend an evening reading a play or script and then analyse its structure, characters and use of language.

Writing On

Monologue

- Choose someone whose habits, mannerisms and speech patterns you know well. You may select real or fictional source material. Try your favourite film star, for example,

Bogart, Woody Allen or Madonna. Make them tell a simple story about something that has just happened to them.

- Some writers respond well to visual stimuli such as photographs, pictures from newspapers and magazines, or postcards and paintings. Find a face that intrigues you and invent a character for it. You might even choose an old family photograph of a parent or relative. Write a monologue which reveals a dark secret about them.

- Obituaries in the broadsheet press may make for melancholy reading but they frequently demonstrate that truth is stranger than fiction and make excellent source material for building up a character. Watch the papers and find a person whose history appeals to you. Write a monologue for them. Locate it at a time that is crucial in their lives; perhaps a turning point or a time when circumstances have forced them to take an unusual decision.

- Many monologues are powerfully confessional: they may show the deepest thoughts and feelings of that character; or show a side that is not revealed to certain other people in their lives. Experiment with the idea of a confession. Why is your character choosing to open up their heart at this moment in time and to whom? Maybe they're confessing something onto tape for someone who will discover it after their death. Or perhaps your character is rehearsing a speech to someone who is to be confronted later. Take a look at Beckett's *Krapp's Last Tape*.

- A device often used by playwrights is the monologue delivered by a child in a simple, naïve language for a subject matter which is disturbing. Claire Dowie's monologue *Adult Child/Dead Child* is one of the most moving pieces on child abuse I have ever come across. Write a monologue by a naïve commentator who is relaying much more than they consciously understand.

- Experiment with the format of an interrogation and create a character who is answering questions to an invisible authority. What charges is your character facing? Are they guilty or innocent or is it not clear-cut? Is the interrogator subtle or brutal? You may find it helpful to write out the questions first and shape your monologue round them. Look at Franca Rame's *I'm Ulrike, Screaming* for a model.

- Write a monologue that employs persuasion. Make your character work hard at justifying an action that they know in their heart is wrong. Explore the areas of truth and deceit. Does the character reveal the whole story? Maybe they contradict themselves or leave tantalising gaps in the narrative.

- Write a monologue using location as your starting point. Place your character somewhere specific and let the writing grow from this. For example, your character may be in a prison cell, a hospital, a car boot, a tower or a tree-house. What are they doing there? Is it a place they revisit often? Why?

- Monologues are often vehicles for comic characters. Look at Alan Bennett's *Talking Heads*, Liz Lochhead's *True Confessions* and Spalding Gray's *Swimming to Cambodia*. Write a monologue for a character who regards themselves as perfectly ordinary but reveals a decided eccentricity in their life-style or their relationship with others.

Dialogue

Many new writers make their dialogue a pure function of plot and use character to expound unwieldy chunks of information. You have to remember that each character has their own agenda when communicating with another character. The crucial point to bear in mind is the *relationship* between the two people speaking: how they relate to each other and what they ask of one another.

- Write a dialogue between a father and son in which the father cannot bring himself to communicate his wife's death and instead tells his son that she's gone to stay with friends. Does the child know that his father is lying? Is the child able to articulate what his father can't? Frequently children are capable of handling tragic news better than adults. Always think beyond stereotypes in your writing: try to make your characters believable individuals. Alternatively, look at April de Angelis' *Ironmistress*. Write a dialogue between a mother and daughter in which the child is seeking to understand the actions of the adult or trying to make sense of a recent event.

- Experiment with a clash between two people who enunciate themselves very differently. You might choose a character who retreats into a rather elaborate language, and someone who speaks before they think. Or you could explore a character who speaks officialese or jargon of some kind and a character who can only speak a few words of English. Where does the power base lie in your dialogue?

- Write a dialogue between a garrulous person and a terse, laconic person. How do the silences affect the balance of your piece? Look at Marie Laberge's *Night* in which the father delivers a rambling speech unconsciously illuminating the years of oppression and verbal abuse to which he has subjected his daughter. When the daughter does eventually speak, her words are a strangled scream, containing years of suppressed violence. Her silent presence on stage has the effect of continually undermining the father's words.

- Watch a romantic movie that you know well, such as *Gone with the Wind*, *Pretty Woman* or *Notting Hill*. Write a piece of stage or radio dialogue between the two lead characters where one is leaving the other; write it within the conventions of the B movie genre and make it as stereotyped as you like. Now take the same dialogue but remove the melodrama and the clichés, update the language and make everything as understated as possible. Ensure that your characters have moved away from their gender stereotypes; you could begin by reversing their roles and seeing what differences it brings to your writing.

- Harold Pinter's stage dialogue frequently betrays a sense of threat and unease between characters; something sinister and motiveless seems to lurk in their minds. Experiment with a dialogue between two people, one of whom is naïve and unsuspecting, and the other malevolent and manipulating. Try to make the fall of the innocent person a gradual, subtle process which opens up further questions about both parties.

- Choose your favourite TV detective as a starting point. Write three sets of dialogue for them.

  (a) With a lover.
  (b) Breaking the news of a death to someone.
  (c) Briefing colleagues on a murder hunt.

  How does their vocabulary vary for each scenario? Remember that each scene should reveal new details about their personality.

- Often comic dialogue comes about through a misunderstanding or a conflict of desires between characters; one character fails to pick up on what another is saying and misconstrues the situation entirely. If you study comedy you will soon deduce how much it rests on a very fine line with tragedy: sustaining the right balance takes a considerable amount of practice. Look at the moment towards the end of Chekhov's *The Cherry Orchard* when Varya is expecting to be proposed to by Lopakhin.

  Imagine that A has invited B for a meal in a lavish restaurant. B thinks that, at last, this is the marriage proposal they have been waiting for. In fact A has booked the table to celebrate a lifetime vow of celibacy which they have recently taken without B's knowledge. How does the information come out? Try and build up the suspense through sustaining the misunderstanding for as long as possible.

Heightened Language

- Increasingly playwrights this century have experimented with heightened forms of language. Many contemporary performance texts are notable for their self-referentiality and self-consciousness. Take a look at Marguerite Duras' play *India Song* in which the notion of character is replaced by poetic voice. Try this stylisation of language for yourself. You could take the following as a beginning.

A: It was such a long time ago.
B: In the Springtime.
C: I can remember the colour of his eyes.
B: The blossom was early.
A: How old was he?
C: And the way he laughed.

Continue the dialogue and evoke a vivid picture of the man A, B, and C are recalling. Try to make each voice serve a function in the telling of the story. A, for example, seems vague on detail and C is precise regarding the man's physical appearance. Do the voices reveal anything else about their individual relationships with this man or each other? Once you have finished it and edited it to your satisfaction show the piece to other people. Is it more suitable for radio or stage? How could it be made visually compelling?

- Examine the language in Frederico García Lorca's play *Blood Wedding*. Write a poetic dialogue trying to evoke a particular mood or landscape.

- Think about the use of language in Sam Shepard's plays. Write a conversation between three people who do not specify the exact topic under discussion, but only hint at it. Read it back to yourself. Is the effect unsettling?

- Look at Samuel Beckett's *Not I* and *Mouth*. Beckett was of the view that words merely punctuate silence. How do these texts bear out his view? Write a scene in which there is some sort of breakdown in communication at a level that the characters do not realise. For example, perhaps they think of themselves as fulfilled people, but it is revealed between the lines that they are terrified of living.

- Consider the concept of stage poetry. Read Ntozake Shange's 'choreopoem' *for coloured girls...* or Guillermo Gomez-Peña's *1992* in *Walks on Water*. Take a poem, perhaps one of your own, and think about its potential for a performance piece.

History and Politics

- Select a political issue about which you feel strongly and compose a dialogue in which two sides of the argument are represented. Try to flesh out the characters and avoid stereotype. You may find Sarah Daniel's treatment of pornography interesting in her play *Masterpieces*.

- Write a monologue by a character who is suffering from an illness or by someone who is overlooked by society. How do you allow that person to speak as an individual with their story and prevent them from sounding as though they are on a soap box? You may find the collections of AIDS plays helpful, as well as the Methuen collections of gay plays and plays for women. Or look at Louise Page's play *Tissue* which is about breast cancer.

- Read David Hare's monologue *Via Dolorosa*, about his impressions of the political situation in Israel. Would this work if it had not been performed by the playwright himself? Write a monologue about a country or situation you have found yourself in that was politically sensitive.

- Many of the Irish playwrights have tackled political issues very eloquently. Look at the work of Frank McGuinness and Brian Friel, especially *Translations*. Anne Devlin introduced a female perspective on the Troubles in her plays *Ourselves Alone* and *After Easter*. Take a current political issue and sketch a five-act structure for a play; try to think of an unusual angle on the story.

- Perhaps you are interested in covering a broad span of time in your play. Look at both Shakespeare's and Bertold Brecht's plays for ways to approach history in theatrical terms. Look at Howard Barker's play *Claw*, which tracks the protagonist's life from birth to death. Write three scenes for a character: one in childhood; one as a young adult; and one in old age.

- Select a historical figure who interests you or whom you admire and write a radio or stage scene for them. Look at Peter Shaffer's play *Amadeus*, Howard Brenton's *Bloody*

Poetry about Byron and Shelley, Brecht's *The Resistible Rise of Arturo Ui* (based on Hitler's rise to power), Alan Bennett's play *The Madness of George III*, or Christopher Hampton's *Liaisons Dangereuses*. Research the language of that era to make your characters sound as authentic as possible.

• Some plays are still politically very sensitive. Julia Pascal's *Thérèse*, about the collaboration of Channel Islanders with their Nazi occupiers during the Second World War, is still banned in Guernsey. Writing about an atrocity such as the Holocaust is an awesome task and playwrights select individual stories to symbolise the larger scale of the horror. Read Joshua Sobol's *Ghetto*, which includes original musical compositions by victims of the Vilna ghetto, and Diane Samuels' *Kindertransport* which examines the life of a German Jewish girl sent into exile. What are the ethical issues and responsibilities involved in writing about such subjects?

Booklist

Aristotle, *Poetics* (Loeb Classical Library, Harvard University Press, 1995).

Barker, Howard, *Collected Plays: Volume One* (John Calder, London, 1990).

Beckett, Samuel, *The Complete Dramatic Works* (Faber & Faber, London, 1986).

Bennett, Alan, *The Complete Talking Heads* (BBC Books, London, 1998).

Brook, Peter, *The Empty Space* (Penguin, London, 1990).

Chekhov, Anton, *Plays* (Penguin, London, 1959).

Daniels, Sarah, *Masterpieces in Plays: One* (Methuen, London, 1994).

De Angelis, April, *Plays: One* (Faber & Faber, London, 1999).

Devlin, Anne, *Ourselves Alone* and *After Easter* (Faber & Faber, London, 1990; 1994).

Dowie, Claire, *Why is John Lennon Wearing a Skirt? and other stand-up theatre plays* (Methuen, London, 1996).

Duras, Marguerite, *Four Plays*, trans. B. Bray (Oberon Books, London, 1992).

García Lorca, F., *Plays One and Plays Two* (Methuen, London, 1990).

Giannachi, G. and Luckhurst, M., *On Directing* (Faber & Faber, London, 1999).

Gray, Spalding, *Swimming to Cambodia* (Picador, London, 1987).

Hare, David, *Via Dolorosa* (Faber & Faber, London, 1998).

Ibsen, Henrik, *A Doll's House and Other Plays* (Penguin, London, 1965).

Laberge, Marie, *Night*, in *Plays By Women*, Vol. VII, ed. Mary Remnant (Methuen, London, 1994).

Levy, Deborah, *Walks on Water* (Methuen, London, 1992).

Miller, Arthur, *Plays One* (Faber & Faber, London, 1990).

Minghella, Anthony, *Plays One* (Methuen, London, 1997).

Norman, Marsha, *Getting Out*, in *Landmarks of Contemporary Women's Drama*, ed. E.S. Kilgore (Methuen, London, 1992).

Oddey, A., *Devising Theatre* (Routledge, London, 1994).

Page, Louise, *Plays: One* (Methuen, London, 1992).

Pascal, Julia, *The Holocaust Plays* (Oberon Books, London, 1999).

Pinter, Harold, *Plays: Volumes One to Four* (Faber & Faber, London, 1991).

Rame, F. and Fo, Dario, *A Woman Alone and Other Plays* (Methuen, London, 1991).

Samuels, Diane, *Kindertransport* (Nick Hern, London, 1995).

Shange, N., *Plays: One* (Methuen, London, 1992).

Shepard, Sam, *Plays I and II* (Methuen, London, 1996).

Stephenson, Shelagh, *An Experiment With An Air Pump* (Methuen, London, 1998).

Stoppard, Tom, *Albert's Bridge*, in *The Plays for Radio 1964–1983* (Faber & Faber, London, 1990).

Stoppard, Tom, *Arcadia* (Faber & Faber, London, 1983).

Stoppard, Tom, *In the Native State*, in *Best Radio Plays of 1991* (Methuen, London, 1992).

Thomas, Dylan, *Under Milk Wood* (Everyman, London, 1995).

10 Journalism

MARY LUCKHURST AND BETTY
PRINCEP

The advancements in electronic and computer technology, the
advent of satellite communications and the speed with which
we can now travel the earth, have combined to produce highly
sophisticated news networks in the press, on radio and on
television. Twenty-four hour news channels are transmitted
in many parts of the world, reports of major events can be
logged within minutes and mass production and distribution
means that an ever-growing volume and diversity of newspapers and journals are appearing on the shelves. This explosion of the news industry has been one of the phenomena of
the twentieth century.

The political ramifications of this are vast and analysis of the
subject has barely begun. What we can say is that currently our
lives are dominated by press and television, indeed many lives
depend upon media publicity whether Hollywood star, political careerist or victim of the war in Bosnia. Madonna, for
example, has developed a skill for manipulating the press
which ensures her enshrinement in Western culture. Reputa-
tions can be made or broken and fame can be bought or sold in
a single article or programme. Wars can be won or lost. Heroes
made and villains exposed. Lies can become truths and truth
lies. This is the era of partnership between Mammon and
Media.

The press, for example, feeds on anything which is likely to
interest specific readers and generate sales. This needn't be
just news items, it can be openly opinionated writing, features,
interviews, investigative journalism, advertisements, obituaries, editorials, review writing and a whole host of other

things. The driving logic behind this spectrum of writing is its topicality: its perceived relevance to a targeted, culture-specific audience. Though who sets the national and international agenda in the press and decides exactly what is 'topical' can vary for political, economic and social reasons. Generally in liberal regimes, newsworthiness is defined by what are currently important debates and issues in the country concerned; by significant new developments in a particular field; and by events that are deemed to have a resonance for the populace. This means that a huge range of subjects from the abolition of the monarchy, or the research into a new contraceptive pill for men, to a film première or the discovery of more crop circles in the west of England will find their way into the pages of newspapers and journals.

How various publications treat these subjects differs according to the market they are aiming for. A magazine like *Cosmopolitan* targets young, professional women, promoting itself as trendy and liberated. *Yachting Monthly*, on the other hand, is appealing to a smaller, more specialist readership and relies on subscription to a greater extent. So-called high and low journalism, supposedly confined to the broadsheet and tabloid press respectively, assume that certain sections of the nation want to read unsophisticated coverage of sex, scandal and sport, whilst other sections want serious, analytical writing on politics and general issues. In practice, however, what is 'high' and 'low' can depend less on content than on style, furthermore readership is by no means defined by class.

Clearly, readers' expectations of journalism are different from their expectations of fiction. We do not read a broadsheet for the same reasons that we read a novel or poetry. We read to discover what is going on in the world; we read to inform ourselves of the 'facts', of what is 'new'. Rarely do we absorb a newspaper from cover to cover, we select the items that rouse our interest, or scan the headlines for a rapid overview. Newspapers are attuned to this in different ways: first by the length of their articles; and second by their choice of analytical content and vocabulary. The writing must be easily digestible. By its nature journalism is ephemeral. Yesterday's news is old news.

A sharp reader will be conscious of authorial manipulation in the articles they read. All publications offer material which is written to a bias and all journalists write from a point of view – whether it is their own or the required slant. A *Times* reader would expect to find articles which present an angle in favour of the right politically. And though *The Independent* may seem to claim an objectivity in its title, it is often taking the middle-ground, the line of consensus politics and therefore of the status quo. This does, of course, mean that the power of the written word can be abused. A certain angle or emphasis can cast an issue in a totally different light or misrepresent a person's views just as a selectivity in the tabling of statistics can mislead. Extreme abuse of this kind is propaganda. The McCarthyite era in the States, for instance, saw a proliferation of journalism focusing on the 'Red Terror' and underlining the imminent threat of invasion by Russia. Jews were the subjects of a barrage of defamatory literature in Nazi Germany.

Looking at the other side of the coin, journalism can do much that is positive. By bringing issues to the public eye newspapers can exert pressure on institutions and governments to change their ways. A recent example of this was the case of John McCarthy, who was kidnapped in Lebanon and held hostage. The government proved reluctant to take any definitive action but the press took it upon themselves to keep McCarthy's name in the news in a way that immortalised him and certainly contributed to the moral squeeze on his captors to release him.

One of the most famous pieces of journalism to appear this century is John Hersey's *Hiroshima*. Sent out by the *New Yorker* in 1946 as the first Western journalist to witness the aftermath of the Hiroshima bombing, Hersey wrote an extraordinary piece, choosing to document the experience through the accounts of certain survivors. Whilst obviously selective in his material, Hersey manages to moderate his presence as a writer behind a cool, understated prose. At the same time he conveys the horror of the scene and allows the irresponsible barbarity of the act to speak for itself. The *New Yorker* decided to devote an entire edition to Hersey's piece, which was the first article to reveal the scale of the devastation and suffering in Hiroshima as well as the reality of nuclear warfare. There are writers who have followed in this tradition such as Shiva Naipaul in his book *Black & White*, which is about the mass suicides of members of the People's Temple in Guyana 1978; and Sidney Schanberg in *The Death and Life of Dith Pran* which documents one man's survival amidst the Cambodian killing fields.

Since the sixties and seventies there has been a boom in the diversity of journalistic styles and forms. One form that has proved to be of devastating consequence is that of investigative journalism. This exploits the basic tenet of any effective article: the idea of exposure, of 'digging up the dirt' on a person or an organisation and revealing them for what they really are. Investigative journalism often involves undercover work; or piecing together what you can 'on the job'. It has become attached to notions of danger and glamour and has ensured that certain journalists have become a part of history. Take Bernstein and Woodward, perhaps the most notorious journalists in this category, who investigated a raid on the Democrat headquarters for the *Washington Post* during President Nixon's term of office. There were suspicions of a conspiracy on the part of the Republicans which were strenuously denied. Painstakingly, over a period of many months, following lead after lead, they tracked those responsible to the Oval Office itself. As a result senior members of the Republican party were tried for corruption and Nixon was forced to resign. At every stage of their investigation Bernstein and Woodward wrote another article for the newspaper, and eventually they wrote their book *All the President's Men*.

The production of books of investigative journalism is a comparatively recent but increasingly common phenomenon. Clive Ponting's *The Right to Know* about the sinking of the *Belgrano* during the Falklands War is another classic example of this. In it he reveals how the Official Secrets Act was used against him as a means of protecting government ministers from public condemnation. But certain questions are raised about journalism when it is packaged in book form: is this not straying into the terrain of 'literature'? And if one of the distinguishing features of journalism has traditionally been its ephemerality, surely it becomes something else as a book? Or is it that some books are crossing into the terrain of journalism?

This perceived divide between literature and journalism was the principal target of a collection of writers in the late sixties and early seventies who were referred to as the 'new journalists'. These writers were known primarily for their reputation as novelists and included in their rank were some of the names of the day such as Truman Capote and Norman Mailer. In an introduction to an anthology called *The New Journalism* Tom Wolfe bemoans the existence of just two kinds of journalists: the scoop reporters and the feature writers. 'The "feature" was the newspaper term for a story that fell outside the category of hard news. It included everything from "brights", chuckly little items... "to human interest stories", long and often hideously sentimental...' Wolfe goes on to condemn the narrowness and formula writing of the journalism of his day and argues for a new form which is *like a novel* and raises journalism to the heights of literature. It was for this reason that Truman Capote's *In Cold Blood* caused controversy at the time. Taking the true story of the violent murder of a Kansas family Capote went and interviewed people connected with the events in some way, he then wrote a fictionalised account of it. This blurring of genres was termed 'faction'.

One proponent of new journalism has developed a working practice entirely of his own. Hunter S. Thompson doses himself up into a narcotic and alcoholic high and then writes his articles. Whereas 'Gonzo' journalism would be professional suicide for the majority, Thompson displays a savage and remarkable insight into American politics and the so-called American Dream. Look out *The Great Shark Hunt* and *Fear and Loathing in Las Vegas* for confirmation of this.

The new journalism movement also paved the way for freer forms of journalism working somewhere in the overlap between *belles lettres* and reportage. It fostered such talents as Joan Didion and Susan Sontag who write what are perhaps best described as long feature essays, meditations on Western culture – Sontag's *On Photography* and *Illness as Metaphor* being particularly fine examples of this art. It influenced writers like Timothy Garton Ash in his book *We the People* which is an eye-witness account of the opening of the Berlin Wall. It allowed for the zaniness of P. J. O'Rourke in such articles as 'How to

Drive Fast on Drugs while Getting your Wing-wang Squeezed and not Spill your Drink'. Not only this, it gave rise to a myriad of styles among travel and review writers and encouraged a more probing style for interview writing. Travel writing, especially, is enjoying huge popularity with writers such as Peter Mayle in the bestseller ranks. Explore this richness of styles for yourself and use the workshops in this chapter as a means of developing your own voice.

Workshop Writing

1 Readership

All journalism requires you to write for specific markets and you will have to target your work accordingly. Knowing your readers is, therefore, a vital part of the journalist's profession. An article on quantum physics, for instance, is clearly not appropriate for the tabloid press; and the sexual exploits of 'Miss Whiplash' are unlikely to make it into the *New Scientist*! Read widely and always try to think about how an article has been pitched. This workshop should help you learn how to analyse certain aspects of journalistic writing.

Below we outline eight steps. You might like to work in pairs or in small groups so that you can try your work out on each other and get feedback.

A Get hold of both broadsheet and tabloid newspapers published on the same day, perhaps the *Independent*, the *Guardian*, the *Telegraph*, the *Sun* and the *News of the World*. Cut out features or news items on an identical topic from each newspaper.
B Compare the set of cuttings you have with one another. What angle have they chosen to take? Is the political agenda different in each? How and why?
C Now compare the language appearing in the articles. Do the writers use formulae or clichés? Are there foreign phrases, jargon or slang? What effect do these have on the tone of the piece? Spend about five minutes on each cutting so that you have a clear idea of the respective 'house-styles'.

D   Now look at the average number of words per sentence and paragraph. What are your findings? Are the words used of three syllables (Latinate) such as 'conference' or of two syllables (Anglo-Saxon) such as 'meeting'? Is the vocabulary sophisticated or everyday?

E   As a test of how much you have absorbed, ask one of the members of the group to choose an article from one of the newspapers. Get them to read a section of it out and see if you can pinpoint the source.

F   By now you should have a sense of readership and corresponding style so try writing a short article for one of the newspapers. Look at your notes before you begin to write. Reread something from that newspaper to refresh your memory.

G   You might like to develop this idea by rewriting the same article for different readerships.

H   Let other writers read your work and see if they can guess which newspaper you have written for; this will be an indication of how successful you have been.

2   Research

Though the idea of research may seem daunting to you, you cannot hope to gain command of all the different sides of a subject without acquainting yourself with as much information on it as possible. Research enables you to make a balanced judgement on a matter and forms the grist to your argument. Even when you think you have covered a topic, it always pays to make the extra effort of yet another telephone call or an interview. You never know what you may uncover. Never be satisfied with a single viewpoint; your article will be unacceptably partisan.

Look at the four modes of research below:

1 Personal, for example, interviews.

2 Written documents.

3 New technology, such as computer databases.

4 Questionnaires, which relate to 1 and 2.

A Bearing the above in mind, take the topics of (a) abortion (b) Beatrix Potter and (c) nuclear reactors and have a collective brainstorming session in your group, discussing every possible research trail you can think of. For example, with the topic of abortion you may immediately think of pro-life and pro-choice arguments. You may then think of ringing helplines advertised in newspapers and magazines and asking for interviews with both sides of the camp. You may think of trying to contact a local hospital. Perhaps you may try to track down some statistics on the issue. How many abortions were carried out in one year? Was there a particularly high teenage abortion rate?

B Divide into pairs and try to devise a questionnaire about local reaction to nuclear power. Is it possible to ensure that you ask questions that are not leading but allow an open response? Does the fact that you are asking questions in the first place generate it as an issue? How might you avoid this?

C Where do you go to find information on Beatrix Potter? Set this as a task for yourselves and see what you come up with for the next meeting. You might be able to locate a biography or obituary, for example. Look at Ann Hoffman's book *Research for Writers*. Once you have all this information what do you do with it? Go on to the next workshop!

3 Finding an Angle

There is no such thing as neutral journalism, no such thing as 'objective journalism', though the phrase is commonplace. Someone has written an article and presented it in a certain way with a certain argument and a certain vocabulary; someone else has also very probably cast an editorial eye over it and made either emendations or deletions. There are, however, degrees of bias and you should remember your responsibility both to your readers and to the subjects of your writing. Finding an effective slant on an article is, therefore, a key factor to its success. Your angle will have to take consideration of the following factors:

1 The publication your article is intended for.

2 Readership.

3 The purpose of the article.

4 Your relationship to the material.

In a feature article, for example, your slant might be arguing strongly for or against a particular issue. In a news item for a broadsheet, however, you are required to stick to the 'facts', though of course bias comes into it in the way you prioritise material and what you choose to highlight. Columnists such as Julie Burchill are specifically employed to give a slant on a subject that is shocking in some way or goes against the grain. Often a slant is not all that it appears to be. A racy article entitled *Ten Ways to Please Your Man* in a women's magazine may be arguing on one level for independence and sexual liberation but on another, even by virtue of its title, is simply reinforcing a notion of women's subservience to men.

Most slants are simply trying to find a way of grasping a subject, or of seeking for a new insight into a particular topic.

A   What would your slant be on the debate about Death Row in the United States, the legalisation of drugs, or the fur trade? Write one article which presents a 'balanced' view of a topic of your choice and read it to the group. Can they detect your own leanings? Now write about the same topic but slam it from the start. Make sure your argument stays cogent and is backed up with things that lend it authenticity such as statistics and citations by leading figures in the debate (make them up if you don't know them).

B   Choose a controversial and unpopular public figure and try writing an article on them for *Hello* Magazine. The whole point of this is to try and find a 'neutral', safe slant on that person, for example their landscaped garden, or the birth of a child.

4   News Articles

What constitutes newsworthiness in a particular culture at a particular time is subject to many factors, often political and economic. Generally, the national news may be seen as the reporting of a significant event in the country in question or elsewhere in the world. But how that 'significant event' is determined is a matter of contention. Very often in Britain a piece of trivia concerning the royal family or a sex scandal will appear on the front page of the press, taking precedence over stories of war or famine in the world. News is a fickle business: what is news one day is not the next. Politicians clearly have their own agendas and exact degrees of censorship in all cultures. There is also the question of sales: newspapers and magazines have to guarantee circulation in order to stay afloat. Hence such infamous headlines as: FREDDIE STAR ATE MY HAMSTER! and WORLD WAR TWO PLANE FOUND ON MOON!

A   Consider the following guidelines for drawing up a news article:

1   Identify what is newsworthy for your particular publication. If, for example, you want to write for a local paper you have to be in touch with the community and the issues that affect them.

2   Identify the facts you wish to put across. Ask yourself the questions: who? what? why? when? where?

3   Prioritise these facts and consider a structure for your article.

4   Remember your responsibility to your readership. For example, in a local paper you don't want to terrify a community about a subject like violent crime but you do want to draw their attention to it and encourage them to see to their personal safety. Think of an appropriate headline.

B   Choose a topic such as the plight of the homeless, joy-riding, noise pollution or vandalism and discuss it in local and national terms. Bearing in mind the list of points above, half the group now writes a piece for the national press and half the group writes something for a local outlet. Think about language and tone. Compare your pieces and discuss the differences in structure.

5   Review Writing

Review writing is about keeping your readers informed about what is going on in the arts world either locally or nationally. Your review might be encouraging or damning: what it shouldn't be is a plot summary or simply a list of things you liked or didn't like. It should be a specialist's opinion of the work seen. It is a given that reviews are personal opinions: you shouldn't feel abashed about giving yours. Do take into account your potential power as a critic, however, and respect the human/s behind the work even if you can't respect their art! Have a look at Michael Billington's reviews in the *Guardian*. The following is a checklist of important points:

1 What did you see? Was it a special occasion of some kind? Who was invited? Was it a play in the tradition of absurdist drama, a piece of music after Berlioz, or an artist clearly influenced by primitive Aztec symbols?

2 Think about context. If you are reviewing a playwright's first play you will make allowances that you might not make for a seasoned writer of national fame. Is the work a new departure for the artist or is it a rehash of their previous work? Do your background work and make sure you have a copy of any accompanying written material, such as catalogues or programmes.

3 What are the artist's aims and have these been achieved? A novelist may claim their book is experimental in some way – is it? A pop group might argue that they are different to their counterparts. Do you agree?

4 Know and critique the technicalities of the work. Did their approach work, if not why not? What were the technical abilities of the performer/artist/writer? What about other technical content? For example, if you are writing on performance consider the use of lighting, costumes, set and sound.

5 What in your opinion is the value of the piece? Is it innovative, different or surprising in any way? Place it in a

historical context if it's relevant. This may give you a clue as to the angle you may take on your piece.

6 Remember to give details of the venue, time and length of run at the end of your review.

A   Take a number of reviews from the press by different critics and compare their methods of approach. Look at Clive James's collections of television reviews for the *Observer* and consider the role of humour in his writing. Or listen to BBC Radio 4's *Kaleidoscope* arts programme. Do any of the critics allow their own egos to intervene too much in their reviewing? How is this avoidable? Brian Sewell, the art critic, has been accused of being unwarrantably opinionated. Read his reviews in *The Reviews that Caused the Rumpus, and Other Pieces*.
B   Using the list above, 'free-write' half a page recording your honest opinion about the work you want to review. Don't worry about polished prose at this point, just record your spontaneous impressions. What emotions did it arouse in you? Did you love it or loathe it? Now choose a publication and put yourself in the place of the reader. What would you want to know? Write your review and read it to the group. Keep a clear throughline, arguing your point.

6 Feature Writing

Features are an opportunity to write an in-depth, researched piece of writing on topical issues and subjects of general interest. They tend to be personalised by the individual style and tone of the writer and allow more room for creativity.

A   Read the Sunday supplements or a selection of maga-zines, concentrating on the feature articles.
B   Write an article about a white witches' coven that has recently been discovered in your locality. You may want to include some history about how the fate of the white witch has changed through the ages. Perhaps you detail their average working day, accompanying one of the witches as she goes about her work. You might describe the house that you visit and give your first impressions. You might describe your first encounter with one of the witches and what it felt like to shake

their hand. You might include sections on eating habits, clothes and whether or not there are any black cats in the vicinity. What are the books on the shelves? Is there any tell-tale evidence of the magic arts?

Now write the first paragraph of a feature article on white witches intended for the local press. Write it in ten minutes and then discuss with each other the different ways in which you started your article and how you sought to pull the reader into your piece.

C Finish the piece. How do you avoid falling into stereotype? It might be an idea to select some common misconceptions about white witches and write an ironic piece that highlights the fact that the truth is actually very different.

7   Travel Writing 1

Travel writing involves and challenges your powers of observation in a different way to other forms of journalistic writing. You must constantly be aware of the small detail. It is very often the way into a gripping travel article. This workshop should assist you in seeing locations as part of a wider landscape. Try to stretch your descriptive abilities.

A   You are sitting next to the pilot in a small aeroplane approaching your home town or village. You can just see the buildings in the distance but they are small and indistinguishable from each other. Your altitude is so great that you have an extensive view beyond the town in all directions, where you might glimpse the sea or a range of mountains. Is the town over a valley, on a plateau or built on a hillside? Write for ten minutes describing the town in relation to its setting.

B   The aeroplane circles and the altitude drops in preparation for landing. As you drop, everything grows larger, the horizon is nearer and you can see more detail. Perhaps you see the glint of a river, a network of roads or a strange outcrop of rocks. Write for ten minutes.

C   You are even lower in the air now and are gaining a three-dimensional perspective. You can distinguish colours and make out people, cars and trees. Write down what you see.

D   The last view, moments before landing, is of a high street. You can see goods in shop windows and read the destination on buses. Take five minutes to write this down.

E   Now compare your observations with others in the group. Have you missed out on certain details and picked up on others? How did your portrayal of the landscape affect your writing about the town? Were you conscious of trying to build up a certain atmosphere?

8   Travel Writing 2

Travel writing aims to give the sense of a place in a way which is exciting, different, new and perhaps humorous. Consider the following checklist.

1 Don't start your travel article in a way which is banal: 'I went to the travel agent and booked my ticket.' Plunge us in to the experience. You don't have to follow a chronological route.

2 Don't use blanket adjectives. For example: The sea was *amazing*, the beach was *beautiful*. What do you really mean? These descriptions give no sense of the unique character of a place. Be specific not general. Don't set out to convey the whole of the Grand Canyon, pick on a detail; perhaps a rock formation that has a curious myth attached to it or an area that was once visited by a celebrity.

3 Use local terms and names. This lends a vividness to your piece. Discover what the history is behind the place name. Specify, for example, what the flowers are: for example Ploughman's Spikenard, Sticky Mouse-Ear or Viper's Bugloss.

4 Do use anecdotes about your journey or ones that you hear the locals relate. This personalises your account and makes it a more real experience for the reader.

5 Do locate yourself as the writer. For example, is this your first time trekking in Nepal? Are you inexperienced and alone? Use everything you can to heighten elements of adventure and risk-taking.

6 Do use irony. You may want to send up a place precisely because it is the most unremarkable spot you have ever seen. You may want to play off your expectations of a place with your actual experience of it. And you may have a thoroughly gruelling and appalling experience that might be humorous in retrospect.

7 Do spice up your writing with sections of dialogue, journal entries, and postcards you may have sent. Include foreign words and phrases that you have learned. Travel writing often focuses on odd encounters and unexpected events.

8 Do try to conjure up an atmosphere but one which is to do with selected observations or character sketches. You are trying to capture the whole feel of a place perhaps in a single image, an encounter or a lasting memory. Read Tim Cahill's excellent collection of travel writing pieces *Pecked to Death by Ducks* for a model of the above points.

A   Using the guidelines above write a piece about a landscape that frightens you. Try to be specific about what it is that disturbs you. Is it the hollow elm whose branches seem to scratch at the skyline? Or is it the inexplicable patch of bare earth on the river bank? Write for ten minutes.
B   Now imagine that someone comes into view whom you immediately distrust. Describe them. What is it about them that makes them stand out?
C   This person approaches you and starts talking animatedly, but you don't understand a word. You remember the local tales you've heard about a spirit or ghost in this area, and wonder if this is a sighting. Write down the dialogue between you. Are you panicking or trying to maintain an air of control?
D   You manage to escape from this scenario and find yourself sitting in convivial company by a roaring fire. You describe the person you met and are told that they are the oldest member of the community and the last remaining person to speak the old dialect. How does this make you feel? What broader issues might you reflect on in this encounter?

9   Interviews

Interviews are arguably a more loyal way of representing a person in that you may simply choose to lay out bare questions and answers. On the other hand, you might select an alternative layout and write both descriptive prose and dialogue: 'The first thing that struck me about him was the fact that he doesn't believe in laundering his clothes.' Of course, your selection of interview questions should be pitched at a specific angle. Why are you interviewing this person at this moment? What is it about them that makes them interesting? You should certainly table your questions carefully, though be prepared to be flexible if they want to spend time on a particular subject. Find out as much about their background as possible; if you haven't done so you will appear unprofessional and what's more the interview will be limited as a result. Use a tape-recorder during the interview if you can. It's a more accurate recording of what they say and will allow you to focus fully on their replies. Remember that you are there to prompt and to listen, not to voice your own views. Tactful, sensitive interviewing that allows the interviewee to open up is quite an art.

A   Interview someone from your family or friends. Find someone with an unusual story to relate, for example someone with a dangerous job such as a life guard or a policeman, or someone who can talk about their experience during the war or at a time of turmoil in the community, perhaps during a flood or riots.

B   How will you shape your raw material? Bring your notes to the workshop and give a five minute outline of which angle you intend to take. What processes are involved in the selection and rejection of elements in your material? Do you have any particular worries about these decisions? Write a first draft in the group, read it out and talk it over.

C   Once you have written up your final draft of the interview show it to the interviewee. Talk about the process you have been through. Do they feel fairly represented? Have you over-elaborated on certain details or not trusted yourself enough?

10   Editing

Editing is vital if you want to present well-crafted work. This is often not the favourite task of many new writers but you will warm to it with practice.

A   Have in front of you a draft of a recent article or review. Count the number of words before you begin so that you can compare it with the number in the final draft.

B   Take a pencil and underline all the adjectives and adverbs. Go through the manuscript again and ask yourself whether you need each of these underlined words. Too often they actually weaken prose. Adverbs can often be incorporated in the verb: 'speaking voicelessly' can be altered to 'whispering' and 'walking quickly' to 'hurrying'.

C   Vague qualifiers drain energies from prose so see if you can delete words such as 'quite', 'seemed', 'rather', and make your writing more direct. Strike out any redundant words: for example, 'He returned the book back to its owner', 'back' is not needed, the meaning is perfectly clear without it.

D   Check that your verbs are in the active voice where possible. This gives writing a charge and dynamism. Verbs in the passive voice make prose cumbersome. 'He loved her' is stronger than 'She was loved by him'.

E   Look at your sentences. Are you joining them continually with commas? Try using the colon and semicolon in some of the longer ones. Have you fallen into the trap of making them all the same length? Try making the short sentences longer by adding conjunctives. Be ruthless and cut the sentences which are just padding.

F   Now write out your final draft. Ensure that you have a smooth and logical flow in your writing. Do your paragraphs connect evenly? Give both your original and final drafts to one of the group to read. Do they agree that the writing is tighter?

G   Consult Keith Waterhouse's book *Keith Waterhouse on Newspaper Style* for general points about style.

Writing On

Practical Hints

- Start a file of newspaper cuttings on subjects that interest you. This way you will have information to hand when you come to your writing.

- Begin another file for smaller items. Stop press, classified advertisements and promotions may provoke ideas for feature articles. Many new writers underestimate their areas of expertise and knowledge. Assess your skills by writing down a list of your strengths. What can you talk about with reasonable confidence? It may be a subject you usually take for granted. Perhaps you are informed about computers, jazz dancing, aikido, a language, science-fiction or folk music. From now on make a conscious effort to keep up to date on these subjects and watch for publications which might accept a freelance article from you.

News

- You are asked to write a 500-word feature for a local newspaper on a village which is unknown to you. How do you obtain your information? And since there is little of obvious interest what angle can you take? You could do a study of the street names and see if they yield a historical angle. You could try and discover the history of the church and see if there are any surprising moments buried in history. Or you could go to the pub and see if there are any unusual characters attached to the village. What other ways in might there be? Write the article.

- Write a spoof article for April Fool's Day to go in one of the broadsheet newspapers. A farmer in Chipping Sodbury has sighted a UFO two nights in a row. You have to write a serious analytical piece on the implications of this to science. Include interview material with fictional experts and quote from invented sources. Show your piece to someone. Are they taken in by it?

• Write a piece on unemployment, the elderly or divorce in your locality. Include statistics to lend weight to your argument. Where might you obtain statistics from? You could try HMSO publications (Her Majesty's Stationery Office) or local councillors and MPs. Interview relevant persons.

• Watch for opportunities to approach your local newspaper with an idea for an article. Are there any significant anniversaries or memorial days coming up? Are there any festivals or celebrations held specifically in your community? Ring up the editorial desk and ask if you can write about them.

• Listen to BBC Radio 4's *From Our Own Correspondent*. Imagine that you have just heard that a war has broken out. First write the stop press for Reuters. Then write a piece that will go on the front page of a broadsheet the following morning.

• You have been made responsible for a page in a national newspaper. The editor wants you to write five articles with the following titles: (a) Prime Minister Snubs France; (b) Gay And Proud! (c) Child Dies In Fire; (d) First Cuckoo of Spring; (e) Torrid Affair Breaks MP's Career! Decide whether you are writing for a broadsheet or tabloid. Prioritise the articles accordingly and think about where you will place the articles on the page, the size of the headlines, and the wordage for each one. Now write one of the articles.

• Write about a demonstration, a strike or a protest by an organisation such as Greenpeace. Try to write an informed, balanced piece which shows no obvious bias. Now write an article from the point of view of the protester, making it passionately rhetorical.

• Write a piece that analyses the current situation of one of the political parties. You might find John Cole's book *The Thatcher Years* helpful.

• Write a profile on a politician or a celebrity. Use Mary McCarthy's *The Mask of State: Watergate Portraits* as a model.

Research

- Select an ordinary domestic item such as a kettle or a vacuum cleaner and write an article on it. When was it invented and by whom? How has it developed? Try looking it up in the *Encyclopaedia Britannica*. You might take a bottle of Glenfiddich whisky and write a leaflet on its prestigious history.

- What were the main events one hundred years ago? Who was born and who died? Find out the news for that year from *The Timetables of History* or Pan's *Book of Dates*. Select one event and research it in depth. Do the same with the year you were born.

- Research the work of your local Citizen's Advice Bureau. Does it give you any ideas about articles of local or national interest?

Style

- Collect ten or fifteen overworked phrases such as a 'highly-acclaimed book', 'angst-ridden artist' and 'once in a lifetime experience' and rewrite them in your own words, trying to find a fresher turn of phrase.

- Practise the art of summarising. Take an especially pompous piece of prose and simplify it down to the bone. 'Pseud's Corner' in the weekly magazine *Private Eye* is a particularly rich source of pretentious nonsense.

- Check the back of a steamy, bestselling paperback book for its blurb. Note the superlative vocabulary and the purple prose. Now rewrite the blurb specifically for: (a) a child's comic; (b) a psychiatrist's case study; and (c) the bishop of the diocese's column in a religious magazine. What considerations do you have to take into account as regards readership? How will this affect your vocabulary?

- Avoid gender stereotypes in your writing. Pick up a traditional romantic novel and select a particularly stereotypical passage which casts both male and female into conventional roles. For example: 'When he strode into the room she felt she might almost swoon...' Rewrite the passage as though it is an item on the nine o'clock news, an article on the front page of a broadsheet or for a specialist magazine.

• Avoid wordiness in your writing. Phrases such as 'at this moment in time' can be simplified to 'now'. 'Ongoing' and 'in point of fact' can often be struck out altogether. Take a newspaper article from one of the broadsheets and replace or delete any unnecessary words. Now do this with a magazine article and then one of your own pieces of writing.

• Note the use of metaphors in journalistic writing. A devastated bridge or building can become the signifier for a tragedy of a much larger scale. A dead, oil-drenched seagull can point to the environmental pollution which wreaks havoc all around us. Search for metaphors in newspapers and develop them further. Create metaphors for six modern constructions, then for six ancient constructions.

• Note the correct, accepted formulae that professional journalists incorporate into their work. For example: 'A man is helping police with their inquiries'. 'Eye-witnesses report seeing an explosion before the aircraft nose-dived.' 'He is said to be in a critical condition.' Why are these phrases used? What is their effect? Begin to compile a list of them.

Travel Writing

• A great deal of travel writing focuses on exotic locations. If you have never been to a distant country, borrow some books from your library and pick up brochures from a travel agent. Try reading Bruce Chatwin's *In Patagonia* or Vikram Seth's *From Heaven Lake* for an account of his travels through Sinkiang and Tibet. Write an article describing a particular aspect of the landscape.

• Examine the tradition of women's travel writing. Look at Freya Stark's *Riding to the Tigris,* Jane Robinson's anthology *Unsuitable for Ladies* and the *Virago Book of Women Travellers.* What issues may arise if you are a lone female traveller? Is male travel writing different to female travel writing? Write a descriptive piece in the voice of a woman travelling in unknown territory.

- Write about a journey on a train, a motorcycle, a camel, an elephant, a jeep, or a canoe. Try to incorporate a sense of the landscape in your piece. Include two snatches of conversation, one that is overheard. You might find Paul Theroux's *Great Railway Bazaar* helpful.

- You are a hitch-hiker alone at night on a highway. Write your journal entry.

- Read P. J. O'Rourke's *Holidays in Hell* in which the writer turns his back on what he sees as the horrors of the traditional tourist trail, and chooses instead the unlikeliest places on earth to spend his time: places such as Chernobyl and the troubled streets of Seoul. Choose a banal or nightmarish holiday experience and write it from an ironic point of view. Look at the role of humour in Bill Bryson's work.

- The details of sensory perception are an important part of travel writing. Imagine that you are sitting beneath a scented plant, perhaps a jasmine or a bougainvillaea, on a Mediterranean evening. What else can you smell? What sounds can you hear? Look at Laurie Lee's *As I Walked Out One Midsummer Morning*.

- Find a landscape photograph of a terrain to which you are unaccustomed, perhaps of the Arctic or a desert. Imagine that you have just arrived there and write 300 words on your first impressions.

Promotion and Publicity

Most of us need to think of this at some point in our lives, even if it's a matter of writing out an advert to go in a shop window, drawing up a CV or working out a programme or leaflet for a community or school play.

- You want to market yourself as a graphic designer, book illustrator, sports instructor, sculptor, odd-job man, translator, cook, or flower arranger. Write 200 words promoting yourself. How do you avoid self-effacement or blatant egotism? Remember to state your qualifications, experience, name, address and telephone number.

- You work for a charity which is trying to draw the community's attention to its needs. Work out a campaign leaflet. How can you appeal to your readers' sensibilities without composing a sob story?

- Write a leaflet on a local or national beauty spot. What practical information do you include?

- Prepare a programme for your favourite stage play, opera, pop group or singer. Include some historical details, biographies and a cast list. Add quotations from current or previous reviews.

- This is a workshop for several contributors. You have been commissioned to produce a catalogue for an art, photography, sculpture or craft exhibition. You are required to write an introduction and to give details of each exhibit. The introduction must identify the movement the exhibition represents. For example, an introduction of Cézanne's paintings might give a potted history of Impressionism. Divide the tasks and see what you come up with.

- You want to promote a new invention. How do you describe its function clearly, using layman's language without being patronising? How do you explain its world-shattering significance with sufficient modesty?

Features

- Write a feature article with a strong feminist line, perhaps looking at women who choose not to have children, women who have opted to remain single or women who are the victims of sexual harassment in the workplace. You might find occasional articles by Germaine Greer in the press to be of interest.

- Write a feature article on racial prejudice in schools, bullying, teenage pregnancies, alcoholism, domestic violence, or alternative therapies. Include evidence of interviews in your article and strongly argue your own opinion of what the situation is, what isn't being done and what should be done. Look at Beatrice Campbell's book *Unofficial Secrets* on child sex abuse.

- Choose a fashion designer, photographer, film star or sports hero and write a feature on them, revealing a side of their life and personality that is not common knowledge.

- Read Joan Didion's famous collection of articles on the American way of life, *Slouching towards Bethlehem*. Choose an aspect of your own cultural background and write about it in an article.

- Look at the women's pages in the broadsheets. Take an aspect of health care and write a feature on it, perhaps post-natal depression, breast cancer, the menopause, or birth.

- Take a liberal magazine intended for a young male audience such as *GQ*. Write a feature from the point of view of a man who has fought against the pressures of his macho conditioning and has gone on to do something rather unusual like becoming a male nanny.

Sports Journalism

- Take a sport of your choice and write up a match. How do you avoid a laborious blow-by-blow account? What can inject energy into the piece?

- Read Nick Hornby's *Fever Pitch* which relates the life and thoughts of a devoted football fan. Write an article from the point of view of a lover of a particular sport.

- Write an account of a football, tennis, chess or rugby match for the tabloid press which reveals exactly where your own allegiances as the writer lie. Now take the same account and write it in a high-flown style so that the prejudice is still there but is camouflaged by elaborate language.

- Write up a match or sporting event that has some historic significance. Learn to describe the moment that becomes inscribed as history in detail, perhaps a legendary catch or a chance piece of luck that alters things entirely. Look at the anthology *The Spirit of Cricket* and note the use of hyperbole and rhetoric in many of the articles, especially by Neville Cardus and C. L. R. James. Does the sport you are writing about have a deeply ingrained significance within the nation?

- Write an article arguing strongly in favour of a sport that is often overlooked by the press and public.

- Write an article that argues for the banning of a particular sport, boxing, for example.

- Write an article that promotes fitness through aerobics, yoga, diet, weight training or running.

- Write a report on the fortunes of the local hockey, football, scuba-diving or abseiling team. Make it humorous.

Booklist

Bernstein, C. and Woodward, B., *All the President's Men* (Quartet Books, London, 1974).

Bryson, B., *Neither Here nor There – Travels in Europe* (Secker & Warburg, London, 1992).

Cahill, T., *Pecked to Death by Ducks* (Fourth Estate, London, 1994).

Campbell, B., *Unofficial Secrets* (Virago, London, 1988).

Capote, T., *In Cold Blood* (Penguin, Harmondsworth, 1993).

Chatwin, B., *In Patagonia* (Picador, London, 1979).

Cole, J., *The Thatcher Years: A Decade of Revolution in British Politics* (BBC Books, London, 1987).

Didion, J., *Slouching towards Bethlehem* (Penguin, Harmondsworth, 1974).

Garton Ash, T., *We the People: the Revolution of '89* (Granta Books, London, 1990).

Hersey, J., *Hiroshima* (Penguin, Harmondsworth, 1946).

Hoffman, A., *Research for Writers* (A & C Black, London, 1986).

Hornby, N., *Fever Pitch* (Gollancz, London, 1992).

James, C., *Television Criticism from the 'Observer' 1976–1979* (Pan Books, London, 1991).

Lee, L., *As I Walked Out One Midsummer Morning* (Penguin, Harmondsworth, 1971).

Martin-Jenkins, C. (ed.), *The Spirit of Cricket: A Personal Anthology* (Faber & Faber, London, 1995).

Mayle, P., *A Year in Provence* (Hamish Hamilton, London, 1989).

McCarthy, M., *The Mask of State: Watergate Portraits* (Harcourt Brace, Jovanovich, London, 1974).

Morris, M. (ed.), *The Virago Book of Women Travellers* (Virago, London, 1994).

Naipaul, V. S., *Black & White* (Sphere Books, London, 1980).

O'Rourke, P. J., *Holidays in Hell* (Picador, London, 1989).

O'Rourke, P. J., *Republican Party Reptile* (Picador, London, 1987).

Ponting, C., *The Right to Know: The Inside Story of the Belgrano Affair* (Sphere Books, London, 1985).

Robinson, J. (ed.), *Unsuitable for Ladies: An Anthology of Women Travellers* (OUP, Oxford, 1995).

Schanberg, S. H., *The Death and Life of Dith Pran* (Penguin, Harmondsworth, 1985).

Seth, V., *From Heaven Lake* (Phoenix, London, 1993).

Sewell, B., *The Reviews that Caused the Rumpus, and Other Pieces* (Bloomsbury, London, 1994).

Sontag, S., *Illness as Metaphor/Aids and its Metaphors* (Penguin, Harmondsworth, 1991).

Sontag, S., *On Photography* (Penguin, Harmondsworth, 1979).

Stark, F., *Riding to the Tigris* (John Murray, London, 1959).

St. Aubin de Terán, L., *A Valley in Italy* (Penguin, Harmondsworth, 1995).

Theroux, P., *The Great Railway Bazaar* (Penguin, Harmondsworth, 1977).

Thompson, H. S., *Fear and Loathing in Las Vegas* (Grafton, London, 1972).

Thompson, H. S., *The Great Shark Hunt* (Picador, London, 1980).

Waterhouse, K., *Keith Waterhouse on Newspaper Style* (Penguin, London, 1993).

Wolfe, T., *The New Journalism* (Picador, London, 1975).

11 Editing and Rewriting

Liz Cashdan, Mary Luckhurst and John Singleton

'Everything is negotiable,' says Michael Donaghy, talking on a BBC tape about writing poetry, which means he thinks you ought to do a lot of negotiating if you want your writing to be successful. Margaret Atwood, trying to explain the writing process in *The Writer on Her Work* by Janet Sternburg, makes nine attempts to answer the question: Why do you write? as a way of showing that the answer itself will need the same kind of redrafting. There's always 'the laborious revision, the scrawled-over, crumpled-up pages that drift across the floor like spilled litter... You look at what you've done. It's hopeless. You begin again. It never gets any easier.'

Great writers have always had to work at their writing: Ernest Hemingway rewrote the first paragraph of one of his novels, *The Sun Also Rises*, forty times. Sometimes the first drafts take place inside the author's head: Jane Gardam spent two years thinking about *The Queen of the Tambourine* before she started writing. Some writers have detailed plans before they begin, others discover as they write. The Norwegian playwright, Ibsen, made detailed scenarios for each of his plays. He rewrote the first draft of *The Doll's House* with so many changes that it became a kind of super-scenario for the succeeding drafts. Sylvia Kantaris reports that sometimes a poem seems to disappear in the drafting process but this is because 'we simply can't grasp where the poem is leading perhaps because we are not yet ready to grasp'.

This chapter will look at the ways in which writers work and at the same time the ways in which the writing itself can help writers to grasp, as Sylvia Kantaris says, where they are

302

being led; or as Michael Donaghy puts it, how to negotiate with the material you have already written.

It is vital to make clear the difference between redrafting and editing. When you edit a piece of writing you are looking not at structure and content or even vocabulary, but at technical skills like spelling and punctuation. They are important because without these skills you may not be communicating what you want to communicate to your reader. In a lot of cases editing need not be done by the original writers themselves: it could be done by copy-editors, whether human as in the case of publishers' editors (though sometimes these editors do more than mere editing!) or mechanistic as in the case of spellchecks on word-processors.

Frank Smith in his book *Writing and the Writer* thinks every writer has to do both composing and transcription. For him composing (drafting and redrafting) is done by the part of the writer that is an author (Frank Smith's term) and includes getting ideas, selecting words and using grammar; transcription (editing) is done by the bit of the writer that is a secretary and includes the physical effort of writing, spelling, punctuation and legibility. He then goes on to divide the composing activity into three parts: pre-writing, writing and rewriting. It is these three activities that really form the basis of the drafting process.

Pre-writing may consist of thinking, reading, talking and listening, possibly leading into some very rambling sort of writing that allows you to experiment. The non-writing bits of pre-writing may also lead into note-making, diagrams, plotting and verbal sketches. Then comes what may be considered your first draft and what Frank Smith would call writing. You might then dip back into the thinking, reading, talking and listening mode before you start on the writing part of rewriting.

What happens when you write? Nobody really knows the answer to this question and it is very possible that different things happen to different people, or different things to the same people on different occasions. You know yourself that sometimes writing comes easily, sometimes it has to be worked for. Sometimes, you can recognise the source of your ideas, sometimes you have no idea what made you write the way you did. But whatever produced the writing in the first place, whether it was carefully planned from beginning to end, or whether it arrived without any conscious planning, it still deserves redrafting. This is where your consciousness takes over. There is often considerable resistance among new writers who claim that their first drafts should be sacrosanct and must be left alone. My argument would be that the more you revere what you have just written the more you should protect it by taking out the weaknesses and faults that otherwise might damage it!

Psychologists have undertaken experiments to try and uncover the writing process. Two American researchers, Gregg and Steinberg, have suggested that 'the act of writing is best described as the act of juggling a number of simultaneous constraints'. They see writing as process rather than product, similar to Frank Smith's three stages of pre-writing, writing, and rewriting. But even the stage model, they argue, is too simple: instead, they choose to compare a writer with a switchboard operator who is dealing with:

Two important calls on hold. (Don't forget those ideas.)

Four lights start flashing. (They demand immediate attention or they'll be lost.)

A party of five wants to be hooked up together. (They need to be connected somehow.)

A party of two think they've been incorrectly connected. (Where do they go?)

And throughout this complicated process of remembering, retrieving, and connecting, the operator's voice must project calmness, confidence and complete control.

In order to try and validate this model the researchers asked student writers to keep protocols or commentaries on what seemed to be happening as they wrote. One of the problems with keeping a commentary on yourself as you write is that the act of commentating may influence what you then go on to write, just as, in any scientific experiment, observation can actually alter the data. Alternatively the protocol may be an inaccurate representation of what is happening. On the other hand, the research did find that once students became conscious of the constraints they were juggling with they were able to adopt strategies for coping.

When Fay Weldon was asked to contribute to a book called *The Agony and the Ego*, on authors' experiences of the process of fiction writing, she decided to make her contribution an actual example of uncovering the process. The chapter is called 'Harnessed to the Harpy' but the subtitle, 'Notes for Aspiring Writers from First to Final Draft or Thinking Aloud on Redrafting', emphasises that redrafting and rewriting are learning processes. You learn about your own strengths and weaknesses as a writer.

She begins by asking the reader/writer to forget why or what they are writing and to concentrate instead on how they 'actually set words upon the page to represent, as simply and gracefully as she or he can, the train of thought which goes on inside the writer's head and which the writer intends by means of the written word, to transfer into the head of a perfect stranger.'

That is how her first paragraph ends; in fact the piece quoted here is the end also of a very long first sentence. Her second paragraph begins like this: 'That sentence is in first draft. The first half's okay – the second half's rotten. The whole goes on for 139 words which is neither here nor there.'

So what Fay Weldon is doing here is really what Gregg and Steinberg asked their students to do; and because Weldon's text is about writing anyway, both original text and commentary are very closely interlinked. Weldon at one point asks would-be writers to consider 'if I, who have been writing for years, still have to carry on in this way, drafting and redrafting, refining and elaborating, searching for proper expression, whether this sort of thing is really how you wish to spend your life.' A serious writer, I suggest, will have to answer Weldon's question in the affirmative.

She takes this for granted and goes on to say that there have to be two personalities in every writer: A, who produces the first drafts, has to be 'creative, impetuous, wilful, emotional, sloppy'; and B, who does what she calls the editing, though I would prefer to call it the redrafting, has to be 'argumentative, self-righteous, cautious, rational, effective, perfectionist, ambitious'. Weldon thent takes a short story by Janice Marriott, called 'The Woman who Flew'. She calls Marriott the A personality, and then she, Weldon, becomes the B personality and starts to redraft. Although this example is of one writer redrafting the work of another writer, Weldon really wants the A and B in each writer to work together so that they can 'hurl this perfect object, this thing they have written, over a great obstacle (publishers etc.) so it lands into the eager hands of the reader'.

Another writer who has tried to uncover what goes on beneath the writing process is Rosalind Brackenbury. In her contribution to Susan Sellers' book on women writing, *Delighting the Heart*, Brackenbury quotes from the writing journal she kept during the composition of her novel called *The Woman in the Tower*. Her comments tend to deal with more overarching matters than Weldon's analysis, but essentially Brackenbury used her journal as the B personality who would analyse and argue about what was going on in what she as the A personality had already written or was about to write. One interesting point made by Brackenbury is that she was surprised when rereading her journal in preparation for writing her article, at how much she had worked on the book. She emphasises this point in order to show that all the work of rethinking and rewriting doesn't have to be a chore that damages the spontaneity of your original writing, but on the contrary, is an essential part of achieving success in the writing process. As Brackenbury puts it: 'In picking out these pieces of journal, I can see clearly what mattered, and matters to me:...not giving up when the going gets rough, working on a piece beyond the place where I feel easily satisfied with it (or nearly) or think that it might "do".'

Sue Roe, in the same book, tells of how alongside the actual text of her novel *Masquerade*, she also wrote on a separate paper headed Novel II Notes. 'Then I wrote notes to myself on how what I had just written would connect with what I was about to write, and how those things would connect with the whole, and then I carried on writing until those things ceased to be Notes and had filtered into the fiction.'

In the next section of this chapter there are some suggestions for trying out this kind of thing for yourself. Writing is not a simple task because language is not a simple contrivance. Language is not transparent: it inevitably carries its own luggage of association, viewpoint and prejudice. As a reader, you can look out for these pieces of luggage and decide what to do with them: keep them, change them or jettison them.

Vernon Scannell is a poet who sees writing as discovery and he has analysed how this worked for him with his poem, 'A Case of Murder'. Scannell explains that someone told him about a nine-year-old boy who had killed the family cat. Scannell was not told any more details, nor the reason for the boy's apparently outrageous action. So he decided to use the writing of a poem as a way of finding out why the boy had done it. As far as the actual incident is concerned, Scannell may not have discovered the truth, but the poem as he wrote it has its own truth. Or as Rose Tremain puts it about novel-writing in her contribution to *The Agony and the Ego*: 'all the studying and reading, all the social fieldwork, all the location visiting, all the garnering of what is or what has been – must be re-imagined before it can find a place in the text. It must rise into the orbit of the anarchic, gift-conjuring, unknowing part of the novelist's mind before it can acquire its own truth for the work in question.'

So even if Scannell did research child psychology or the behaviour of cats, the interesting thing he did was to put the boy on his own with the cat and see what the 'anarchic, gift-conjuring, unknowing part' of his mind produced. What did happen in his writing was the emergence of a smug, satisfied cat, and a desperately lonely, dissatisfied boy. The boy attacks the cat half in fun, half in earnest and when the cat is caught in the door and killed, the ghost of the cat becomes the boy's guilty conscience. That is what Scannell discovered as far as storyline goes, but because he makes it clear in his explanation that he loves playing with words and sounds he comes up with phrases like 'snug in its fur, hot blood in a muff' for the cat, and for the boy: 'he felt his skin/prickle with sparks of dry delight' and 'His eyes squeezed beads of salty prayer'.

Another poet whose drafts are well worth studying is Thomas Kinsella, to be found in Robin Skelton's book *The*

Practice of Poetry. The way in which Kinsella's poem changes through the series of drafts makes clear that although he had an image to start with he did not know exactly what form he wanted to write in until he had toyed with a lot of different versions. To go back to Michael Donaghy's phrase, Kinsella was negotiating through twelve drafts. Ian McMillan once said you have to be prepared to change the whole wardrobe, not just straighten the tie.

It is important to emphasise Rose Tremain's point about the unknowing part of the writer's mind acquiring its own truth. When you are writing, you don't have to tell it how it happened. The sort of writing that is being talked about here is writing as craft, not therapy (though it may have a therapeutic spin-off). It is not the sincerity of your emotions that is going to be judged, nor indeed the supposed accuracy of your reporting, but your skill as a writer. This means you can play about with your material. If you write skilfully, the reader will be convinced of your integrity. A very useful question to ask yourself when your writing has come to a standstill for whatever reason is: What if I change things in some way?

In his book of short stories, *Eight Plus One*, Robert Cormier explains how he came to write each one of them. Most of them arose out of his own experience, but for each one, he took the outline story and then said: What if I change it in some way? So a visit to an elderly relative in a nursing home becomes the story of a nineteen year old visiting his grandmother. In her confusion she thinks her grandson is her own husband as a young man when they were first going out together. The grandson is left with the dilemma of deciding whether to humour his grandmother or to try to explain the real situation to her. In another story, the narrator's day out with his daughter becomes the story of a girl who only sees her father on certain occasions because her parents are separated.

Whether Cormier actually wrote the first draft of his story and then said: 'What if?' is not clear, but the What if? technique could become a very useful tool for a first draft that has got stuck or doesn't seem to be going in the right direction.

Dorothea Brande's book, *Becoming a Writer*, has some very good advice for would-be writers. Although Brande doesn't use the same terms as Fay Weldon, she nevertheless presupposes a first-draft writer who gets on with the writing without bothering too much about self-criticism, who then becomes a second-draft writer for whom self-criticism is all-important: 'Your workaday self has been standing aside while you were about the business of teaching your unconscious to flow whenever you could find a moment for it; you will find now that it has been closely following the process, remarking your successes and failures, and getting ready with suggestions.'

To improve your skills as a second-draft writer you need to read as widely as possible. The writers on the BBC tape *Ways with Words*, some of whom left school without any further education, describe how wide reading enabled them to become good writers. Sue Townsend, author of *Adrian Mole* and *The Queen and I*, says that she has read three hours a day ever since she was eight years old. You may not have time to keep up with Sue Townsend but you need to think about writing as a reader and reading as a writer.

Wallace Hildick's book, *Word for Word*, analyses how well-known writers have rewritten their material, and makes the point that there are three different kinds of alteration: substitution, insertion, and deletion. Hildick then goes on to show how each of these can be divided into five different subgroups (given here in a slightly different order): (a) the structural group where you might change from short story to novel; (b) the power group which includes things like accuracy, clarity, attention to images, timing, place and viewpoint; and closely linked (c) the tidying-up group or its inverse roughening-up; (d) the ideological group which would include political and religious considerations; and (e) a more miscellaneous group linked to the ideological which might be based on fashion, competition rules, legal requirements.

The next section concentrates on what Hildick above calls the power group and offers some simple ways of improving your work. The features considered next are fundamental to good writing but are in no way exhaustive. Your group should devise its own style sheet, an in-house guide to clear and effective expression.

Workshop Writing

1 Wordiness

Your first concern in your writing should be clarity. What are you trying to communicate and have you done so effectively? New writers often make the mistake of assuming that elaborate turns of phrase and sentence structure guarantee a 'literary' pedigree. Look at contemporary writers and you will see that their styles are largely characterised by lucidity and simplicity. The art is in making it look easy, in hiding the craft: Alice Walker is a model writer in this sense. Use the following as a checklist in your own writing.

Periphrasis or circumlocution

Avoid tortuous modes of expression and say what you mean in the appropriate narrative voice. For example: *On the whole, arachnids tended to engender him with a feeling akin to perturbation...* is a sentence that could equally read: *He was terrified of spiders.* The first version is ornate and far less hard-hitting. It could work but only if the narrative voice were ironic and self-consciously mocking. On the other hand: *She raised her gaze and directed her pupils fixedly in front of her at the house...* is a sentence that is both cumbersome and unclear. It can be reworked to: *She stared at the house.* Take a piece of elaborate nineteenth-century prose and rewrite it in a clear-cut contemporary style. Now go through a piece of your own writing, rephrasing anything that is awkward or long-winded.

Purple prose

It was a sunrise to end all sunrises, golden skies stretching out to infinity. Beware superlatives and beware the attempt to describe a panorama in a sentence, you'll always end up sounding melodramatic.

Repetition

Critics have long been divided over the prose of D. H. Lawrence for its reliance on repetition: some have taken this to be a sign of poetic daring, and others have seen it as crude and uncrafted. In general, trust the image and associations of a word. 'Blood', for instance, conjures up notions of violence and death: its use just once will have a powerful impact in a sentence or paragraph. Repeat it too many times and you risk overstating your intention and rendering the passage absurd. Now choose a word with immediate resonances like *scandal, sexual, body, bride* and work it into a short paragraph at least five times. Take the same paragraph and cut all but one occurrence of the word. What are the different effects of the two paragraphs? Which do you prefer and why?

Metaphors and similes

Don't clutter your writing with overworked metaphors; if it is appropriate follow through one or two and develop them. Don't reach for fantastical similes just for the sake of it – unless you're writing comedy. Don't settle for clichés like *as old as the hills*. You are looking for bold, simple images which cast someone or something in an unusual light. Consider Marguerite Duras' description of a six-year-old boy: *He was thin. You could see his body plainly. He was too tall and seemed to be made of glass, like a windowpane – you could already see how he would turn out ... And the head, emerging like a tangent, a beacon, the culminating tip of a flower.* Now try to describe someone, developing no more than two metaphors.

Adjectives

Contrary to popular thinking, a descriptive piece of writing is not necessarily one that is overladen with adjectives. Writers such as Angela Carter often use an abundance of adjectives because they are consciously parodying a tradition: see her gothic collection *The Bloody Chamber* and look particularly at the first paragraph of the title story, which resonates with associations of virginity, sex and marriage. If your narrator is contemporary then your use of adjectives should be restrained. The overuse of adjectives in *the livid gruesome horrible wound*, for example, is negating the potential power of the image. You might decide to keep just 'livid' or you may decide to cut them all out and rely solely on the strength of the noun 'wound'. Write a passage using as many adjectives as you can to describe an object. Now rewrite it replacing the adjectives with nouns and verbs where possible. Compare the passages, noting the way meanings are changed.

Redundant subclauses
Unless you are deliberately moulding a pompous narrator cut out clauses that are simply padding. *I am yours* sounds more powerful than: *I am, as it were, yours.* And *I disagree* or *you're wrong* are stronger than: *Not to put too fine a point on it, I beg to differ.* Take ten phrases from a piece of fiction that you regard as 'redundant' and find their equivalents in clear, concise English.

2   Abstraction

Always write about a specific instance or person in your writing. Specificity authenticates your writing and makes it different from other poems, prose works or scripts.

A   Avoid blanket description such as: *The beach was amazing. The mountains were truly magical. The sea was gorgeous.* Generality is useless; the adjectives here are so overused that they convey nothing of the particular characteristics of the landscapes. As soon as you find yourself creeping into this mode of description stop and ask yourself what you mean. Perhaps: *The sand was a strip of glaring white bone.* Or: *Only I was real. The mountains had to be cut-outs, or perhaps just pictures from magazines, the ones I had snipped out and stuck in my scrapbook as a child.* Study the techniques of various travel writers. How do they avoid falling into stereotype and cliché? Or look at the novels of writers such as Thomas Hardy. How does he manage to convey entire landscapes? Concentrate on an aspect of the landscape or person you are trying to describe – perhaps the dead elm tree on the hill, or the single, blazing poppy in the hedgerow, and write a paragraph on it.
B   Avoid cosmic writing. By this we mean writing that launches off into the realms of vague or lordly universality. Out go constructions like: *She felt her soul awaken and rise up towards the stars.* Or: *Outside, in the dusk, he saw that all life was spread before him.* Or even: *There are no words that could possibly*

convey the beauty of what he saw before him. Don't pontificate and don't legislate as a writer. If your narrator does that is a different matter. Do focus on detail, don't brush over it airily. Be aware too of the resonances that words like 'soul' currently carry with them; secularism in the West has challenged the very concept of the soul and your writing could sound precious if you haven't thought it through.

C   Avoid over-formality. Some new writers find it difficult to adjust themselves to the freedom that creative writing offers. They feel that they cannot let themselves go and flinch from the idea of saying anything concrete. These are writers who turn out an essayistic style of writing which avoids the business of making hard decisions. If you are someone who often writes words and phrases such as: *moreover, furthermore, on the other hand, nevertheless, thus, therefore* strike them out, decide on your story and narrator and stick to them ruthlessly. Creative writing is not about balance and detachment; it is about pitching in, deciding what you think and feel about someone or something and then fashioning that material into an effective narrative and form. If you sit on the fence as a writer your work will be insipid and uninspiring.

3   Active/Passive

A   New writers often have difficulties negotiating their way through time and tenses. The most immediate, active tense is the present which places the reader in the here and now and lends an extra edge of uncertainty to it because anything can happen. Compare these two versions: (a) *I have three hours to live. My last wish is to write these lines, my last hope that you may one day read them.* And (b) *I was given three hours to live. These lines were written as my last wish, your reading of them was my last hope.* Note how in (b) the passive voice changes the meaning. In (b) we understand that the narrator has survived the threat of death and there is a feeling of reassurance in this. In (a) we are left guessing. Explore using the present tense in diary formats or epistolary forms such as Amos Oz's novel *Black Box*. Always write your stage plays and scripts in the present tense, otherwise they will sound like prose that should be read rather than performed.

B   The passive tense can be cumbersome and remove pace from your writing. Ask yourself whether it is really what you want. *He was shot by her*, for instance, is much less snappy than: *She shot him.* And *he was proposed to* does not have the same clarity as: *She proposed to him.* You may, of course, want to play on this style of formality and reportage. Look at Gabriel García Márquez' novella *Chronicle of a Death Foretold*, which exploits the passive tense in order to mimic the language of official reports and testimonials in the reconstruction of a murder.

C   Remember that you can switch tenses to bring a certain section of prose to life. For example, your main narrative may be in the past tense, but you might move to a dialogue which is conducted in the present.

He could never concede a point. For the purposes of argument, black was white and white black, it didn't bother him.
   'I saw you do it,' I say. 'I heard you.'
   'Come off it!' he says.
   'There's no mistake.'
   'You've always got to be fictionalising!'
   'What?' I say, getting riled now.
   'You heard.'

Make particular note of any tense changes that you come across in any book you read from now on. For instance try Margaret Atwood's novel *Life Before Man*, especially passages from Part 5 of the book. Or the first pages and other passages from Michael Ondaatje's novel *The English Patient*. Ask yourself what effect each writer is aiming for. Write a prose piece which experiments with a change from past to present tense.

4   Diction and Vocabulary

A writer should choose words carefully and for a clear purpose. It is a matter of diction. In writing where the diction is faulty words are used inappropriately or overabundantly. Diction is the right word in the right place for the right reason.

   Diction is part of style. If you want a lean, sparse style then rich, ornate polysyllabic phrasing will not do. If you are after a poetic, meaty, metaphoric style a succession of short sentences dominated by monosyllables will not do either. This is poor diction not because the words are used in an ungrammatical way but because they do not realise the purpose of the writer.

On the other hand, a writer may choose to create one verbal effect to counter it with the opposite. These counterpoints range from comic deflation to more subtle forms of irony. Consider the following.

A The opening of William Trevor's novel *The Children of Dynmouth* describes a small south-coast resort. Read the first paragraph and comment on the phrasing. What impression of the town do the words create? Now consider the shift in vocabulary in the second paragraph. Contrast selected phrases. For example '... later developed prettily as a watering place...', '...it was now considered unspoilt...', '...shingle gave way to sand...' (para. 1) with '...were scheduled to be manufactured...', '... with a view to developing a plant there' (para. 2). These sets of phrases represent contrasting vocabularies. What is William Trevor's purpose in doing this?

B Contrast this group of words – 'nestled', 'lace-making', 'ornamental lamp-posts', 'modest pier' (para. 1) with this group – 'tile-works', 'public lavatories', 'plastic lampshades' (para. 2). Discuss the reasons why Trevor sets up these verbal oppositions.

C Suppose William Trevor had used the word 'loos' or 'toilets' or 'conveniences' instead of the word 'lavatories', would they be just as effective and appropriate? Comment on the differences each substitution would make.

D Read the third paragraph of Angela Carter's novel *The Wise Children*. Seventy-five-year-old Dora Chance is sitting in the bedroom of her house in Brixton reminiscing. The paragraph starts off with an eight-line sentence and contains phrases like 'verdure' and 'urban deprivation'. But it ends with 'fish and chips'. This is a hybrid vocabulary. Would a poorly educated but intelligent cockney woman use words like 'Diaspora'? What is the writer's purpose do you think? Comic? Is Dora mimicking the 'posh' language of the 'rich', who in good sociological diction she also calls the 'affluent', in order to deflate its pretension by linking words like 'Diaspora' and 'diesel' in one incongruous phrase?

E   East End slang, music hall idioms and colloquialisms make up an appropriate language for Dora. It is also appropriate for the monologue form if your intention is to create a sympathetic character. Other forms demand different vocabularies and sets of words. The academic essay requires an objective, scholarly language. There is *no* place for slang here. You don't write – *Macbeth bumped off Duncan.* Unless your purpose is to write a spoof Shakespeare. But there *is* a place for technical terms like 'metaphor' and 'binary' and 'pentameter'. This is the diction of critical discourse.

Other discourses such as religion and education have their special dictions and verbal etiquette. Professions have their distinct vocabularies too. Their use depends on readership/listener, context and purpose. So, if I am a doctor I might use the words 'tummy ache' to a child or nervous adult instead of the more intimidating 'dyspepsia'. I might go somewhere midway between the homely and the technical by using the term 'indigestion'. If, however, I talk of 'gastric malfunction' I'm turning technicalities into jargon to intimidate or impress. And if I diagnose an 'occlusion of the gastric peritoneum' this is only appropriate if I'm talking to a fellow clinician.

Appropriateness is a principle governing all word usage whether fiction or non-fiction. If you are creating character you must get the words right. The talk of a 1960s Liverpool teenager obviously differs from a black New York adolescent in the Bronx: a cockney grandmother and a retired colonial officer from the Gilbert and Ellis Islands don't speak the same language: a first generation black social worker might not understand an ex-patriot Tynesider living in Marbella; a Bosnian refugee in London speaks differently from a Welsh hill farmer and both would have trouble with the speech of an Orcadian fisherman.

F   Take any short passage of prose written in the first person and rewrite it for a different character using an appropriate language. Here are some suggestions:

as a seventeenth-century seaman;
as a non-native speaker;
as a slightly inebriated, retired schoolteacher;
as an ex-Harrovian, ex-Guards officer;
as an adolescent;
as a mentally retarded person;
as an eighty year old using a local dialect;
as a different gender.

G Try with dialogue between two characters both of whom have very different 'languages'. Keep swapping characters so you can develop further dialogues.

H P. D. James in her detective novel *A Mind to Murder* uses words like 'malodorous' and 'minatory' instead of 'stinking' and 'threatening'. Can you explain such choices? Are they appropriate in a popular fictional genre like the whodunnit?

This habit of using the unfamiliar word so it sticks out like a sore thumb is the prose equivalent of 'poetic diction', a term used pejoratively. Verse that is inflated with puffs of big words and vacuous phrasing like *dark perplexity tortures my supine thoughts,* is just self-important. And conferring a false antiquity on poetry with archaisms like *hoary locks, o'er, ne'er, dost, hast, bygone, thou* and so on, should be avoided. Scan your work for signs of mock-Tudor writing.

I Raymond Chandler in a letter to a magazine editor complained about a copy-editor who kept correcting his language in favour of grammatical and stylistic correctness. He went on to describe his style as 'a sort of brokendown patois which is something like the way a Swiss waiter talks, ... when I split an infinitive, God damn it, I split it so it will stay split, and when I interrupt the velvety smoothness of my more or less literate syntax with a few sudden words of bar-room vernacular ... it is done with the eyes wide open and the mind relaxed but attentive.' In other words break the rules but have a good reason for doing so.

J Read Carol Ann Duffy's poem 'Mouth, with Soap' for examples of social and psychological factors at work in word usage. Or read Tony Harrison's poems 'Wordlists 1, 2, 3.', 'Them and (uz) 1, 2.' and 'The Queen's English'. In these poems he explores the different languages of his educated self and the dialect of his father's generation of Yorkshire men and women. Collect some comparable examples of language use and language clash from your own experience or that of your workshop group.

5   Sentences

Length, word order (syntax) and structure are the defining features of sentences. Control them and you control your writing. So when you rework passages of your writing start with the sentences.

A   The two words *I write* are an example of a basic sentence unit. Short though it is, it can be increased by a bewildering variety of add-ons and insertions. Try increasing this sentence to 10 words, then 15, then 20. See if you can get to 50 without losing control. You can insert an adjectival clause introduced by 'who' after the pronoun 'I'. You can add adverbs and adverbial phrases after the verb. You can join on another sentence by using a conjunction like 'and' or 'but' or 'yet'. You could insert a parenthesis or a long list of nouns as the object of the verb 'write'.

Whatever you do, you will have altered the telegrammatic terseness of that opening sentence. If I were to increase it to *I write easy, languorous and nonchalant prose* I would have created a sentence that drifts at a slow-motion pace. If, on the other hand, I increase it to *I write flat, dead prose* then with its repeated accentuated monosyllables and hard, clipped *t* and *d* sounds it now plods pedestrian fashion in mimicry of its meaning.

Since sentences in English are so flexible it is possible to twist them round and rearrange the syntax. For instance, the word order of *I write flat, dead prose* can be reversed to *Flat, dead prose I write*. How many other permutations can you devise? Often such changes create clumsy versions but by putting the words *I write* at the end delays the full meaning in this instance and adds suspense to an otherwise undistinguished sentence.

Writers play with sentences, with their internal anatomy, to create a wide variety of effects and you have to work on the dynamics of sentences to get the best out of them. It is not just a matter of getting each separate sentence shaped and balanced. Each sentence has to work with the other ones around. There is in fact a dynamic of the paragraph and experienced writers exploit the larger rhythms, the braking and acceleration of phrase and sentence, the internal tensions of clause and clause, the rise and fall, pull and tug of syntactic energies.

B   Take a simple example. Look at Thomas Hardy's poem 'The Self Un-Seeing'. The slow pace of the first verse quickens in the second and fairly rattles along in the third only to be stopped in its tracks in the last line. Work out how these energies are released in the poem.

C   You should read carefully selected paragraphs from any good writer and listen for the rhythms and momentum of the writing. Does a short sentence follow on from a long one? Are there a succession of short sentences? Why? Does the paragraph surge, trip, plod, speed up and slow down? Is the pace stately, suitable for a solemn occasion? Is it lively and jaunty, appropriate for an informal subject?

Here are three examples of accomplished sentence and paragraph making: the opening pages of E. M. Forster's novel *A Passage to India* or chapter 12, the opening two pages of Cormac McCarthy's novel *All the Pretty Horses*, and the final page of Pat Barker's novel *Blow Your House Down*. Start with the Pat Barker and examine her sentences, length and make-up. Try and work out the effects of her variation of these elements. Go on to consider the opening of the McCarthy novel. The fifth paragraph starts with a 9-word sentence, is followed by a 100-word one and ends with one 9 words long. Can you explain the variation? Now look at sentences, read some paragraphs aloud to feel the large rhythms of his prose. Compare them with any section of a Hemingway story, say 'The Battler' or 'A Well-lighted Place'. After all this take a careful look at examples of your own sentences. Does the syntax vary or not? Are they all similar in length? Have you created a dynamic to your paragraphs or are they a monotone without rise and fall, without quickening and slowing? Do sentences peter out or do they end on a strong note, a rising inflexion and a concrete image? Now revise them!

Booklist

Atwood, M., 'Nine Beginnings', in *The Writer and her Work*, ed. J. Sternburg (London, Virago, 1992).

Atwood, M., *Life Before Man* (Virago, London, 1982).

Barker, P., *Blow Your House Down* (Virago, London, 1984).

BBC Tape, *Ways with Words* (BBC Publications, London, 1994).

Boylan, C. (ed.), *The Agony and the Ego* (Penguin, Harmondsworth, 1993).

Brackenbury, R., 'The Woman in the Tower': Notebook in *Delighting the Heart*, ed. S. Sellers (Women's Press, London, 1989).

Brande, D., *Becoming a Writer* (Macmillan, London, 1983).

Carter, A., *The Bloody Chamber* (Penguin, Harmondsworth, 1981).

Carter, A., *Wise Children* (Virago, London, 1991).

Chandler, R., *Raymond Chandler Speaking*, ed. D. Gardiner & S. Walker (Penguin, Harmondsworth, 1988).

Cormier, R., *Eight Plus One* (Teen Tracks, London, 1988).

Donaghy, M., Interviewed in *Ways with Words* by J. Bailey and N. Clarke, *BBC Guide to Creative Writing* (BBC Publications, London, 1994).

Duffy, Carol Anne, *Selling Manhattan* (Anvil, London, 1987).

Duras, M., *Yann Andrea Steiner* (Hodder & Stoughton, London, 1995).

Forster, E. M., *A Passage to India* (Penguin, Harmondsworth, 1961).

Gardam, J., 'Angels and Daemons – The Anatomy of a Novel', in *The Agony and the Ego*, ed. C. Boylan (Penguin, Harmondsworth, 1993).

Gardner, J., *The Art of Fiction* (Vintage Books, New York, 1985).

Gregg, L. W. and Steinberg, E. R., *Cognitive Processes in Writing* (Laurence Erlbaum, New York, 1980).

Hardy, T., *Selected Shorter Poems*, ed. J. Wain (Macmillan, London, 1988).

Harrison, T., *Selected Poems* (Penguin, Harmondsworth, 1984).

Hemingway, E., 'The Battler' and 'A Well-Lighted Place' in *The Essential Hemingway* (Granada, London, 1977).

Hemingway, E., *The Sun Also Rises* (Macmillan, London, 1982).

Hildick, W., *Word for Word* (Faber, London, 1965).

James, P. D., *A Mind to Murder* (Penguin, Harmondsworth, 1984).

Kantaris, S., 'Poetry and Academe', in *Delighting the Heart*, ed. S. Sellers (Women's Press, London, 1989).

MacMillan, I., quoted in Sansom, P., *Writing Poetry* (Bloodaxe, Newcastle-upon-Tyne, 1994).

Márquez, G. G., *Chronicle of a Death Foretold* (Picador, London, 1989).

Ondaatje, M., *The English Patient* (Vintage, New York, 1992).

Oz, A., *Black Box* (Vintage, London, 1993).

Roe, S., 'No Discernible Life-Model', in *Delighting the Heart*, ed. S. Sellers (Women's Press, London, 1989).

Sansom, P., *Writing Poetry* (Bloodaxe, Newcastle-upon-Tyne, 1994).

Scannell, V., 'A Case of Murder', in Higgins, D. S., *Wider Aspects of English 3* (Cassell, London, 1974).

Skelton, R., *The Practice of Poetry* (Heinemann, London, 1971).

Smith, F., *Writing and the Writer* (Heinemann, London, 1982).

Sternburg, J. (ed.), *The Writer and Her Work* (Virago, London, 1992).

Townsend, S., in BBC Tape *Ways with Words* (BBC Publications, London, 1994).

Townsend, S., *Adrian Mole: from Minor to Major* (Mandarin, London, 1991).

Townsend, S., *The Queen and I* (Methuen, London, 1994).

Tremain, R., 'The First Mystery', in *The Agony and the Ego*, ed. C. Boylan (Penguin, Harmondsworth, 1993).

Trevor, W., *The Children of Dynmouth* (Penguin, Harmondsworth, 1982).

Weldon, F., 'Harnessed to the Harpy', in *The Agony and the Ego*, ed. C. Boylan (Penguin, Harmondsworth, 1993).

Recommended Reading

The following are books that we think you will find particularly useful and may be referred to elsewhere in the Handbook.

General

Boylan, C. (ed.), *The Agony and the Ego* (Penguin, Harmondsworth, 1993).

Goldberg, N., *Writing down the Bones* (Shambhala Publications, Boston & London, 1986).

Goldberg, N., *Wild Mind: Living the Writer's Life* (Bantam Books, London, 1990).

Hildick, W., *Word for Word* (Faber, London, 1965).

Legat, M., *The Nuts and Bolts of Writing* (Robert Hale, London, 1989).

Sellers, S., *Delighting the Heart* (Women's Press, London, 1989).

Sternburg, J. (ed.), *The Writer on her Work* (Virago, London, 1992).

Poetry/Verse

Attridge, D., *The Rhythms of English Poetry* (Longman, London & New York, 1982).

Chisholm, A., *A Practical Poetry Course* (Allison & Busby, London, 1994).

Ciardi, J., *How Does a Poem Mean?* (Riverside Press, Houghton Mifflin, Boston, 1959).

Everett, B., *Poets in Their Time* (Clarendon Press, Oxford, 1989).

Ricks, C., *The Force of Poetry* (Clarendon Press, Oxford, 1984).

Sansom, P., *Writing Poems* (Bloodaxe, Newcastle-upon-Tyne, 1994).

Play- and Scriptwriting

Brenner, A., *TV Scriptwriter's Handbook* (Silman-James Press, Los Angeles, 1992).

Dancyger, K., and Rush J., *Alternative Scriptwriting* (Butterworth-Heinemann, Stoneham, MA, 1991).

George, K., *Playwriting: The First Workshop* (Butterworth- Heinemann, Newton, MA, 1994).

Horton, A., *Writing the Character-centered Screenplay* (University of California Press, London, 1994).

Howard, D. and Mabley, E., *The Tools of Screenwriting* (St. Martin's Press, New York, 1995).

Seger, L., *Making a Good Script Great* (Samuel French, London & New York, 1987).

Fiction

Braine, J., *Writing a Novel* (Methuen, London, 1974).

Gardner, J., *The Art of Fiction* (Vintage, New York, 1985).

Lodge, D., *The Art of Fiction* (Penguin, Harmondsworth, 1992).

Steadman, C., *Essays on Writing Autobiography and History* (Rivers Oram Press, London, 1992).

Journalism

Waterhouse, K., *Waterhouse on Newspaper Style* (Penguin, Harmondsworth, 1993).

Biographical Notes

The Co-editors

Mary Luckhurst is an award-winning playwright and performance writer. Her latest play, *Kretschmer's Diary*, was premiered at the Theatre Celetne in Prague to great acclaim. She formerly ran the writing for performance courses at Manchester Metropolitan University and is now Lecturer in Modern Drama at the University of York. She has also edited *On Directing* for Faber & Faber.

John Singleton was formerly Head of Writing at Manchester Metropolitan University where he continues to teach creative writing. His publications include short stories, a children's novel and textbooks for secondary schools.

The Contributors

Liz Almond teaches creative writing at Manchester Metropolitan University. Her latest work has been published in *The Long Pale Corridor*, a Bloodaxe anthology, and in *Generations*, a new Penguin anthology. Crocus Books (an imprint of Commonword in Manchester) has published a short collection of her poetry called *Art Is Only A Boy's Name*.

Geoff Sutton has taught creative writing at Manchester Metropolitan University and is now an Open University Arts Tutor-counsellor. He writes poems and travel journals.

Ailsa Cox is a tutor with the Open University and teaches at Manchester Metropolitan University. Her short stories have appeared in numerous anthologies and magazines including *The Virago Book of Love and Loss, Stand One, Critical Quarterly* and *Writing Women*. She has also been co-editor of *metropolitan*, the acclaimed short story magazine.

Elizabeth Baines has taught creative writing in schools, to Adult Education students, on BA university courses and most recently at the University of Manchester. Her short stories have appeared in numerous literary magazines and anthologies and her published novels are *The Birth Machine* (Women's Press) and *Body Cuts* (Pandora). She is an award-winning radio playwright and was founder editor of *metropolitan*.

John Lennard is the author of *But I Digress* (Clarendon, 1991) and *The Poetry Handbook* (Oxford, 1996). From 1991 to 1998 he was Fellow in English at Trinity Hall and Newton Trust Lecturer in Practical Criticism in the Faculty of English at the University of Cambridge. He now has a Leverhulme Award to finish work on a Shakespeare project.

Meriel Lland teaches creative writing at Manchester Metropolitan University. She has published essays on the American novelist Willa Cather and the British poet Roy Fisher. Her interdisciplinary practice combines text and image as in her recent exhibition, *Archaeopteryx*.

Robin Nelson is a Principal Lecturer responsible for research and graduate study in the Department of Contemporary Arts at Manchester Metropolitan University. Besides publishing on aspects of theatre, media and contemporary arts, he has published two books on television drama: *Boys from the Black Stuff: the Making of TV Drama* (with Bob Millington) and *TV Drama in Transition* (Macmillan, 1997).

Betty Princep has taught creative writing at Manchester Metropolitan University. She writes and publishes travel and feature articles.

Liz Cashdan teaches creative writing at Sheffield Hallam University and Derby University. Her poetry has appeared in *New Women Poets*, published by Bloodaxe. Her most recent work includes *Trouble with Cattle*, a joint collection, published by Smith Door Stop and *Laughing All the Way*, Five Leaves Press.

Acknowledgements

The editors would like to thank all the students who helped them with this book.